COMPARATIVE MARKETING SYSTEMS

COMPARATIVE MARKETING SYSTEMS

Edited by
Erdener Kaynak and Ronald Savitt

Library of Congress Cataloging in Publication Data
Main entry under title:

Comparative marketing systems.

Bibliography: p.
Includes index.
1. Marketing—Addresses, essays, lectures. 2. Export
marketing—Addresses, essays, lectures. I. Kaynak,
Erdener. II. Savitt, Ronald.
HF5415.C54736 1984   380.1   83-24468
ISBN 0-03-062604-8 (alk. paper)

Published in 1984 by Praeger Publishers
CBS Educational and Professional Publishing
a Division of CBS Inc.
521 Fifth Avenue, New York, NY 10175 USA

© by Praeger Publishers

456789 052 0987654321

Printed in the United States of America
on acid-free paper

FOREWORD

This book reflects the editors' dedication to a search for "marketing universals," generalizations about marketing behavior and its consequences that apply in human societies around the world irrespective of their economic, political or cultural organization. To seek marketing universals, the editors, Erdener Kaynak and Ronald Savitt, have chosen to focus on comparisons between marketing behavior systems. As Erdener Kaynak notes in Chapter 16, entitled, "Comparative Marketing Systems: Past, Present and Future," a comparative marketing study "examines relationships between marketing and its environment in two or more countries."

Application of the systems concept is explained in the paper on "Comparative Marketing Systems Analysis Revisited" by Adel El Ansary and Marilyn L. Liebrenz. In Figures 3.1 and 3.2 and the accompanying discussion, the authors show how comparative studies can be linked to the systems paradigm that bridges the behavioral sciences by identifying commonalities or "universals." Thus, by collecting papers offering comparisons between marketing systems, Kaynak and Savitt show how patterns of marketing behavior can be generalized over time and across cultures.

Beyond substantive findings on comparative marketing systems, the editors' efforts are also distinguished by their search for a methodology for learning to learn about comparative marketing. In seeking to give coherence to contributions from such disparate fields as cross cultural comparisons and historical analyses of longitudinal time-bound marketing processes, they have focussed the content on research methodology. Kaynak and Savitt have approached this task by assembling papers into groups concerned with related issues. Readers will be able to identify these issues by referring to Table 1.3 which provides the conceptual framework for this book. Table 1.3 permits readers to select individual papers without losing sight of the book's major themes of theoretical-abstract conceptualization on the one hand and empirical research on the other.

Readers interested in marketing performance measurement may wish to examine Parts 3, 5, and 6 first. These deal with macro-development issues in agriculture, changes in marketing processes, and evolutionary changes in command economies compared to market-directed economies. Readers most concerned with research methodology may prefer to examine first Part 2, which reviews the present state of knowledge, then Part 4, which sets priorities for exploring research techniques for further study and Part 7 which sets forth the editors' own evaluation and agenda for future research.

Viewed in the context of comparative marketing literature, Kaynak and Savitt's emphasis on methodological issues to be surmounted does not lead to neglect of substantive content. Samli, for example, deals with marketing evolution in Eastern Europe; Mun Kin-chok compares the planned command allocation system in command and market-directed programs in the Peoples' Republic of China, and William Lazer's "Insights into Japanese Marketing" would be of value to participants in Executive Development Programs. Problems introduced by state intervention in market direction of resource use are chronicled in Szabo's "Marketing and Marketing Research in Socialist Countries."

Together the papers included in this volume document "marketing universals": the effectiveness of markets and marketing in producing social benefits including transfer of new technologies, the promotion of economic development, and the allocation and mobilization of resources to those ventures for which demands warrant risks and investment. Also evident is the mirror image of the undesirable social costs of state interventions in marketing including inefficiency and ineffective interference with provisioning technologies of marketing by central allocation plans that result in shortages of desired supplies and gluts of unsaleable products.

Any human effort is of course subject to improvement. One benefit derived from exposure to this collection of papers is the reader's sense that other materials could improve its contents. Indeed, reading this book provides exactly the incentive to scholars that could result in the production of additional comparative literature. The editors express their awareness of this in one of the most ambitious statements available anywhere on "The Future Directions of Comparative Marketing: An Agenda for Research Priorities". In this final chapter the editors, Kaynak and Savitt, express thirteen methodological concerns and present an agenda of six topics and issues for further research. Recognizing that theirs are not the final words on comparative marketing, they conclude with a question: "Comparative analysis demands answers to the question: relevant compared to what?"

George Fisk

PREFACE

During the past thirty years comparative marketing issues have become the focus of an increasing and intensive research effort. This effort is reflected in the growing number of publications on comparative marketing systems. Greater involvement of North American companies as well as public policy makers in international trade has also created the need and has provided some of the data for comparative marketing studies. Another important factor contributing to the development of comparative marketing as a field has been the growing interest of academics in developing general or universal theories and conceptual frameworks for application in solving marketing problems, most notably those dealing with international marketing.

The book presents an integrated view of the field of comparative marketing, growing out of a concerted effort to systematically assemble and develop materials that define and appraise its contents, describe research methods, present important findings, and synthesize generalizations. It was conceived and developed with an eye toward expanding the field of comparative marketing; to reach that goal it was necessary to commission original materials from a group of individuals selected both for their diversity, and their distinct contributions to the field. The materials in this book reflect a systematic effort by all concerned to give full meaning to a broad field of study.

Unlike past writings on comparative marketing, this book seeks to identify and explore comparative issues in and among nations by using a systems perspective, considering comparative marketing in both its macro- and micro-dimensions. It is our sincere hope that this book will be a valuable asset to academics interested in developing their understanding of marketing in diverse environments as well as broadening their research. It is also hoped that the book will be of value to managers involved in expanding their markets and faced with the problem of dealing with different marketing systems. Finally, it is hoped that public policy makers and international organizations presented with the day-to-day issues of developing marketing systems will find this volume a useful guide.

ACKNOWLEDGEMENTS

The authors gratefully acknowledge the contributors of materials to this volume, many of whom stopped in the midst of other projects to pay heed to a topic that they saw as important. The coeditors could not have succeeded in this undertaking without such support. The book is a sample of the many excellent papers that were submitted. Unfortunately, we were unable to include all of the manuscripts; however, we are extremely gratified to know that there is such great interest in comparative marketing and that the level of work in the field is so high.

We are extremely pleased with Praeger's foresight in allowing us to undertake such a project at this time. They have identified international marketing as a strategic area and have been willing to support such ventures as this.

We also acknowledge the support of our respective universities in providing the intellectual environments in which scholarly work of this nature can be accomplished. Specifically, we wish to thank Mrs. Debbie Smicer, Ms. Kay Hus, and Ms. Kim Oliver for their support in many phases of the project.

Last but not least, the coeditors are grateful to their families for being generous in understanding the demands of scholarly activity.

We of course take all responsibility for any errors or commission.

Erdener Kaynak
Halifax, Nova Scotia

Ronald Savitt
East Lansing, Michigan

CONTENTS

Part VII:
Comparative Marketing Systems: An Evaluation

LIST OF TABLES

LIST OF FIGURES

I

INTRODUCTION

The purpose of this part is to assess the current status of research on comparative marketing systems issues and to suggest areas that are "ripe" for immediate research. To this end, a critical review of comparative marketing studies is undertaken to identify what has already been achieved by way of conceptual frameworks, including typologies in the process of systematically detecting, identifying, classifying, measuring, and interpreting similarities and differences among marketing systems around the world. Descriptive, normative, and diagnostic approaches to comparative marketing systems studies are examined, and a methodology is suggested in order to provide an adequate framework on which to base comparative marketing studies. It is felt that there is an urgent need for mutually supportive theoretical and empirical research in comparative marketing studies both at macro- as well as of micro-levels. A comparative marketing study requires a generalized system of concepts that will enable the researcher to rigorously compare and contrast marketing phenomena in different cultures/countries. Although a universal marketing taxonomy does not exist, it is reasonable to expect that there are universal patterns of marketing behavior and structure. The identification of such patterns is the essential purpose of comparative marketing systems study. The first step in applying such a framework involves identification of the functional prerequisites of marketing. These refer to the institutions and processes that are extant in every marketing system and that are necessary to its survival.

1

COMPARATIVE MARKETING: INTEGRATIVE STATEMENT

Erdener Kaynak and Ronald Savitt

Introduction

Despite recognition that international marketing operations are important to the survival and growth of an increasing number of North American and European companies, the study of foreign markets has lagged considerably behind developments in domestic marketing.[1] This lack of study may be caused by difficulties in researching multi-country marketing issues. Most of the problems stem from the complexity of multi-national environments, which involves monetary variations, scheduling conflicts, language and culture variations, plus operational and technical difficulties associated with the conduct of multi-country comparisons.

The purposes of this volume are: a) to explain the significance of comparative marketing systems research; b) to outline the current status of comparative marketing systems research; and c) to indicate and predict the direction which comparative marketing systems research might take in the immediate future as well as in the long run. In essence, this volume recognizes the growing importance of comparative marketing systems research as a subject area of marketing. It is also a point of departure for scholars and practitioners interested in contributing to the development of comparative marketing systems research and practice. It will establish priorities by asking what regions, countries, periods, and sectors should be studied; what type of marketing problems, internal or external to the company, should be examined; and how should these problems be examined and with what resources. It will suggest suitable typologies and analytical conceptual schemes of analysis. It will design and develop methodologies and working propositions which can be used and applied in more than one country or geographical region over a period of time. It will evaluate and interpret existing and ongoing research. It will make predictions for future research in comparative marketing systems and attempt to determine the best research methods and techniques.

What Is Comparative Marketing Systems Research?

The comparative approach to the study of marketing systems is generally aimed at systematic detection, identification, classification, measurement, and interpretation of cross-cultural or cross-institutional similarities and/or differences in various marketing practices and systems in two or more countries or within the confines of a single country in which substantial cultural differences exists.[2] For this reason, it is not adequate to describe the marketing system in each country or region. The critical issue in comparative marketing systems research is the manner in which the experiental, conceptual, and methodological understanding as well as observational data gained in two or more countries are analyzed, interpreted, related, and generalized for model or theory-building purposes.[3]

The focus of the comparison in comparative marketing research should be either upon time, space, or among different sectors of the economy.[4] As for the different sector comparisons, temporal (historical) comparisons deal with differences and/or similarities among marketing phenomena removed in time but otherwise identical or similar as far as space and sectors of the economy are concerned.[5] Spatial (geographical) comparisons focus on differences and/or similarities among phenomena located in spatially removed units such as cultures, nations, regions, and cities but otherwise identical or similar as far as time or sectors of the economy are concerned.[6] Sectoral (subcultural) comparisons, on the other hand, concentrate on differences and/or similarities among segments of a single spatial unit (e.g.: a nation) at a single time (or period).[7]

Comparative marketing systems research provides a systematic framework for comparing new and different marketing situations and develops an awareness and understanding of the organic unity of a country's marketing system or culture. Such an approach provides an intellectual appreciation of the impact of environment on the marketing system.[8] This approach breaks the tradition-bound thinking of practitioners as well as academicians. It determines, as well, whether conceptual frameworks, constructs, and theories developed and tested in one country have relevance and applicability in other countries and under varying conditions.

As has been pointed out before, comparative marketing deals with the development of marketing systems under different historical and environmental characteristics. The question of what should be compared, and how, is the major issue in a comparative marketing systems research. Comparative marketing systems research focuses on some features of the functional area and some environmental factors. The selection of the features should be based on a systematic framework as shown in Figure 1.1.* The relationship of functional areas of marketing to the environment is reflected in some of the problems of comparative marketing systems. Thus, how do marketeers compare in terms of who they are, what they do, how they relate to other people, what they contribute, and how they interact with all aspects of the marketing environment.[9]

Research designs for comparative marketing systems studies must be carefully developed. They must accommodate three interrelated research objectives: a) detailed descriptions on a country-by-country basis that analyze the national system—its intrarelationships and interrelationships; b) a study of certain elements or particular issues of the marketing systems in terms of their structural and functional characteristics, and c) explanations and evaluations of the significant differences between or among the marketing systems. A conceptual framework for comparative marketing systems process is shown in Table 1.1. The ultimate purpose of comparative marketing systems studies is to form a solid foundation for international marketing, and to provide a useful perspective for understanding domestic marketing systems.

Dimensions of Comparative Marketing Systems

Comparative marketing systems research is the tool for generation and interpretation of the macro- and micro- constructs that guide decision making about product, price, promotion and distribution policies in a number of countries. The relationship among approaches, methods, and techniques

---

*For fuller treatment of this subject see: Erdener Kaynak, "The Introduction of a Modern Food Retailing Institution to Less-Developed Economies: Problems and Opportunities", in M. G. Harvey and R. F. Lusch, eds., *Marketing Channels: Domestic and International Perspectives*, Dallas, Texas, March 17–19, 1982, pp: 52–58. Several factors must be taken into consideration as comprising the environment within which urban food retailing of less-developed countries operates. Among these factors are consumer-related impediments, the backward nature of the supporting food industry and the infrastructure, as well as small and inefficient food manufacturers. In order to be successful, retailing institutions must anticipate social, economic, and technological trends as well as adapt to rapid and somewhat unpredictable changes in the consumer market.

FIGURE 1.1

Impact of Environment on the Distribution System of Developed versus Less-Developed Countries

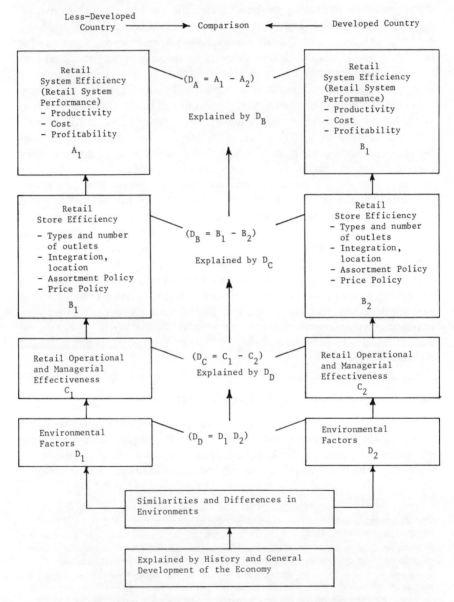

Source: Erdener Kaynak, "The Introduction of a Modern Food Retailing Institution to Less-Developed Economies: Problems and Opportunities" in M. G. Harvey and R. F. Lusch, eds.), *Marketing Channels: Domestic and International Perspectives,* Dallas, Texas, March 17–19, 1982, p. 54.

TABLE 1.1
Conceptualizing Comparative Marketing Systems Process in Multiple Environments

	Descriptive Studies	Generalizing Normative Studies	Analytical Interpretive Studies
One-Dimensional Micro construct of Marketing Systems	Leff (14) Demetrescu (10)	Buzzell (12) Douglas (15) Dholakia & Dholakia (20)	Keegan (23) Anderson, et al. (26) Anderson, et al. (27)
Multi-Dimensional macro construct of Marketing Systems	Luqmani et al (28) Kaynak & Mitchell (29) Demetrescu (10) Kaynak & Samli (11) Boddewyn (30) Hilger (16)	Henley (13) Meissner (15) Preston (15) Wadinambiaratchi (15) Lipson (17) Harrison et al (18) Riley (18) Slater (18) Kaynak & Cavusgil (21) Moyer (22)	Henley (24) Riley (24) Slater (24)

used in comparative marketing systems research would vary from one country to another.[10]

Past empirical research studies conducted on comparative marketing systems can be categorized into at least three general groups: a) descriptive studies, b) normative studies, and c) analytical studies. There are both micro- (one-dimensional) and macro- (multi-dimensional) studies in each of these three groups.

At macro level, descriptive studies try to identify a marketing system as well as define the institutional structure of the marketing institution. This type of comparison does not tell us anything about how marketing in different countries functions or how to distinguish among different macro-marketing systems of the world. Much of the descriptive research has been concerned with issues involving the conditions of process, structure, conduct, and performance predicted by the perfectly competitive market model. The major problem with this relatively static macroframework is that it underplays the potential impact of marketing institutions and systems in achieving socio-economic and marketing development goals including efficiency, produc-tivity, growth, and welfare.[11]

Comparative marketing is concerned with the effect of environmental as well as managerial variables on operating results and performance. Unfor-tunately, much of the comparative marketing literature has been comprised of primarily descriptive macrostudies of marketing environments. Little progress has been made in relating environmental factors to differences in market behavior and marketing management performance of companies in multiple environments.[12] In comparative marketing systems studies, a number of difficulties exist in defining and measuring environmental variables and relating them to performance. Of course, the greatest needs are to recognize similarities and differences in various market systems and areas, to develop coordinated strategic plans, and to manage and control the world-wide marketing effort.[13] As a result of this, a number of useful and insightful micro-descriptive studies have been undertaken. In part, these have been conducted by geographers interested in the economic activities of marketing institutions. This type of study is important for the development process because it provides knowledge of a country's functioning institutions. However, much of this research suffers from the inability to offer normative solutions to problems concerning the policy and planning of marketing systems at different stages of socioeconomic and technological development.[14]

Normative studies emerge as the second stage in the succession of comparative marketing studies. These studies use selected empirical data to generalize or to make normative, prescriptive assertions. Most of these studies recommend the transfer of relatively capital-intensive marketing technology to third-world countries. Horizontally and vertically integrated systems were prescribed to create economies of scale, shorten distribution channels, and increase purchasing power for consumers.[15] However, Hilger argues that few of these studies or their public policy implications have led to real generalizations about how to affect structural, institutional, or behavioral change in market systems. The author continues:

> We have yet to put the descriptive conclusions into a conceptual model of public and private roles in system development. What may be needed at this point is a change in the types of institutions or products or market locations. There is truly an absence of these studies in the comparative marketing literature and our ability to build generalizations about how to cause market system change is likewise limited.[16]

Some of the microstudies described the domestic system, then suggested that the system should look more like the U.S.A. model.[17] A number of research centers carried out broadly based studies in order to provide support for normative models.[18]

The barriers to changing marketing systems from the way they are to the way they should be are immense. In addition to cultural, socioeconomic, technological, and political barriers, less developed countries faced high levels of unemployment plus capital shortages. It is also conceivable that each will pursue the development of a marketing system most suitable to its own needs and desires. Whatever system is developed or adopted by an LDC, one point is clear: There is a need for closer international linkages among these countries.[19] Cooperation will serve three purposes: to learn from each other's experiences, to provide a collective front in negotiating with strong industrial nations, and to create an atmosphere of equality for the underprivileged.[20]

Although normative approaches to comparative marketing may encounter a substantial degree of difficulty during implementation, they are very important and realistic in terms of evaluating marketing system performance. Market systems in this context are measured against what might be considered most desirable in fulfillment of broader socio-economic development goals.[21]

Analytical-interpretive studies are the third stage in the succession of broader assessments of marketing systems. These studies focus on an evaluation of empirically verified data. They provide necessary inputs to policy and program development in a more dynamic and individualistic manner. In most of these studies, there has been a tendency to utilize secondary macrodata to test the structure, process, development, and performance of marketing institutions. Thus, although they provide good inputs at the macrolevel, they do not focus on the microbehavior of marketing institutions in multiple environments.[22] In comparative marketing

TABLE 1.2
Conceptual Framework of the Book*

COMPARATIVE MARKETING RESEARCH
Basic Orientations

THEORETICAL-ABSTRACT	EMPIRICAL	
C Barksdale & Anderson (2)	O Lazer (14) Kin-chok (15)	Descriptive
O	N Dawson (10)	
N Douglas & Craig (6)	E	
C		
E	D	
P	I Goldman (4)	Generalizing
T	M Etgar (5)	Normative
U	E	
A	N	
L	S	
I	I	
Z	O	
I	N Future Research	Analytical
N	A Areas	Interpretive
G	L	
S El-Ansary & Liebrenz (3)	M Hazard (12) Szabo (8)	
Y	U Samli (13)	Descriptive
N Cavusgil & Kaynak (7)	L	
T	T	
H Savitt (9)	I	
E		
S Kaynak (16)	D Future Research	Generalizing
I	I Areas	Normative
Z	M	
I	E	
N	N	
G	S	
	I	
	O Future Research	Analytical
	N Areas	Interpretive
	A	
	L	

Source: Adopted from Hans Schollhammer, "Current Research on International and Comparative Management Issues," Management International Review, Vol. 15, No. 2 and 3, 1975, p. 35.

---

*Chapter numbers are indicated in brackets.

system studies, there are a number of conventional variables that can be used to measure performance, such as market share, sales growth, gross and net marketing margin, and price realization. These all appear to be acceptable for comparative marketing studies. However, differences in competitive practices, marketing institutions, a host of environmental factors and the product life cycle in country-markets will have their effect on profit.[23]

Broader analytical interpretive assessments of marketing systems in overseas markets have provided input to policy and program development and to an evolving conceptual and analytical framework for future research and development effort. The Food and Agriculture Organization of the United Nations as well as a number of research centers have carried out more broadly based studies of marketing systems of foreign countries.[24] A major problem with the research frame developed in most of these diagnostic studies is the lack of concern for the dynamic impact which marketing services can have on production and consumption. In most of these studies, there is the tendency to utilize secondary, usually macrodata for examining conditions of structure, development, and performance of institutions. These types of data do not permit focusing on the micro-behavior of marketing institutions in different socio-economic and cultural environments.

The following scheme is the summary of a typology used in this book for the purpose of clarifying and analyzing the different contributions to this volume.[25] For the purpose of categorizing comparative marketing research according to its research orientations, the chapters included in this volume are designated either theoretical-abstract or empirical. (See Table 1.2).

Notes

1. Erdener Kaynak, "Future Directions for Research in Comparative Marketing," *The Canadian Marketer*, Vol. 11, No. 1, 1980, pp: 23–28.

2. Robert Bartels, "Methodological Framework for Comparative Marketing Study" in A. Greyser, ed., *Toward Scientific Marketing* (Chicago: American Marketing Association, 1964), pp: 383–90.

3. Yoram Wind and Susan P. Douglas, "Comparative Methodology and Marketing Theory", in *Theoretical Developments in Marketing* (Chicago: American Marketing Association, 1980).

4. For more information on this see: J. J. Boddewyn, "The Comparative Approach to the Study of Business Administration," *Academy of Management Journal*, Vol. 8, No. 4, December 1965, pp: 261–67.

5. Ronald Savitt, "A Historical Approach to Comparative Retailing", *Management Decision*, Vol. 20, No. 4, 1982, pp: 16–23.

6. John A. Dawson, *The Marketing Environment*, Croom Helm, London 1979 and *Commercial Distribution in Europe* (Croom Helm, London 1982).

7. Vern Terpstra, *The Cultural Environment of International Business* (Cincinnati, Ohio: South Western, 1978).

8. Jean Boddewyn, "The Comparative Approach to the Study of Business Administration," *Academy of Management Journal*, Vol. 8, December 1965, pp: 261–67.

9. For an outline for Comparative Marketing Analysis see: Robert Bartels, *Comparative Marketing: Wholesaling in Fifteen Countries*, Homewood, Illinois, Irwin 1963, pp: 297–308.

10. Mihail C. Demetrescu, "Comparative Marketing Systems—Conceptual Outline," in Dov Izraeli; D. N. Izraeli and F. Meissner, eds., *Marketing Systems for Developing Countries," Journal of Business Research*, Vol. 11, No. 1, March 1983.

11. Erdener Kaynak and A. Coskun Samli, "A Conceptual and Methodological Approach to the Study of Marketing Practices in Less-Developed Countries," *Journal of Business Research*, Vol. 11, No. 4, December 1983.

12. For a pioneering effort in this area see: Robert D. Buzzell, "Can You Standardize Multinational Marketing?" *Harvard Business Review*, Vol. 45, November–December 1968, pp: 102–113.

13. Donald S. Henley, "Evaluating International Product Line Performance", in Dole A. Anderson, M. Luqmani, and Z. A. Quraeshi, eds., *International Business—1979: A Selection of Current Readings*, East Lansing, Michigan 1979, pp: 338–50.

14. Nathaniel H. Leff, "Multinational Corporate Pricing Strategy in the Developing Countries," *Journal of International Business Studies*, Fall 1975, pp. 55–64.

15. Edna Douglas, "Size of Firm and the Structure of Costs in Retailing, *Journal of Business*, April 1962, pp. 158–80; Frank Meissner, Capital-Intensive Super Market Technology, Can't Serve Needs of Poor in Third World or U.S., *Marketing News*, November 27, 1981, p. 13; Lee E. Preston, "Market Control in Developing Economies," *The Journal of Development Studies*, July 1968, pp: 481–96; and George Wadinamblarachi, "Channels of Distribution in Developing Economies," *The Business Quarterly*, Winter 1964, pp: 74–82.

16. Marye Tharp Hilger, "Factors Inhibiting the Development of Comparative Marketing." Paper presented at the Seventh Macro Marketing Seminar, University of Colorado, Boulder, August 1982.

17. Harry A. Lipson, "The Impact of Double Digit Inflation Upon the Modernization of the Retail Structure in Developed Economies, in Edward M. Mazze, ed., 1975 *Combined Proceedings*, Series No. 37, AMA 1976, p. 315.

18. Kelly Harrison, Donald Henley, Harold Riley, and James Shaffer, *Improving Food Marketing Systems in Developing Countries: Experiences from Latin America*, Research Report No. 6, Michigan State University, East Lansing 1974; Harold M. Riley, *Improving Internal Marketing Systems as Part of National Development Plans*, Department of Agricultural Economics, Michigan State University, May 1972, p. 24; and Charles C. Slater, "Marketing Processes in Developing Latin American Societies," *Journal of Marketing* Vol. 32, July 1968, pp: 50–55.

19. N. Dholokia and F. A. Firat, "The Role of Marketing in the Development of Non-Market Sectors and Conditions Necessary for Success," in Dov Izraeli, Dafna N. Izraeli and Frank Meissner, eds., *Marketing Systems for Developing Countries* (New York: John Wiley Sons, 1976), pp: 50–62.

20. Nikhilesh Dholakia and R. R. Dholakia, "A Framework for Analyzing International Influences on Third World Marketing Systems," Working Paper No. 80-8, Kansas State University, May 1980.

21. Erdener Kaynak and S. Tamer Cavusgil, "The Evolution of Food Retailing Systems: Contrasting the Experience of Developed and Developing Countries," *Academy of Marketing Science Journal*, Vol. 10, No. 4, Fall, 1982, pp: 249–68.

22. Reed Moyer, "The Structure of Markets in Developing Economies," *MSU Business Topics*, Autumn 1964, pp: 43–60.

23. Warren J. Keegan, "Multinational Product Planning: Strategic Alternatives," *Journal of Marketing*, Vol. 33, January 1969, pp: 58–62.

24. Donald S. Henley, "Marketing and Economic Integration in Developing Countries," in Reed Moyer and Stanley Hollander, eds., *Markets and Marketing in Developing Economies* (Homewood: Richard D. Irwin, 1968), pp: 70–86; Charles C. Slater, "Marketing Processes in Developing Latin American Societies," *Journal of Marketing*, Vol. 32, July 1968, pp: 50–55; Harold M. Riley, *Improving Internal Marketing Systems as Part of National Development Plans*, Department of Agricultural Economics, Michigan State University, May 1972.

25. Hans Schollhammer, "Strategies and Methodologies in International Business and Comparative Management Research," *Management International Review*, Vol. 15, Nos: 2–3, 1975, pp: 29–45.

26. R. D. Anderson, J. L. Engledow, and H. Becker, "Advertising Attitudes in Germany and the U.S.A.: An Analysis Over Age and Time," *Journal of International Business Studies*, Winter 1978, pp: 27–38.

27. R. D. Anderson and J. L. Engledow, "A Factor Analytic Comparison of U.S. and German Information Seekers," *Journal of Consumer Research*, Vol. 3, March 1977, pp: 185–96.

28. Mushtaq Luqmani, Z. A. Quraeshi, and L. Delene, "Marketing in Islamic Countries: A Viewpoint" *MSU Business Topics*, Vol. 28, No. 3, Summer 1980, pp: 17–28.

29. Erdener Kaynak and L. A. Mitchell, "A Study of Comparative Media Usage in Canada, the United Kingdom, and Turkey," *European Journal of Marketing*, Vol. 15, No. 1, 1980, pp: 1–9.

30. Jean J. Boddewyn, "Comparative Marketing: The First Twenty-Five Years," *Journal of International Business Studies*, Vol. 12, No. 1, Spring-Summer, 1981, pp: 61–79.

parameters and variables? What is to be done with the findings? In sum, contributors to this part review the field of comparative marketing in terms of scope, types, and depth of study, methodological issues, conceptual and managerial pay-offs, and teaching approaches. After nearly three decades as an international business topic, comparative marketing is still considered relatively new.

2

TOWARD A CONCEPTUAL FRAMEWORK FOR COMPARATIVE MARKETING

Hiram C. Barksdale and L. McTier Anderson

Comparative Marketing as a Field of Study

The emergence of comparative marketing as a separate subject is generally traced back to the 1950s when the American Marketing Association appointed a committee to formulate a study program.[1] However, there were some publications, prior to that period, which document earlier interest in the subject area.[2]

A brief review of the literature published over the past 25 years reveals the progress that has been achieved and, at the same time, indicates the problems and difficulties that represent major obstacles to further conceptualization and development in the field. The existing body of literature concentrates on six distinct topics. They are: a) development of comparative marketing; b) marketing institutions and activities; c) environmental conditions; d) consumer behavior; e) methodological considerations; and f) conceptual frameworks for comparative marketing.

Space does not permit an exhaustive review of the literature.[3] However, highlights of the work published in each of the first five areas will be outlined. The sixth area, conceptual frameworks for comparative marketing—the topic of primary interest in this paper—is discussed in greater depth.

Development of Comparative Marketing

There are a number of excellent survey papers that discuss the development of comparative marketing as an area of inquiry. These papers provide an overview of the field and describe many of the problems encountered in comparative marketing studies.

The first papers, and still among the most important, are those by Bartels,[4] Shapiro,[5] and Cox.[6] Bartels played a pioneering role in defining comparative marketing by explaining its importance. He mainly emphasized the environmental context of marketing, and perhaps more than anyone else, deserves credit for developing the structure and setting the directions that comparative marketing has taken.

Shapiro focused on the relationship between marketing and economic development. He examined the possibility of classifying marketing systems of countries by stage of development and emphasized the need for a framework for comparative marketing analysis. Shapiro further argued that these are basic problems that have to be resolved before comparative marketing can make important advances.

Cox believed that the greatest weakness in comparative marketing was the shortcomings of the concepts used. In comparing marketing systems, Cox stated that researchers should search for universals, generalizations about marketing that can be applied to every society. In the absence of true universals, or as complements to them, Cox recommended that researchers should seek "limited generalizations" which come as close as possible to universals and which can provide a basis for classifying societies according to their marketing systems.

In 1969, Boddewyn reviewed the concept and methodology of comparative marketing and concluded that very few comparative studies had been published.[7] Boddewyn also emphasized the need for classification systems, conceptual frameworks and measurement methods if the similarities and differences among marketing systems are to be explained. In a more recent paper, Boddewyn assessed developments in comparative marketing during its first 25 years. In this formative period, comparative marketing has not stimulated much interest in academic circles, and the subject has never been in the mainstream of marketing thought. Various dimensions of the subject have been probed, but theoretical and practical problems continue to plague the field. The debate continues on the content and structure of comparative marketing. Basic methodological questions have not been resolved and priorities for research have been difficult to establish. The difficulty of financing comparative research continues to be a major obstacle. After reviewing the first quarter of a century of comparative marketing, Boddewyn reported some advances—but no major breakthroughs.[8]

Marketing Institutions and Activities

The first comparative studies focused on marketing institutions and activities and discussed the similarities and differences from one country to another. Hall, Knapp, and Winsten examined the structure of distribution in Great Britain, Canada, and the U.S.A.[9] Using census data for the three nations, they compared sales-productivity in retailing and wholesaling. Jefferys and Knee analyzed retailing in 18 countries in Western Europe and speculated about future developments.[10] Hollander explored the problems of multinational retail organizations and discussed the contributions that these firms make in the countries where they operate.[11] A study edited by Bartels described wholesaling in 15 countries.[12] Recently, Samli outlined the marketing system of seven eastern European countries.[13]

In addition to these general studies on comparative marketing, there are several publications that describe marketing institutions and activities in a single nation.[14] Although these are not comparative studies, collectively they provide considerable insight into the marketing institutions and activities of different countries of the world.

Environmental Conditions

Numerous writers have discussed the connections between environmental conditions and marketing processes. Many of these discussions concentrate on the contributions of marketing to economic growth and development. In a classic article, Drucker asserted that marketing plays a critical role in economic growth.[15] According to Drucker, marketing makes possible economic integration and full utilization of the productive capacity that developing nations possess. McCarthy contented that effective marketing institutions were needed to progress from one stage of economic development to the next.[16] He further argued that marketing institutions were not only necessary, but also sufficient, for economic development.

A collection of essays edited by Moyer and Hollander suggests that the connections between marketing and economic development are more complex and controversial than some writers envision.[17] These authors express different opinions about the influence of marketing on economic growth. Although there is consensus that marketing is an important component in economic growth and that it is not given sufficient attention in economic development plans, they do not agree that marketing is a prerequisite or leading factor for economic development.[18]

Empirical research on the connections between marketing and economic development has produced mixed results. For example, Wadinambiarachi found that marketing institutions and channel structures of a country reflect social and economic conditions within the nation.[19] Using secondary data to estimate social, cultural, and economic conditions in eight countries, Wadinambiarachi found "regular" patterns of distribution that were more or less unique for different levels of economic development. Cundiff has reported that the adoption of innovations in 19 nations was directly related to stage of economic development.[20] Also, Arndt studied retailing in 16 countries, relatively homogeneous in terms of sociopolitical characteristics, and found support for the notion that the structure of retailing is a function of selected environmental factors.[21]

The Marketing Science Institute examined a large number of environmental variables and classified countries according to selected environmental characteristics.[22] Using the data from this study, Douglas tested the hypothesis that the marketing system of a nation is closely related to its level of development.[23] Based on this analysis, Douglas found little support for the proposition that marketing parallels the social, economic, and technological characteristics of a country.

Sethi has demonstrated the use of cluster analysis to classify world markets.[24] After analyzing 91 countries, using 29 variables, Sethi reported that the countries could be classified—but not on a single dimension of development. Furthermore, Sethi's analysis did not reveal a well-defined continuum of economic development.

Another stream of research that should be mentioned is the pioneering work of Slater and his associates.[25] They developed a general model of demand-driven, market systems which was then used as a framework for studying the impact of different market strategies on the economy of several developing countries. Slater's work is important because of the approach that it takes and the methodological directions that it suggests.

Buyer Behavior

Studies of this type concentrate on the similarities and differences in consumer attitudes and buying behavior. Goldman analyzed spending patterns of American and Soviet consumers.[26] He attributed the similarities that he found to increases in Soviet wages and to changes in the volume of consumer goods produced in Russia. Goldman predicted that a continued rise in Soviet incomes would lead to greater similarity between Soviet and U.S. consumers.

Sommers and Kernan emphasized the influence of cultural values on buying behavior.[27] According to Sommers and Kernan, the cultural values of a nation can be used to predict product success and offers clues to marketing strategy. Douglas and Dubois also examined the connection between consumer behavior and cultural variables.[28] Using examples, they illustrate the pervasive influence of culture on purchase behavior and marketing strategy.

Green and Langeard studied consumer habits and characteristics of innovators in France and the United States.[29] They attributed differences between French and American consumers to the social and environmental factors that characterize the two nations. In the same view, Cosmas and Sheth used multidimensional analysis—in an exploratory study—to examine perceptions of opinion leaders in five cultural groups.[30]

Wind and Douglas have discussed the importance of international market segmentation and reviewed some of the problems encountered in segmenting international markets.[31] Linton and Broadbent illustrated how life-style research can be used to identify target markets in different countries and develop advertising and marketing strategy.[32]

After studying the buying behavior of working and non-working women in France and the United States, Douglas reported that the cross-national differences were, on the surface, greater than the within country differences.[33] Urban analyzed mass media exposure in the same two countries.[34] She found similar patterns of media exposure and concluded that there were underlying consistencies in advertising media usage in France and the United States.

Sheth and Sethi have outlined a tentative theory of cross-national buyer behavior.[35] By integrating concepts from anthropology and diffusion theory, they developed a general explanation of buying behavior.

Methodological Considerations

Comparative studies across different nations present many problems not encountered in research projects confined to a single country. Yet, marketing scholars have devoted relatively little attention to the methodological issues involved in comparative research.

The most fundamental consideration in comparative research is the isolation of true differences in the phenomena being studied from variations caused by differences in research methods. Green and White identified equivalence as the basic methodological issue in cross-national research.[36] They discuss the questions of functional and conceptual equivalence and explain the use of emic (culturally specific) and etic (culturally universal) approaches to comparative research. They also describe the problems of translation and sample design.

Wind and Douglas have emphasized the importance of methodology in comparative marketing.[37] They point out that comparative studies require specific research designs, just as any other marketing research project, and propose a six-stage procedure for cross-national studies. The first stage is to set objectives for the comparison. The next step is to determine the scope of the analysis by identifying the categories of marketing systems to be studied. The third stage is identification of the components and properties of the marketing systems that will be analyzed. The fourth task is to develop appropriate transformation rules and functionally equivalent measures of the properties to be compared. The fifth step is to develop propositions, specify the comparisons to be made. The sixth phase is to design the research project. As an extension to this, Lamb discusses the methodology of comparative marketing studies.[38]

In general, scholars in other disciplines have been more concerned, than marketing researchers, with the methodological problems of cross-national studies. As a result, there is a large number of publications discussing the unique problems of comparative research in specific disciplines. Anyone interested in comparative marketing would probably find the specific publications of psychology anthropology and sociology as useful introductions to the methodological issues in cross-national research.[39]

Conceptual Frameworks

Bartels developed the first formal set of guidelines for comparative marketing.[40] He viewed marketing as a social process and argued that heterogeneity of environmental conditions was the key element in comparative marketing. Based on this proposition, he developed a detailed list of environmental factors that should be included in comparative studies. Essentially, Bartels thought that environmental conditions of a nation determined its marketing system. Furthermore, his analytical framework assumes that detailed analysis of environmental conditions would lead to explanations of the environmental-marketing relationship. Comparative marketing would focus on these relationships and explain the similarities and differences from one country to another.[41]

Boddewyn thought that Bartels overemphasized environmental conditions.[42] According to Boddewyn, even though it is correct to say that marketing systems are influenced by their environments, it does not follow that comparisons of marketing systems require detailed analyses of their environments. Boddewyn contended that comparative studies should focus on aspects of marketing systems other than their environments. Therefore, he identified five dimensions of marketing—function, structure, process, actors, and environment—and argued that comparative studies could center on any of these dimensions, or contrast the relations among them, or compare changes in these elements and their relationships through time.

Fisk recommended a general systems approach to comparative marketing.[43] According to Fisk, comparative marketing should focus on the goals, organization, productivity, and the major constraints placed on marketing by different political-economic forms of organization. Fisk saw government as the institution with the greatest impact on marketing, in both developed and developing countries, and thought that the purpose of comparative marketing should be to guide public as well as private decision makers. Fisk believed that the systems framework would accommodate the analyses using different bases of comparison. He identified two bases for comparing marketing systems: "stage of development" and "political-economic organization." Regarding the stage of development, Fisk stated that comparisons of productivity were meaningful only for countries at roughly the same level of development, but he did not think that this restriction was necessary for comparing marketing goals. Regarding political-economic organization, Fisk emphasized the differences between centrally planned and market-directed systems.

A flow approach to comparative marketing was first mentioned by Cox in 1965, but he did not explain how it could be applied. Jaffe, after studying marketing in Israel, proposed the flow approach as a framework for comparative marketing.[44] Jaffe developed a systems model of marketing consisting of the following six parameters: inputs, process, outputs, goals, constraints, and feedback. Using this model, Jaffe stated that the primary focus of comparative research should be the marketing process and the relevant marketing flows—ownership, physical possession, communication, financing, and risking taking. Jaffe termed these flows "invariant points of reference, essential parts of all distribution channels and all marketing systems."

A brief review of the literature leads to one major conclusion. Comparative marketing is not a well-developed field of study at present. There are important differences of opinion about the boundaries of comparative marketing and even less agreement about the conceptual structure of the subject. Barnes concluded, recently, that the literature of comparative marketing was "remarkably empty."[45] Perhaps this assessment is too severe, but a review of the literature suggests that we have looked at a lot of trees without developing a clear vision of the forest. Without a generally accepted framework or paradigm to guide research, the facts generated have vague reference points and limited meaning.

A Framework for Comparative Marketing

Efforts to develop marketing as a separate field of study started early in the twentieth century in the United States. As a result, the basic concepts of marketing were developed primarily within the framework of capitalism—assuming private property and self-regulating markets.

When the study of comparative marketing began in the late 1950s, it was recognized from the outset that marketing concepts developed in the United States could not be applied to other nations without some modification.[46] It was also argued that environmental conditions played a dominant role in shaping the marketing system of a nation.[47] Following this line of thought, it was assumed that differences in environmental conditions provide the key to understanding the differences in marketing systems. These propositions have set the directions and determined the priorities for research in comparative marketing over the past 25 years.

The pioneers who first stimulated interest in the field thought that comparative studies of marketing systems would make important contributions to our knowledge of marketing.[48] However, the research that has been published during the ensuing years has not produced significant breakthroughs. Among those who have reviewed this literature, there is a consensus that the published research does not add up to very much.[49] Among the reasons for the slow progress are these: 1) the environmental approach overemphasized environmental conditions and underemphasizes the marketing process; 2) limited funds have restricted the scope of research efforts and many research projects have been modest in design and execution; 3) much of the research has been determined by travel plans and convenience rather than the intellectual and conceptual requirements of the field; and 4) comparative marketing has never been in the mainstream of marketing thought. Regardless of the reasons, the current body of knowledge does not reflect a logical progression and the research findings are not additive. The country-by-country comparisons that have been reported present a quagmire for anyone who tries to take stock of the field and attempts to synthesize the accumulated knowledge.

The major thrust in every discipline is to explain the phenomena that comprise its subject matter. If comparative marketing is to make significant progress toward this goal, more attention must be devoted to theory and model building and hypotheses testing. Drawing upon the experience of other, more advanced disciplines, certain priorities must be set to make the effort allocated to this task more productive. Among these priorities, none is more important than the adoption of a paradigm that will structure the subject and focus research on topics that will contribute to the conceptual development of the field.

The framework suggested here provides a basic classification scheme that can be used to partition marketing systems into more or less homogeneous groups. This framework is considered complementary, rather than competitive, with existing concepts. It is not intended as a replacement for other models. Rather, it should be viewed as a conceptual scheme that establishes a framework for comparing marketing systems.

Classification of Marketing Systems

Classification is a fundamental activity in the development of disciplines. The most important function of any classification system is to establish groupings about which generalizations can be made. The ability to group objects, events, or things into relatively homogeneous categories plays a vital role in developing generalizations and explanations in all fields of study. In some instances, the creation of a powerful, new classification system has been the basis for major conceptual advancement within a discipline. For example, invention of the periodic table revolutionized the field of chemistry; and acceptance of the four P's as a classification of marketing activities transformed the composition of marketing.

The value of any classification system is dependent upon the connection between the explanatory objectives and the classification variables. In other words, if a classification system is to be informative and useful, it must be based upon some proposition that establishes the connection between the classification variables and the explanatory objectives.[50]

The classification system proposed here is based upon the observation that every society has a conglomeration of people that require an assortment of goods and services and a group of organizations that produce and supply the products that the people consume. Furthermore, in each country—at any given time—there is a particular pattern of ownership between the organizations that supply the goods and services and a characteristic set of procedures for making production/marketing decisions.

In economics, political science, and comparative marketing, countries are traditionally classified along a continuum—ranging from those that rely on self-regulating markets at one end to those that use central planning on the other. Nations that contain elements of both are placed somewhere between the extremes. Historically it has been the practice to associate market direction of production and distribution with private ownership, while government direction is coupled with public ownership of production/marketing facilities.

If these two variables—ownership of production/marketing facilities and managerial decision procedures—are uncoupled, they can be treated as separate variables. Then using the two basic systems of ownership—public and private—and the two fundamental approaches to production/marketing decisions—self-regulating markets and government direction—it is possible to construct a 2×2 matrix and group countries of the world according to these basic characteristics (Figure 2.1) This classification system is based on the hypothesis that the basic variables—ownership of production/distribution facilities and managerial decision procedures—determine the organization and operation of all marketing systems. The four cells of the matrix represent

FIGURE 2.1
Two-Dimensional Classification of Production—Marketing Systems

	Capitalism	Market Socialism
Market Directed		
	(United States)	(Yugoslavia)
Decision Procedure	Administered Capitalism	Communism
Government Directed	(Japan)	(Soviet Union)
	Private	Public

Ownership

production/marketing systems with different operating philosophies and different configurations of constraints on managerial decisions. Here is a brief description of each category in the matrix:

Capitalism—Private Ownership and Market Direction.

Organizations that produce and supply products are privately owned and production/marketing decisions are based on the preferences buyers express in the market. The role of government is regulatory and, in theory, is limited to maintaining competition among individual organizations and protecting the welfare of consumers. Under this system, market choices feed directly into managerial decisions. To be successful, individual organizations must be responsive to market demand and sensitive to changing requirements. The system encourages the production and distribution of any product that people are willing and able to buy at prices that make production profitable.

Communism—Public Ownership and Government Direction.

Resources, production facilities, and distributive organizations are owned by the public and the production and distribution of goods and services is centrally planned. The government plays a predominant role in social and economic affairs. Under this system, the choices that consumers make do not feed directly into the production/distribution decisions of individual enterprises. Rather, production and distribution are controlled by government planning agencies and products are produced only if the administrative authority decides that they should be manufactured. The planning agencies set the goals for industrial development, allocate resources, and make production/distribution decisions according to some general concept of social needs. In other words, government planners—rather than market demand—determine the kinds and quantities of goods produced and fix the structure of relative prices.

Market Socialism—Public Ownership and Market Direction.

Production and distribution facilities and all resources are owned by the state. However, state-owned enterprises compete for sales and production/ marketing decisions are based on preferences expressed in the market. Market socialism creates a balance between state authority, which specifies national goals, and decentralized decision making based on market demand. Within established guidelines, individual enterprises are free to choose the markets they will serve and decide the quantity, quality, and price of the products produced.

Administered Capitalism—Private Ownership and Government Direction.

The government, in consultation with private business firms and labor, develops indicative plans that provide guidance and incentives for industrial development. There is no formal, centralized plan that provides specific instructions to individual organizations, rather, there are general plans intended to guide private enterprise towards long-term goals. Specific decisions about what to produce are based on consumer preferences, but the government takes an active role in setting goals and in this way exerts some influence on production/distribution decisions.

Drucker[51], Shapiro[52], and others have emphasized the relationship between marketing and economic development. Recognizing this relationship, the matrix may be extended by adding "stage of development" as a third dimension (Figure 2.2.). This addition transforms the traditional one-dimensional classification into a three-dimension scheme. In theory, the proposed classification system should yield well-defined sets or categories. As a practical matter, however, the classifications are fuzzy. All nations of the world have a mixture of characteristics. None is pure in the sense that all

FIGURE 2.2

Three-Dimensional Classification of Production—Marketing Systems

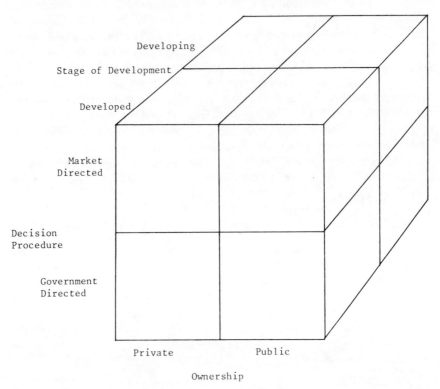

Ownership

segments of all industries have the same patterns of ownership and follow the same decision procedures. Thus, the classification of countries according to this plan must be based on a majority rule. In other words, the categories represent the dominant form of organization within each country and category membership is not precise or clear cut. If this point is not recognized, it is possible to overlook the diversity that exists in every nation.

The proposed classification scheme identifies alternative ways of organizing the production/marketing system of a country. The organizational alternative followed by a nation not only determines the structure of marketing, it also defines the managerial context of marketing operations and suggests the procedures for planning and controlling marketing activities. In this sense, the organizational alternative that a nation adopts has profound consequences for marketing because it determines the basic organization and operating characteristics of the country's marketing system. Using the proposed classification scheme, all marketing systems of the world can be placed into a small number of categories. This should make comparative analysis in marketing more manageable than the traditional country-by-country comparisons.

Suggestions for Future Research

The next question concerns the directions that comparative marketing research should take in the future. This question focuses attention on the areas of study that are likely to be most productive and the characteristics or properties of marketing that must be clarified if comparative marketing is to become an important field of inquiry.

Although any component or characteristic of marketing can be the subject of comparative analysis, the areas of research that are likely to be most productive are shown in Figure 2.3. They are:

1) Philosophy-Management—The philosophy of marketing and the managerial processes that direct and control marketing systems.

FIGURE 2.3
Framework for Comparative Marketing

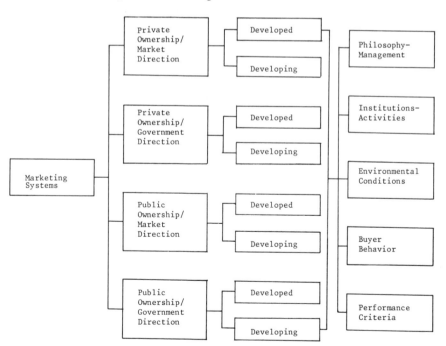

2) Institutions-Activities—The institutions involved in marketing and the activities that they perform.

3) Environmental Conditions—Environmental conditions and the relations and interactions between the environment and marketing operations.

4) Buyer Behavior—Patterns of behavior and the impact of marketing operations on purchase decisions.

5) Performance Criteria—Standards for measuring the performance of marketing and evaluating its contribution to society.

Most of the published research in the field of comparative marketing deals with institutions and activities, environmental conditions, and consumer behavior. Much of this work is based on limited comparisions of some "other" country with the United States. In addition, there is wide variance in the findings. Factors found to be important in one study are reported to be less important—and sometimes not important at all—in other studies. In spite of considerable effort by some competent people, the existing body of research is a hodgepodge of exploratory studies that provides some interesting insights but does not make any significant contribution to the conceptualization of comparative marketing. The main challenge in each of these areas is to move beyond demonstration projects and concentrate future effort on generating and testing hypotheses that have theoretical significance.

The main thrust of these suggestions is the recommendation that comparative marketing shift its focus from the environment–centered approach that has dominated the field from its beginning to a marketing-systems, managerially oriented approach. Attention would then be directed toward explaining how marketing operates and adapts to environmental conditions. In other words, by changing focus we can stop comparing environmental conditions and start comparing marketing systems.

Conclusions

There is perhaps no enterprise in the modern world on which so much energy and effort is expended and about which so little is known as marketing. Comparative marketing is an area that offers great potential for expanding our knowledge. Comparative studies, properly focused, should lead to better explanations of the philosophy, organizational processes, and performance of marketing systems.

Progress in developing a coherent body of knowledge in comparative marketing will be slow and halting until an acceptable paradigm or conceptual framework is developed to guide research and substantial advances are made in developing and testing hypotheses. Until this turning point is reached, comparative marketing will continue to flounder in a trickling stream of disjunctive research and discrete facts.

Notes

1. Robert Bartels, ed., *Comparative Marketing: Wholesaling in Fifteen Countries* (Homewood: Richard D. Irwin), 1963.

2. Malcolm P. McNair, Stanley F. Teele, and Frances G. Mulhearn, *Distribution Costs—An International Digest*, Boston: Harvard Business School, 1941.

3. David Carson, *International Marketing: A Comparative Systems Approach* (New York: John Wiley & Sons, 1967) and David Carson, "Present State of the Art of Comparative Marketing," in *Increasing Marketing Productivity*, Thomas V. Greer, ed., Chicago: American Marketing Association, Proceedings, 1974.

4. Robert Bartels, "Comparative Marketing".

5. Stanley J. Shapiro, "Comparative Marketing and Economic Development," in *Science in Marketing*, George Schwartz, ed., (New York: John Wiley and Sons, 1965), pp: 398–429.

6. Reavis Cox, "The Search for Universals in Comparative Studies of Domestic Marketing Systems," in *Marketing and Economic Development*, P. D. Bennett, ed., (Chicago: American Marketing Association, Proceedings, 1965).

7. Jean J. Boddewyn, *Comparative Management and Marketing* (Glenview: Scott, Foresman and Company), 1969.

8. For an exclusive review of the literature see: Jean J. Boddewyn, "Comparative Marketing: The First Twenty-Five Years," *Journal of International Business Studies*, 12, Spring/Summer 1981, pp: 61–79.

9. Margaret Hall, John Knapp, and Christopher Winsten, *Distribution in Great Britain and North America* (London: Oxford University Press, 1961).

10. James B. Jefferys and Derek Knee, *Retailing in Europe: Present Structure and Future Trends* (London: Macmillan, 1962).

11. Stanley C. Hollander, *Multinational Retailing*, East Lansing, Michigan State University, Institute for International Business and Economic Studies, 1970.

12. Robert Bartels, ed., "Comparative Marketing: Wholesaling".

13. A. Coskun Samli, *Marketing and Distribution Systems in Eastern Europe* (New York: Praeger, 1978).

14. Marshall I. Goldman, *Soviet Marketing: Distribution in a Controlled Economy* (New York: Free Press, 1963); Thomas V. Greer, *Marketing in the Soviet Union* (New York: Praeger, 1973); Mitsauki Shimaguchi and Willilam Lazer, "Japanese Distribution Channels: Invisible Barriers to Market Entry," *MSU Business Topics*, 27, Winter, 1979, pp: 49–62; and M. Y. Yoshino, *The Japanese Marketing System: Adaptations and Innovations* (Cambridge: MIT Press, 1971).

15. Peter F. Drucker, "Marketing and Economic Development," *Journal of Marketing*, 5, February 1958, pp: 29–33.

16. E. Jerome McCarthy, "Effective Marketing Institutions for Economic Development," in *Toward Scientific Marketing*, Stephen A. Greyser, ed., (Chicago: American Marketing Association, Proceedings, 1963).

17. Reed Moyer and Stanley C. Hollander, *Markets and Marketing in Developing Economies* (Homewood: Richard D. Irwin, 1968).

18. Marye Tharp Hilger, "Theories of the Relationship Between Marketing and Economic Development: Public Policy Implications," in *Macro-Marketing Distributive Processes from a Societal Perspective*, Charles C. Slater, ed., (Boulder: Business Research Division, University of Colorado, 1978) and Edward W. Cundiff and Marye T. Hilger, "Marketing and the Production-Consumption Thesis in Economic Development," in *Macromarketing: Evolution of Thought*, George Fisk, Robert Nason, and Phillip D. White, eds., (Boulder: Business Research Division, University of Colorado, 1980); and A. A. El-Sherbini, "Behavioral Adjustments as Marketing Constraints on Economic Development," in *Macromarketing:*

Evolution of Thought, George Fisk, Robert Nason, and Phillip D. White, eds., Boulder: Business Research Division, University of Colorado, 1980.

19. George Wadinambiarachi,"Channels of Distribution in Developing Economies," *Business Quarterly*, 30, Winter 1965, pp: 74–82.

20. Edward W. Cundiff, "Concepts in Comparative Retailing," *Journal of Marketing*, 29, January 1965, pp: 59–63.

21. Johan Arndt, "Temporal Lags in Comparative Retailing," *Journal of Marketing*, 36, October 1972, pp: 40–45.

22. Bertil Liander, ed., *Comparative Analysis for International Marketing*, Boston: Allyn and Bacon, 1967.

23. Susan P. Douglas, "Patterns and Parallels of Marketing Structures in Several Countries," *MSU Business Topics*, 19, Spring 1971, pp: 38–48.

24. S. Prakash Sethi, "Comparative Cluster Analysis for World Markets," *Journal of Marketing Research*, 8, August 1971, pp: 348–54.

25. Charles C. Slater, "A Theory of Market Processes," in *Macro-Marketing: Distributive Processes from a Societal Perspective*, Charles C. Slater, ed., (Boulder: Business Research Division, University of Colorado, 1977) and Charles C. Slater, "Toward an Operational Theory of Market Process," in *Macro Marketing: Distributive Processes from a Societal Perspective: An Elaboration of the Issues*, Philip D. White and Charles C. Slater, eds., (Boulder: Business Research Division, University of Colorado, 1978).

26. Marshall I. Goldman, "A Cross-Cultural Comparison of the Soviet and American Consumer," in *Changing Marketing Systems*, Reed Moyer, ed., (Chicago: American Marketing Association, pp: 195–99, 1967).

27. Montrose Summers and Jerome Kernan, "Why Products Flourish Here, Fizzle There," *Columbia Journal of World Business*, 11, March–April 1967, pp: 89–97.

28. Susan P. Douglas and Bernard Dubois, "Looking at the Cultural Environment for International Marketing Opportunities," *Columbia Journal of World Business*, 12, Winter 1977, pp: 102–109.

29. Robert T. Green and Eric Langeard, "A Cross-National Comparison of Consumer Habits and Innovator Characteristics," *Journal of Marketing*, 39, July 1975, pp: 34–41.

30. Stephen C. Cosmas and Jagdish N. Sheth, "Identification of Opinion Leaders Across Cultures: An Assessment for Use in the Diffusion of Innovations and Ideas," *Journal of International Business Studies*, 11, Spring/Summer 1980, pp: 66–73.

31. Yoram Wind and Susan P. Douglas, "International Market Segmentation," *European Journal of Marketing*, 6:1, 1972, pp: 17–25; Yoram Wind and Susan P. Douglas, "Some Issues in International Consumer Research," *European Journal of Marketing*, 8:3, 1974, pp: 209–217; Yorman Wind and Susan P. Douglas, "Comparative Methodology and Marketing Theory," in *Theoretical Developments in Marketing*; and Charles W. Lamb, Jr. and Patrick M. Dunne, eds., (Chicago: American Marketing Association, Proceedings, 1980).

32. Anna Linton and Simon Broadbent, "International Life-style Comparisons," *European Research*, 3, March 1975, pp: 51–55 and p: 84.

33. Susan P. Douglas, "Cross-National Comparisons and Consumer Stereotypes: A Case Study of Working and Non-Working Wives in the U.S. and France," *Journal of Consumer Research*, 3, June 1976, pp: 12–20.

34. Christine D. Urban, "A Cross-National Comparison of Consumer Media Use Patterns," *Columbia Journal of World Business*, 12, Winter 1977, pp: 54–63.

35. Jagdish N. Sheth and S. Prakash Sethi, "A Theory of Cross-Cultural Buyer Behavior," in *Consumer and Industrial Buying Behavior*, Arch G. Woodside, Jagdish N. Sheth, and Peter D. Bennett, eds., New York: North Holland, 1977, pp: 369–86.

36. Robert T. Green and Phillip D. White, "Methodological Consumer Reseach," *Journal of International Business Studies*, 7, Winter 1976, pp: 81–87.

37. Yoram Wind and Susan P. Douglas, "On the Meaning of Comparison: A Methodology

for Cross-Cultural Studies," *Quarterly Journal of Management Development*, 1, July 1971, pp: 106–21.

38. Charles W. Lamb, "Domestic Applications of Comparative Marketing Analysis," *European Journal of Marketing*, 9:2, 1975, pp: 167–72.

39. Richard W. Brislin, Walter J. Lonner, and Robert M. Thorndike, *Cross-Cultural Research methods*, New York: John Wiley & Sons, 1973; Robert Holt and John E. Turner, eds., *The Methodology of Comparative Research* (New York: Press Press, 1970); and Bert Kaplan, ed., *Studying Personality Cross-Culturally* (New York: Harper and Row).

40. Robert Bartels, "A Methodological Framework for Comparative Marketing Study," in *Toward Scientific Marketing*, Stephen A. Greyser, ed., (Chicago: American Marketing Association, 1964), pp: 383–90.

41. Robert Bartels, "Are Domestic and International Marketing Dissimilar?" *Journal of Marketing Research*, 3, May 1966, pp: 149–53.

42. Jean J. Boddewyn, *Comparative Management and Marketing* (Glenview: Scott, Foresman and Company, 1969).

43. George Fisk, *Marketing Systems: An Introductory Analysis* (New York: Harper & Row, 1967).

44. Eugene D. Jaffe, "Comparative Marketing Revisited," *Marquette Business Review*, 20, Winter 1976, pp: 143–53.

45. W. N. Barnes, "International Marketing Indicators," *European Journal of Marketing*, 14:2, 1980, pp: 90–136.

46. Robert Bartels, "Comparative Marketing: Wholesaling."

47. Robert Bartels, "A Methodological Framework," pp: 383–90; David Carson, "International Marketing"; and George Fisk, "Marketing Systems."

48. Eugene D. Jaffe, "Are Domestic and International Marketing Dissimilar?" *Management International Review*, 20:3, 1980, pp: 83–86; and Robert Bartels, "Are Domestic and International."

49. Hiram C. Barksdale and L. McTier Anderson, "Comparative Marketing: A Review of the Literature," *Journal of Macromarketing*, 2, Spring 1982, pp: 57–62; W. N. Barnes, "International Marketing," pp: 90–136; and Jean J. Boddewyn, "Comparative Marketing," pp: 61–79.

50. Carl G. Hempel, *Aspects of Scientific Explanation* (New York: Free Press, 1965).

51. Peter F. Drucker, "Marketing and Economic", pp: 29–33.

52. Stanley J. Shapiro, "Comparative Marketing," pp: 398–429.

3

COMPARATIVE MARKETING SYSTEMS ANALYSIS: REVISITED

Adel I. El-Ansary and Marilyn L. Liebrenz

The late 1950s and the 1960s were marked by increased interest in the comparative study of various domestic marketing systems.[1] However, the interest in comparative marketing declined significantly in the 1970s. Such a marked decline can be attributed, in part, to confusion about macro-marketing. There is a lack of agreement on several aspects. What constitutes comparative analysis? What are the parameters and variables? What is to be done with the findings?

Profiles of Comparative Marketing

This chapter attempts to develop a construct for comparative marketing. Emphasis is on the analytical aspects. The construct is comprehensive, integrating earlier efforts by leading scholars in comparative marketing. To ensure conceptual clarity, the construct is composed of three profiles, much as an object may be viewed in three dimensions. The focus throughout the discussion will be on applications of comparative analysis in multinational marketing management.

Profile I: A General Construct for Comparative Marketing

Comparative marketing is a term that is sometimes used so generally that its particular meaning is obscured. Comparative marketing, as illustrated in Figure 3.1, is based upon a number of propositions stemming from the process of comparison. Profile I integrates these propositions by illustrating the flows that occur between different markets (countries, regions, or other delineated areas) as well as the flows which take place *within* each market. Assessment of the output resulting from each market provides an indication of similarities and/or differences. Analysis of these results provides information for future marketing efforts, because this construct is designed as a comparison of markets. The propositions underlying Figure 3.1 include the following:

FIGURE 3.1

A General Construct for Comparative Marketing

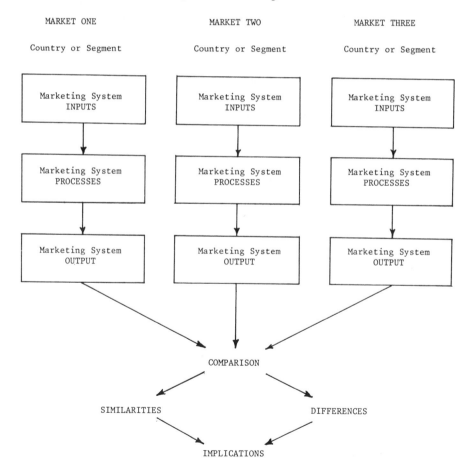

1. The focus of comparative marketing is the analytical comparison of marketing system *inputs*, *processes*, and *outputs* in different countries in a systematic manner.

2. When countries are subjected to comparative analysis, the focus should be on *markets* and *segments* in each country, not on the country as a whole. Multinational marketing by multinational corporations, increased communications and the emergence of international consumer segments have resulted in the emergence of cosmopolitan markets with similar structures and behavior across countries. Indeed, many marketing institutions and practices in the cosmopolitan, urban, capital city markets of different countries are similar, despite great differences along many other dimensions.

3. It is not sufficient for comparative analysis to help in the detection of similarities and differences between the domestic marketing system subject to this analysis. It is also necessary to determine *why* these systems are similar or different.

4. It is important to explore the results of comparative analysis upon marketing theory development and marketing practice. For example, comparative studies using cluster analysis might help identify variables or dimensions relevant to the planning, implementation, and control of marketing programs. Therefore, a multinational corporation operating in sixty different countries would not need to develop sixty different marketing plans or programs if comparative analysis revealed that the sixty countries clustered into eight groups.

Specific examples of the benefits of comparative marketing are numerous.[2] One company studied by Liander attempted to measure marketing performance among its key European operations.[3] The objective was to determine the relative sales performance of each affiliate by measuring the degree to which each had penetrated the potential market. The project was assigned to a member of the marketing staff and was confined to three major product lines. A comparative study greatly facilitated the analysis. The investigator estimated the potential market for the selected product among eight key countries by calculating a composite weighted index of seven factors which were found to be highly correlated with the demand for the product. These eight countries were then ranked in terms of the potential market as measured by a weighted index. The countries were also ranked on the basis of actual sales. The rankings of both potential and actual sales were compared to identify the areas of discrepancy. The company executive emphasized that this approach was far from conclusive in measuring relative performance of each unit, but provided a useful starting point. To complement the analysis, another senior marketing staff member undertook a thorough review of marketing operations and competitive conditions in each of the key countries. The investigation provided useful qualitative information to interpret the result of the quantitative analysis.

Profile II: A Technical Construct for the Comparative Analysis of Marketing Systems

Profile I prescribed a systems analysis approach to the comparative analysis of marketing systems, using an input-processing-output paradigm. Profile II spells out the components of the marketing system subject to analysis as shown in Figure 3.2. All the classic frameworks spell out the marketing system variables that should be examined. It is equally important to systematically develop the relationships *between* these variables of the system. The systems analysis view presented here examines the components of the construct using the same three major categories as before: the marketing system's inputs, processes, and outputs.

Marketing System Inputs

Marketing system inputs encompass a lengthy list of variables. Individual scholars differ on how to categorize these variables, but the following assortment is felt to be the most realistic and comprehensive:

1. The actors:[4] profile of consumers (population characteristics) and profile of decision makers (executives in private and public sectors).
2. The resources:[5]
   GNP and its distribution,
   Technology,
   Stock of capital goods.
3. Environmental conditions:[6]
   Geography and typography,
   Urbanization,
   Ethnographic diversity,
   Racial homogeneity and identification,
   Religious homogeneity and identification,
   Linguistic homogeneity,
   Political stability.
4. Executive Behavior:
   a. Decision making in the government and the public sector,
   Imposition of price controls,
   Price subsidies,
   Control of promotion practices,
   Consumer protection laws,
   Environmental protection laws.
   b. Decision making in the private sector,
   R & D expenditures,
   Promotional budgets,
   Physical distribution expenditures,
   Price discount structure.

FIGURE 3.2
A Technical Construct for Comparative Analysis of Marketing Systems

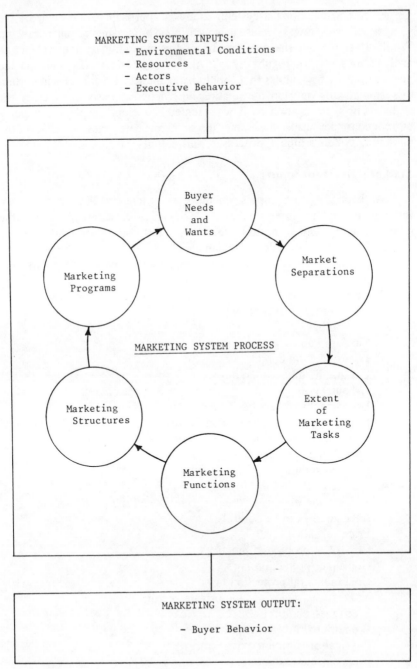

Marketing System Process

The characteristics of the actors, the resources of the system, the environmental conditions, and the executive behavior in the system all contribute to the formation of buyer needs and wants. Satisfaction of these wants and needs requires bridging gaps or separations that exist between producers and consumers. These gaps or separations are created by possession, time, space, information, and valuation. The extent of these gaps and separations determines the extent of the marketing tasks to be performed.

Marketing functions are performed to bridge market gaps and separations. Examples include buying and selling to bridge the possession gap; warehousing and risking to bridge the time gap; transportation to bridge the space gap; promotion to bridge the information gap; and pricing and credit to bridge the valuation gap.[7] Marketing institutions evolve as marketing functions are identified and performed. These institutions, in turn, develop marketing programs designed to bring about the desired exchanges, thus satisfying the needs and wants of consumers and other actors.

Marketing System Output

Buyer behavior, including both the final consumer and intermediary organizations, is viewed as a marketing system output. This "buyer behavior" output, however, is passed back to the marketing process and the input segments of the construct, forming feedback that completes the loop. Modifications in the system in both the short and long run may take place, depending on the system's sensitivity to this feedback and the degree of the attitude towards tradition of its actors. Should the system be relatively entrenched and static, little variation may occur. If, however, circumstances have changed to the point where the traditional is highly undesirable or virtually impossible to maintain, modifications will take place even in the most tradition-bound situations.

Comparative analysis is a taxing undertaking because of the large number of variables involved. When relationships among the variables are not adequately delineated, it becomes necessary to examine the entire marketing system in order to understand any of the parts thereof. The purpose of Profile II is to specify the relationship between the system variables in order to be able to isolate sectors of the system that are of interest to researchers. For example, one may be able to examine the hoarding of goods, an aspect of buyer behavior in developing countries, using Profile II. The phenomena may easily be related to:

1) Strong need by buyers along with feelings of insecurity to satisfy those needs because of chronic shortages of goods held, i.e., the buyer needs and wants variable in marketing process; 2) Inadequate inventory capacity in

the institutional structure, i.e., the marketing structure variable in the marketing process; 3) Limited foreign exchange allocated for importation, i.e., decision making by the government is a marketing system input; and 4) Inadequate subsidy budget for goods in question, i.e., the resource variable of the marketing system inputs.

Profile III: Generic Interactions Construct

Research and problem solving can become even easier if the interactions in the marketing system are viewed more generically.

This construct specifies the technical variables in terms of interactions between three generic sets of variables, i.e., the structural, decision, and manifest behavior variables as shown in Figure 3.3 and explained below.

1. *Structural variables*: consumer profile in a country, wholesale and retail structure, resources of the country, and environmental conditions.

2. *Decision variables*: marketing program decisions, consumer decisions to buy, and executive decisions in the public and private sectors.

3. *Manifest behavior variables*: total advertising expenditure, public policy regulating marketing decisions, consumer information dissemination, codes of marketing conduct by associations, availability of goods and number of brands in the market.

FIGURE 3.3
Generic Interactions in the Technical Construct

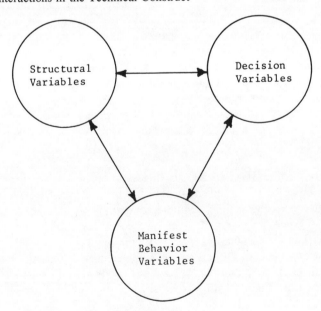

This paradigm was applied successfully in a comparative study of cigarette marketing in seven countries.[8] Figure 3.4 illustrates the structural, decision, and manifest behavior variables in the model developed for the study.

These three profiles have been used to depict comparative marketing in such a way as to make it clearer and more comprehensive than former models. Profile I might be viewed as the horizontal axis—the general construct for comparative marketing. Profile II might be taken as the vertical axis, looking at the variables which comprise the marketing system input, process, and output. It is important to mark the interaction between Profiles I and II, since all the selected markets are to be examined on the basis of all variables. Profile III encompasses another form of interaction, as it details the structural, decision, and manifest behavior variables. These variables provide a pictorial or graphic view of comparative marketing that is constantly shifting, changing, and evolving. It is the ultimate interaction between the three profiles that captures more of the total essence of comparative marketing than former studies or analyses. (See Figure 3.5).

It is insufficient, however, to stop at this point. Regardless of the comprehensive nature of any framework or model, application to the area of comparative marketing requires that the variable be identifiable and, in some instances, quantifiable. Thus, measurement becomes a crucial factor for the comparative marketing framework.

Measurement Issues

The three-dimensional framework offered on the preceding pages encompasses comparative marketing. Successful application of such a model, however, requires adequate measurement techniques. An assessment of comparative analyses within the multinational realm highlights aspects that would benefit from additional development.

Survey of Measurement Techniques

Measurement appears to come down to two issues: the selection of indicators to be examined, and the groupings that result when certain indicators are employed on a global or subglobal basis. Use of these two elements, in combination, has provided the bulk of the current information available to those involved with multinational marketing.

Selection of indicators may be relatively brief, such as the thirty item assortment identified by Sherbini in a preliminary study for the 1967 work.[9] Others may be lengthy, detailed, and specific, such as those listed by Bartels in his early work on wholesaling in fifteen countries.[10] Several authors and researchers have provided outlines for global analysis, usually on a country-by-country comparative basis.[11]

FIGURE 3.4

An Illustration of the Technical Construct: A Model of the Cigarette Marketing
System in the Third World

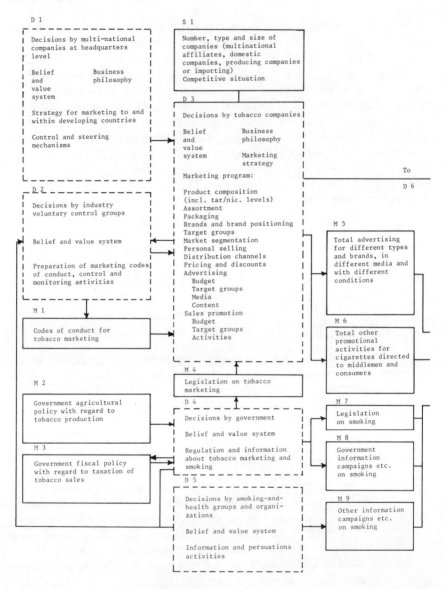

Source: Bo Wickstrom. Cigarette Marketing in the Third World: A Study of Four
Countries. Goteborg, Sweden: University of Gothenburg, Department of Business Administration, 1979, pp. 22–23

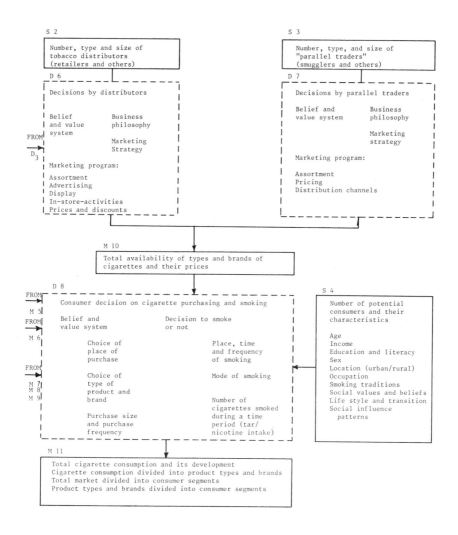

FIGURE 3.5
Interaction among Profiles I, II, and III

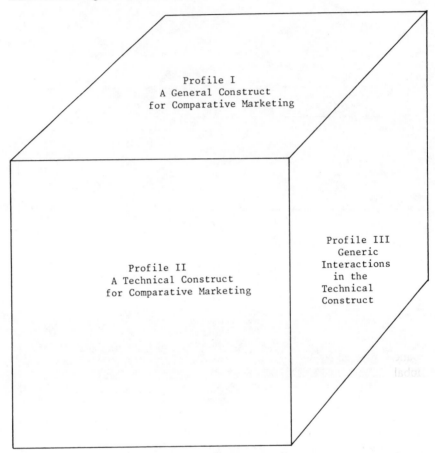

Most of the indicators may be grouped into two categories: general indicators of the socio-economic conditions of the country, and specific marketing factors encompassing both marketing institutions and practices in that area. These indicators are illustrated in Figure 3.6. A blend of these indicators is provided by Wind and Perlmutter in their guidelines for multi-national marketing decisions.[12] Such information is equally relevant and necessary whether the marketing decision is made on a national or an international basis. Likewise, Ayal and Zif provide a combined list of generalized indicators titled product/market factors to be employed in market operations culminating in either diversified or concentrated marketing strategies.[13]

FIGURE 3.6
Selection of Indicators for Multinational Marketing Analysis

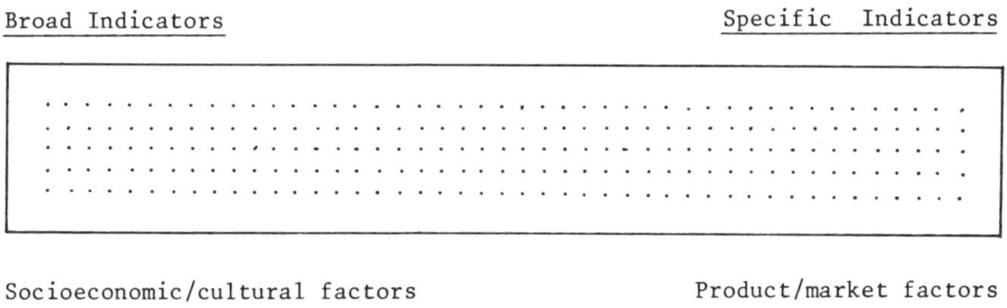

Broad Indicators   Specific   Indicators

Socioeconomic/cultural factors   Product/market factors

The ability to identify common traits throughout a region (or worldwide) that might legitimately aid international marketing has been disputed. One observation is that "there is no such thing as a global market . . . each country has its distinct needs and must be treated individually."[14] However, opinions to the contrary exist. Whether considered on a worldwide or regional basis, it appears most desirable to identify similarities and differences among selected areas with hopes of maximizing market opportunities.

Sherbini's use of the nation state, reflecting the use of geographical area analysis to determine similarities and differences, is one of the more common approaches. However, such areas have also been identified by smaller boundaries such as metropolitan areas, or larger ones encompassing entire global regions. Sheth noted that a "world-wide assessment of buyer needs and expectations should be done to establish a longitudinal panel of select geographical areas clustered on similar environmental factors."[15]

Geographical groupings are not the only ones that have been employed. Wind, Douglas, and Perlmutter approached their analysis from the framework of Perlmutter's four global orientations: regiocentric, ethnocentric, polycentric, and geocentric.[16] Keegan identified five groupings on the basis of host country development combined with political and/or resource factors.[17]

Value systems, although more difficult to study and quantify, have formed the basis of other clusters. Sommers and Kernan provided an early study back in 1967 on value orientations over four English-speaking countries using the comparative scale developed by Parsons and Lipset.[18] England, a decade later, provided a 2,500 manager value study across five relatively diverse cultures: Australia, Japan, Korea, India, and the United States. (See Figure 3.7).[19]

Selection of certain indicators, with their subsequent identification within a certain area or globally, has provided the basis for most clusters.

FIGURE 3.7

Clusters/Groupings Formed through Indicator Analysis

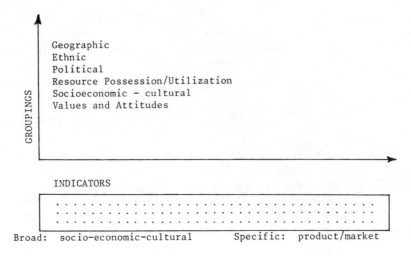

These clusterings could be utilized in isolation, but the more common approach has been to consider several different analyses together. For example, Sherbini described three approaches that, particularly when utilized in unison, were useful in highlighting marketing opportunities.[20] These approaches were:

1. Development approach/cluster analysis—structured countries into one of five economic and technological levels on the basis of demographic and societal factors deemed significant for marketing decisions. The objective was to provide a developmental basis for comparison instead of a geographical one.

2. Regional typological approach—considered five major regions, world-wide, and provided socioeconomic factors for developmental levels within each region.

3. Two-dimensional, direct-score approach—a two-axis approach that compared socioeconomic factors against internal cohesion and stability.

Sherbini found that, when possible, the results of one approach tended to approximate those received through the other approaches.[21] He noted, however, that variations would occur because different characteristics were involved in each of the approaches. His opinion was that "consistent results . . . confirmed a particular cluster or grouping. Inconsistent results did not necessarily negate it since the several methods of analysis were used for different purposes and reflected diverse consideration." Variations derived from various clustering techniques have formed the basis for most comparative analyses, whether on a global or regional basis. Application of computerized analysis, greatly improved since Sherbini's work in the late 1960s, has expanded the clustering techniques.

Moyer, in 1968, provided direction for computerized international market analysis through his study of demand patterns based on multiple factor economic indicators.[22] Other similar approaches were provided by such researchers as Armstrong,[23] with his application of econometric models or Ajiferuke and Boddewyn and their use of multiple regression analyses in comparative management based on Haire's socioeconomic indicators.[24] Haire's work provided the basis for the 1970 Boddewyn work and also for the 1977 value analysis conducted by Ronen and Kraut.[25] Their research culminated in their "smallest space analysis" country clusters. Their conclusion was that such clustering permitted marketers to concentrate on certain areas without having to survey the entire globe for similar markets.

A somewhat different clustering approach was taken by Johansson and Moinpour in their study of Pacific rim countries.[26] Their intention was to identify similar traits among all countries in this region, and to provide a comparison between objective and subjective variables. Geographic as well as economic factors were involved with the objective assessment, while subjective variables were seen as providing a form of judgment over whether or not to accept the objective conclusions.

Problems in Measurement

The researcher is responsible for the selection of the countries and characteristics to be examined, the selection of the comparative techniques to be employed, and the collection of the information. Each of these responsibilities carries its own type of problems. Selected indicators may or may not be the most accurate ones for the problem at hand. Correlation of all data, either through objective or subjective means, may result in logical but erroneous conclusions. Incomplete and unreliable information often forms the basis for comparison across regions or nation states. Data collection is improving, but incomplete and unreliable aspects persist. Unfortunately, these difficulties are most apparent in the developing countries where the marketing opportunities sometimes appear more appealing.

Bases for absolute comparison between countries or regions are still often inaccurate, if not impossible. Moyer suggested some techniques to provide a reliable basis for comparison without access to the total scope of required or desired information.[27] These techniques are becoming more refined, and providing a higher degree of predictability, but are still in developmental stages.

These observations are based in idealism. Realistically, total market information or knowledge is unlikely. Executives involved in decision-making within multinational corporations often amass information in nonsystematic ways. Keegan pointed this out in his 1974 study of multinational information scanning.[28] His research documented marketing decisions made on the basis of several information sources. In 60 percent of the instances, survey-based information (often highly subjective) constituted approximately two-thirds of the total information package. Thus, several major problems remain in the area of information collection for comparative marketing. First, the identification of indicators remains an unsolved problem for the marketer—particularly in light of time and financial constraints. Indicators that concentrate on socioeconomic factors help to identify possible marketing opportunities, but cultural variations that may not appear in such an analysis might distort these conclusions. Marketing institutions and the practices available in that country, region, or area, also have a great impact upon marketing success, but apart from early listings by authors such as Bartels, no comprehensive guidance has been offered in this area. Little help has been provided in the selection of those marketing features that might prove most crucial among all marketing system variables.

Second, the marketer is faced with the decisions on groupings or cluster selection. Limiting research to one region or area may help in facilitating common traits, but other market opportunities may therefore escape attention. Consideration of marketing opportunities on a global basis is far more difficult, both because of the amount of information involved and because of the margin of error accompanying data selection and collection.

Current market research correlation techniques provide analyses that were unavailable only a decade ago. However, since these analyses are based only on the information provided for such a correlation, the conclusions are based only on that information. As pointed out by Johansson and Moinpour, subjective judgement is still a necessary part of these analyses.[29]

Conclusion

The ultimate test for comparative marketing constructs lies in their potential contribution to advancing marketing practice and marketing theory. Profiles I, II, and III presented in this chapter capitalize on the strength of the classic comparative marketing analysis frameworks. Their analytic power is furthered through system variables. The incorporation of interaction enables analysts to focus on specific variables or sectors of the system, or to view the impact of one variable upon another.

The review of measurement provides an overview of the techniques available today. However, no one technique to date has proved all-encompassing. A combination of clustering and subjective analyses appears to be the safest and most dependable approach so far. Duplication appears to help in validating results. Additional study needs to be done in the area of measurement to adequately apply the comparative marketing model to multinational marketing decisions and strategies. The constructs and the analysis of measurement techniques provide a basis for future discussions and research. Let us hope they provide a step in the right direction.

Notes

1. Robert Bartels, ed., *Comparative Marketing: Wholesaling in Fifteen Countries* (Homewood, Illinois: Richard D. Irwin, 1963); Robert Bartels, "A Methodological Framework for Comparative Marketing Study," in Stephen A. Greyser, ed., *Toward Scientific Marketing* (Chicago, American Marketing Association, 1964), pp: 383–92; Robert Bartels, "Are Domestic and International Marketing Dissimilar?" *Journal of Marketing*, July, 1968, pp: 56–61; Jean J. Boddewyn, "A Construct for Comparative Marketing Research," *Journal of Marketing Research*, 3, May 1966, pp: 149–53; Jean J. Boddewyn, *Comparative Management and Marketing*, Glenview, Illinois, Scott, Foresman and Company, 1969; Reavis Cox, "The Search for Universals in Comparative Studies of Domestic Marketing Systems," in Peter D. Bennett, ed., *Marketing and Economic Development*, Chicago: American Marketing Association, 1965, pp: 143–62, and Bertil Liander; V. Terpstra; M. Y. Yoshino and A. A. Sherbini, *Comparative Analysis for International Marketing* (Boston, Allyn and Bacon, 1967).

2. Robert D. Buzzell, "Can You Standardize International Marketing?" *Harvard Business Review*, November–December 1968, pp: 102–13; and Bertil Liander, V. Terpstra, M. Y. Yoshino and A. A. Sherbini, "Comparative Analysis," pp: 16–19, 26–27, and 37–39.

3. Bertil Liander, V. Terpstra, M. Y. Yoshino, and A. A. Sherbini, "Comparative Analysis," p. 37.

4. Jean J. Boddewyn, "Comparative Management," pp: 109–12.

5. Bertil Liander, V. Terpstra, M. Y. Yoshino, and A. A. Sherbini, "Comparative Analysis," pp: 64–65.

6. *Ibid*, pp: 65–69.

7. Robert Bartels, eds., "Comparative Marketing," pp: 301–2.

8. Bo Wickstrom, *Cigarette Marketing in the Third World* (Goteborg, Sweden, University of Gothenburg, Department of Business Administration, Marketing Section, 1979).

9. Bertil Liander, V. Terpstra, M. Y. Yoshino, and A. A. Sherbini, "Comparative Analysis," pp: 146–47.

10. Robert Bartels, ed., "Comparative Marketing."

11. David Carson, *International Marketing: A Comparative Systems Approach* (New York: John Wiley and Sons, 1967); and Warren J. Keegan, *Multinational Marketing Management* (Englewood Cliffs, New Jersey: Prentice-Hall, 1980.

12. Yoram Wind and Howard Perlmutter, "On the Identification of Frontier Issues in Multinational Marketing," *Columbia Journal of World Business*, Winter 1977, p. 134.

13. Igal Ayal and Jehiel Zif, "Competitive Market Choice Strategies in Multinational Marketing," *Columbia Journal of World Business*, Fall 1978, pp: 72–80.

14. "Why a Global Market Doesn't Exist," *Business Week*, December 19, 1980, pp: 140–43.

15. Jagdish N. Seth, "A Conceptual Model of Long-Range Multinational Marketing Planning," *Management International Review*, 12:4–5, 1972, pp: 3–11.

16. Yoram Wind, Susan P. Douglas, and Howard V. Perlmutter, "Guidelines for

Developing International Marketing Strategies," *Journal of Marketing*, 37, April 1973, pp: 14–23.

17. Warren J. Keegan, "Strategic Marketing: International Diversification Versus National Concentration," *Columbia Journal of World Business*, Winter 1977, pp: 119–30.

18. Montrose Sommers, and Jerome Kernan, "Why Products Flourish Here, Fizzle There," *Columbia Journal of World Business*, March–April, 1967, pp: 89–96.

19. George W. England, "Managers and Their Value Systems: A Five-Country Comparative Study," *Columbia Journal of World Business*, Summer 1978, pp: 35–44.

20. Bertil Liander, V. Terpstra, M. Y. Yoshino, and A. A. Sherbini, "Comparative Analysis," p. 47.

21. *Ibid*, p. 143.

22. Reed Moyer, "International Market Analysis," *Journal of Marketing Research*, 5, November 1968, pp: 353–60.

23. J. Scott Armstrong, "An Application of Econometric Models to International Marketing," *Journal of Marketing Research*, 7, May 1970, pp: 190–98.

24. Musbau Ajiferuka and J. Boddewyn, "Socio-economic Indicators in Comparative Management," *Administrative Science Quarterly*, December 1970: pp:453–58.

25. Simcha Ronen, and Allen I. Kraut, "Similarities Among Countries Based on Employee Work Values and Attitudes," *Columbia Journal of World Business*, Summer 1977, pp: 89–96.

26. J. K. Johansson, and Reza Moinpour, "Objective and Perceived Similarity of Pacific Rim Countries," *Columbia Journal of World Business*, Winter 1977, pp: 65–76.

27. Reed Moyer, "International Market," p. 354.

28. Warren J. Keegan, "Multinational Scanning: A Study of the Information Sources Utilized by Headquarters Executives in Multinational Companies," *Administrative Science Quarterly*, September 1974, pp: 411–21.

29. J. K. Johansson and R. Moinpour, "Objective and Perceived Similarity," pp. 66–70.

III

COMPARATIVE MARKETING
AND
ECONOMIC DEVELOPMENT

In this part macrodevelopmental issues related to agricultural sector are discussed. It is stated that the building of an adequate marketing infrastructure is a necessary condition of intensive agricultural development. Goldman reports a case of an economic development program in Israel where the importance of marketing to the success of the economic development plan was recognized early and where marketing considerations were successfully incorporated into the development plan. Such studies are needed if we are to create the basis of empirical research and findings that will, eventually, make possible the development of theory and generalizations called for by the critiques of the areas of comparative marketing in economic development. The last chapter in this part, by Etgar, reviews the issues of governmental involvement in marketing commodity exports through the analysis of the experience of one developing country with two export commodities—coffee and cocoa. The experience of Ivory Coast with the development of a marketing system for these two commodities may have implications that are relevant not only to that particular country but to other developing countries as well.

4

THE DEVELOPMENT AND IMPLEMENTATION OF A MARKETING-BASED ECONOMIC DEVELOPMENT PROJECT IN THE AGRICULTURAL SECTOR—AN ISRAELI CASE

Arieh Goldman

Introduction

The interest in the role marketing can play in economic development arose as a result of a number of failures of economic development plans reported in the 1950s and the 1960s.[1] Since then the idea that marketing considerations should be incorporated into the planning and implementation of economic development plans seem to have been generally accepted by the various development agencies. However, when marketing experts are being invited to contribute to economic development projects, they face a situation where there is little empirical and theoretical basis on which they can draw.

The areas of marketing and economic development and of comparative marketing urgently need a large number of such studies in order to move out of their current infancy state. While the various "state of the art" papers that have become popular recently are important, they are not substitutes for field studies.[2] The fields of comparative marketing and the role of marketing in economic development will develop from the bottom up, by pulling together and making sense of the experiences, insights, and findings reported in specific studies. Knowledge in this area is more likely to develop through theory-based field studies and not through "arm-chair developed grand theories."

This chapter reports a case of an economic development program in Israel where the importance of marketing to the success of the plan was recognized early and where marketing considerations were successfully incorporated into the development plan. Furthermore, the marketing team was able to make a major contribution to the success of the project because it viewed the problems facing it not in isolation but in a broader perspective. Consequently, the conceptualization of the problems and the planning of the field studies were based on available findings from studies in other developed countries and on marketing theory. This approach not only improved the performance of the marketing team in the specific situation but also makes it possible to relate back the findings and lessons of this case to a more general body of findings and theory.[3]

The Problem

Poultry is the single most important meat product consumed in Israel. Per capita yearly consumption in the early 1970s was around 80 pounds and poultry meat was responsible for some 15 percent of the total volume of the fresh agricultural products marketed in the country. Most of the poultry consumed is "fresh," that is, sold to consumers a relatively short time after slaughtering without undergoing any freezing or chilling process.

The industry suffered, for many years, from large fluctuations in the quantities supplied and in price. The poultry system displayed a high level of instability with many periods of excess supply or excess demand occurring. The fluctuations on the supply side resulted mostly from diseases and climatic effects that were magnified by the structure of the industry. Those on the demand side were caused by factors such as holidays, tourism, and the price of imported red meats. The large price fluctuations of such a basic commodity negatively affected the efforts of the government to secure for consumers a consistent supply of basic food items at reasonable prices. It also had a negative effect on poultry growers and the well-being of an important agricultural sector. Consequently, the government established the Poultry Board, a statutory body empowered by a special law to plan and control the production and marketing of poultry products.[4]

In the 1960s, the board developed and implemented an elaborate administrative control system intended to stabilize the system and reduce price fluctuations. Each year a production and marketing quota of poultry meat was determined for the whole country. It was based on demand projections carried out by the board's economists. The national quota was then allocated among the individual growers, who were allowed to produce each month 1/12 of the yearly quota. The main production control mechanism used by the board was its power over the centralized system of hatcheries, which allocated chicks to growers only in accordance with the plan. Also, the board supervised the allocation of subsidized feed, which was distributed on the basis of the quota. In addition, a market control system based on "promised" (minimum) prices was established. Each grower was entitled to receive a minimum price from the board for the amount of poultry meat marketed within his planned quota. In case the actual price received in the market was below that of the "promised" price, the grower received a price supplement.

Finally, the board instituted the policy that when the price dropped below a certain level, it would purchase the excess supply, which was then processed into frozen poultry and warehoused. In periods of shortages, mostly holidays, it offered this frozen poultry for sale. However, since frozen poultry was considered an inferior product by consumers, it was sold at a price below the actual costs of the product. In spite of the low price, there was little demand, and it was sold mostly to institutional buyers (army, hospitals) and to lower-income consumers, and most of the sales were through special outlets.

In the early 1970s, it became apparent that the control system operated by the Poultry Board was not working well. The costs of administering the program had become very substantial and the government had to subsidize the board's operations by as much as 10 percent of the total poultry industry revenues. In addition, many growers found ways to circumvent the system while others took risks and often produced above their allocated quota. Consequently, the system continued to suffer from instabilities and high levels of price fluctuations.

This situation has led the Poultry Board in 1973 to establish an independent team of experts to analyze the operation of the total system, both on the supply and marketing side, and propose less expensive and more effective methods of controlling the system and reducing price fluctuations. The team eventually made a number of recommendations that involved major changes in the nature of the administrative control mechanisms and had a major impact on the system.[5] Among the alternative methods considered for increasing the stability of the system was the idea of enlarging the role of frozen poultry in the system. This issue is the focus of this chapter.

In the late 1960s frozen poultry had little effect on the system. It was purchased mostly by institutional buyers and lower-income consumers. While it was offered in supermarkets, it was not available there on a regular basis and was considered by them as a marginal product. Furthermore, the quality of the frozen product was generally low. The size of the birds being frozen, their age, and the quality of the meat was highly variable. Since the growers were paid by the board for the surplus birds according to weight, they tended to divert for freezing the larger, lower-quality birds. In addition, processing and freezing were conducted by facilities using outmoded technology and the quality of procesing was generally low. The product was poorly packaged, unlabeled, and was generally known as "Board's poultry." This term connoted an image of a low-quality, surplus product. In the early 1970s the board realized that, since frozen poultry can be kept in inventories, it can be used as an active mechanism to regularly intervene in the market and reduce price fluctuations. Consequently, it attempted to make the frozen product a full substitute for fresh poultry. The board economists (the planners) realized that the frozen product faced both demand and distribution problems. The planners assumed, however, that low prices, a better quality frozen product, and regular availability of the product in retail outlets should be enough to change the negative image and make it a substitute for fresh poultry for most consumers.

The plan they developed emphasized that the supermarkets should be the major outlets for the product. While the small specialized butcher shops were responsible for some 85 percent of all poultry meat sold in the country, it was felt that only the supermarkets had the modern facilities needed to handle the frozen product. It was believed that once the traditional outlets realized that frozen poultry was making inroads and demand was increasing, they would have no choice but to carry it and actively seek to sell it also. In order to prepare for the expected increased demand and improve the quality of the product, a program of major increase in the production capacity of frozen poultry and of modernization of production facilities was implemented. In the early 1970s, nine modern slaughtering house facilities were built, with the capacity to process some 25 percent of the total poultry consumed in the country.

By 1973, however, it became clear that this program was not working well. While frozen poultry was now available on a more regular basis in most supermarkets and even in some of the traditional butcher shops, consumer demand was very limited. The slaughtering houses were operating at about 50 percent of their capacity, storage facilities were full to capacity with frozen poultry and it was clear the frozen product was not widely accepted as a substitute for fresh poultry and consequently the board could not use it to effectively control the system.

The agricultural economists that analysed the system in 1973 realized that the failure of the frozen product to serve as a major stabilizing mechanism of the system was a marketing one. Consequently, in 1973 a team of marketing researchers was added to the project and was given the task of analysing the reasons for the failure, evaluate the demand potential for frozen poultry, and recommend ways to increase the level of consumption for the product.

The Marketing Problems: An Overview

Marketing failures of economic development programs reported in the literature can be classified into two general types.[6] The first is represented by the situation where the economic development plan has led to the development of new products but no demand exists for them. The second involves the situation where final demand does exist but because of inadequate distribution system and the lack of related infrastructures, the product can not get to its market.

The issue in the present case was more complicated than in the cases commonly discussed in the economic development literature. Frozen poultry was not a complete failure. It did sell at a level of around 8 to 10 percent of the total poultry sales. Given this situation it was not clear whether the problem was that of distribution, which could be solved by making the product more accessible to consumers, or whether the product faced a low level of trial by those consumers who had easy accessibility to it, or whether it had a low repeat rate. This issue had to be resolved at the onset before any commitment to a program of research was made. Since the statistical data available could not resolve the issue, a quick survey of a sample of supermarket shoppers was undertaken. It was found that, in spite of the availability of frozen poultry on a regular basis, many of these consumers did not use frozen poultry. It was concluded that the product faced both a demand and a distribution problem and both had to be dealt with. Finally, it was realized that those two issues are interrelated. A high propensity of consumers to adopt the product was likely to create pressures on the traditional butcher shops to offer the product in their assortment. In turn, making the product available through the butcher stores was likely to increase the number of people trying it and consequently increase the level of adoption.

The Demand Issue

The paradigm of Diffusion of Innovations as developed by Rogers and Shoemarker was used to analyze the demand problem frozen poultry faced.[7] While other diffusion of innovations paradigms are available in areas such as economics and geography, the Rogers Paradigm is the one that focuses on consumer behavior and the demand side of the process. A larger consumer study was carried out to assess consumer's reactions to frozen poultry. For the purposes of the study, three categories of consumers were identified: 1) "Full Adopters" of frozen poultry who have used the product regularly for an extended period of time; 2) "Triers," consumers who have tried the product but discontinued usage and 3) "Non-Triers," consumers who did not try it.

The sample was drawn from areas served by supermarkets that carried frozen poultry and included consumers in all three categories. These categories were compared and contrasted in terms of their images and perceptions of frozen poultry vis-a-vis other types of meat products, their attitudes towards the frozen poultry and their preferences, the profile of the ideal poultry product and how it differed from the frozen product, their knowledge level about the frozen product, the reasons for adoption, trial, discontinuation of use or rejection of the frozen product. In addition, the shopping and buying habits of the consumer were studied as well as their consumption patterns and the role the poultry in general, and frozen poultry in particular, played in it. Information was gathered, among other things, about the types of retail institutions in which consumers shopped for poultry and meat, sensitivity to poultry prices, and perceptions regarding the "just" price. Finaly, extensive social, economic, and demographic information was generated about these consumers.

The study results revealed that the product had a relatively high rate of penetration. About 45 percent of the respondents tried it but only 25 percent became regular users and there was a large group of consumers who discontinued usage. The low price of the product induced trial but was not enough to support regular usage. The users of the frozen product used it intermittently with fresh poultry and regarded it as an almost full substitute for the fresh product. As expected, frozen poultry was purchased mostly in supermarkets (63 percent) while for most other meat products the role the supermarket played was quite limited (around 20 percent). However, some 18 percent of the purchases of the frozen product were made in butcher shops, which indicated some penetration into the traditional outlets. Analysis of the demographic and socioeconomic data revealed the typical profile of the "triers" and regular users of the frozen product. Both groups tended to be higher in income and wealth (better neighborhoods, larger apartments, car ownership, etc.) better educated, the women in the family tended to work outside the home, and most were of Askanazi origin rather than Sepharadi. However, this information was not considered of much long-term value because this profile exactly matched that of typical supermarket shoppers, where the frozen poultry was mostly available. Of much more interest was the perceptual information generated. Frozen poultry had a generally negative image. It was characterized as low-grade quality, "not healthy," and not "fresh." Consumers did not understand the freezing process and believed that the chickens being frozen were of lower grade and that freezing produced a lower-quality product. In addition, the packaging of the frozen product, variations in the size of the birds being frozen, and the general appearance of the frozen product were cited as factors supplementing the negative image. In many respects the frozen product represented the opposite of the picture of the ideal poultry product described by the respondents. Even the regular users of the product were hard pressed to cite major advantages of the frozen poultry over the fresh one. They used it because they believed it was not very different from the fresh one and it was convenient to have it around.

The Taste Experiment

Among those who discontinued usage of the frozen product a high proportion had complained about its poor taste, smell, and about an unpleasant aftertaste. Similar complaints were voiced by some regular users. When these findings were presented and discussed in the regular meetings of the project team with the board planners, a debate ensued. It turned out that, because of kosher requirements for all meat products in Israel, the meat had to be soaked in salt water for a number of hours after the birds were slaughtered. Production engineers and food technicians had to modify the freezing process, compared to the process used in the U.S.A. and Europe, in order to adjust for the added saltiness and soaking. While they believed the modified freezing process currently used went a long way toward solving the problem, they argued for a continued program of research into the technology of poultry freezing in order to further improve the taste of the product. This group viewed the findings of the consumer survey as providing support for their view that the reluctance of consumers to adopt the frozen product can be overcome by producing a better product. They wanted resources allocated to allow further R & D efforts aimed at improving the physical quality and the taste of the frozen product. The marketing team counter-argued that the survey evidence was not conclusive. While a real taste and quality problem may indeed have existed, consumers complaints about taste may have simply been another indicator of the overall negative image they held of the frozen product. If this was indeed the case, the problem had to be dealt with through image change methods rather than through a product improvement program. Since a major commitment of resources and time was at stake, it was decided to conduct a blind taste experiment to resolve the issue.

In the taste experiment, a sample of consumers evaluated the taste and other product attributes of two poultry dishes. The poultry portions in each of the two dishes consumed by each subject were the same and were also cooked in the same manner. One was prepared from frozen poultry and the other from "fresh" poultry. The order in which they were presented was randomized and only the researchers knew which was from frozen poultry and which was prepared from the "fresh" product. The study clearly indicated that consumers could not discriminate on the basis of the blind test between the portions prepared from the frozen poultry and those prepared from the "fresh" product. Both types of products were evaluated as being of similar quality. It was, therefore, concluded that the frozen product faced an image problem and did not require a product improvement program.

Implementation

The consumer study yielded a number of important inputs. It ended the debate whether to continue to invest in R & D in an effort to improve taste and quality, and it showed that the main obstacle to the product adoption was the negative image of the frozen product. It identified the profile of the likely triers and adopters. It supplied a large amount of information on the nature of the ideal poultry product and how it differed from the current image of the frozen product. It identified the price ranges considered by consumers to be "fair" for frozen poultry and the "fair" price differential between frozen and fresh poultry.[8] It showed the importance of differentiating between the goal of penetrating the market and achieving regular usage. While the product achieved a relatively high level of trial, many of the triers did not become regular users. The effect of some factors (e.g. price and availability in the butcher shops) was found to be mostly on the trial rate while other factors (e.g. perception of benefits of the frozen product and advantages over "fresh" poultry) were found to affect mostly the rate of regular usage. Finally, based on extrapolations of the factors analyzed, it was possible to provide rough estimates as to levels of trials and of regular usage that will ensue from changing various marketing factors such as price, and number of outlets carrying the product.

The major obstacle to regular usage of the frozen poultry was the negative image and the lack of perception by consumers of positive benefits to be derived from it. An image change campaign is a very difficult marketing undertaking and involves the investment of a large amount of resources, effort, and time. Perhaps the single most important contribution of the marketing team to the project was the idea that the vehicle for achieving such an image change is that of developing a "new" frozen poultry product that will conform to the consumer's expectations regarding the ideal poultry product. In order to succeed this product must be differentiated from the other frozen poultry products consumers were familiar with, such as the surplus low-quality "Board" product and the more recent frozen poultry produced by the new slaughtering facilities that suffered from inconsistency in quality. Instead of changing the image of the frozen poultry product consumers were familiar with, the idea was to push forward and market a frozen poultry product that did not suffer from the problems the earlier products suffered from, is of consistent high quality, and incorporates many of the characteristics of the "ideal" poultry product.

The idea was accepted and implemented within a relatively short period of time. First, the nature of the new product was decided upon, based on the findings of consumer surveys. Most consumers characterized the ideal poultry product as "young" birds, small to medium size, "fresh," good outside appearance, and lean. A grading system for birds and a quality control system based on it was instituted and all processors agreed to abide by it. Only birds of a certain quality were used for the new product. In addition, the responsibility for the new product was given to one organization—Tnuva, which is the largest wholesaler of agricultural products in Israel. It is a cooperative organization owned by the cooperative settlements in Israel (Kibbutizm and Moshavim) that are responsible for most agricultural production in the country. Since most poultry production was conducted by the cooperative settlements and the poultry processing and freezing facilities were owned by the regional organizations of these cooperatives, the selection of Tnuva as the coordinating organization was clear. Furthermore, Tnuva had a lot of experience in marketing, whereas the individual processing facilities and their parent regional organizations that at the time of the study marketed frozen poultry had relatively little marketing expertise. A unifying brand name was instituted for the "new" frozen poultry as well as a special colored packaging. A strict system of rules was instituted and control mechanisms established not only regarding the nature of the types of poultry inputs but also regarding processing and packaging. The emphasis was on producing a standardized, consistent high-quality product. All participating processing facilities agreed to adhere to these rules and the responsibility for controlling it was given to the marketing organization. Finally, a major advertising campaign was undertaken. It announced the appearance of the new frozen product, and explained why frozen poultry is better than fresh. The underlying theme was that frozen is "fresher" than fresh because freezing "captures" and conserves freshness. It tied in well with a similar campaign for frozen vegetables introduced in the 1960s into Israel. It emphasized the high quality of the birds being frozen and the sophistication and reliability of the processing and freezing process. The focus was on developing an image of a high-quality consistent modern product with characteristics that echoed the picture of the ideal product consumers held. The brand name was emphasized as the anchor for the new image and as a vehicle for differentiating the new product from the "other" frozen poultry products.

The implementation of the new product idea and of the marketing effort supporting it took about a year and was very successful. By 1975 most consumers were aware of the existence of the new poultry frozen product, and believed that it was different and of better quality than the others. The proportion of consumers who used the product regularly increased in a major way, and frozen poultry became a major factor helping to stabilize the poultry meat system in the country.

The Distribution System

Parallel to dealing with the demand issue the marketing team also concentrated on the distribution problem faced by frozen poultry. Poultry meat in Israel was sold in the early 1970s mostly through small poultry butcher shops. These accounted for some 85 percent of the poultry sold. Supermarkets that were introduced in the late 1950s were responsible for some 15 percent, which was below their general share of the food market.

Poultry butcher stores in Israel traditionally sold "fresh" poultry. These are birds typically slaughtered in small nonautomated slaughtering houses, delivered immediately to retailers, and offered for sale on the same day. Butchers receive whole birds and clean and cut them in their stores. In contrast, frozen poultry is mass-produced by large automated slaughtering houses. It comes to the store already prepackaged and the retailers simply display it.

In 1973, most supermarkets in the country carried the frozen product produced by the modern processing facilities (but not the surplus "Board poultry"). However, the product faced difficulties in gaining acceptance by poultry butcher stores. Few butchers adopted the product, others tried and discontinued it but most refused even to try the new product. This result was totally unexpected. The board planners assumed that most butchers would adopt it since almost all the butcher stores already had the necessary refrigeration equipment needed and the new product was expected to reduce the butcher's work load and increase sales. Consequently, the purpose of the study carried out by the marketing team was to understand the reasons for the rejection of the product by the traditional distribution system and suggest ways to make the product more available through the butcher and thus make it more accessible to consumers.

The study design was based on the idea of comparing butcher stores that adopted the product to those that did not. A sample of 94 poultry butcher stores were studied and a sequential sampling procedure was employed that ensured that about a third of the stores would be those that tried to sell the frozen product but discontinued it, about a third were stores that adopted it, and about a third of the sample were stores that refused to try the new frozen product.

Each of the poultry store owners was interviewed at his store by trained interviewers. The poultry retailers were asked about various aspects of the store operation, policies, and developments. In addition, personal, demographic, and attitudinal data were collected from the owners. The interview was supplemented by a long period of observation in the store and discussions of store policies with the retailers.

The adoption of frozen poultry by butcher stores can be conceptualized in terms of two perspectives. The first is that of the diffusion of innovations, which focuses on the innovators and their characteristics.[9] The second is that of the theory of development of a food retail store, emphasizing how the frozen product fits within the development path of the store.

Diffusion of Innovations Approach

Heavy emphasis is given in the diffusion of innovations studies conducted in developing countries to the identification of the entrepreneur's characteristics associated with innovativeness. Socioeconomic variables such as education, literacy, income, age, and attitudinal varibles such as attitudes towards change, achievement, motivation, and satisfaction with the present situation, are often used in such analyses.[10] For example, a study of innovative small food retail stores in Puerto Rico has found that the operators of the more innovative food retailing establishments were younger and better educated.[11] The proponents of this approach believe that the characteristics of the retailer are the most important factors determining whether the small store will adopt new innovations.

The Store Development Strategy Approach

Most researchers and planning agencies interested in economic development and comparative marketing view the small food stores as inefficient distributors of foods and recommend their replacement by larger modern institutions such as the supermarkets.[12]

This attitude has resulted in a preoccupation with modernization through transplantation of "modern" retailing institutions and in a general lack of interest in the small traditional stores. The general failure of large modern retailing institutions in the developing countries and the political and social realities of the continued existence of the traditional system have brought many developing countries to focus attention on the small store and attempt to assist small food retailers to modernize their operation.[13] However, because of the preoccupation of researchers with the large, modern retailing systems, little attention has been given in the literature to the study of the autonomous development of small retail stores. In his studies of the evolutionary development of the supermarket in the U.S.A.[14] and of the development path of small food stores in LDCs[15] the author focused on the issue of the expansion of store assortments by small store retailers and viewed it as one of the major avenues for growth available to small retailers. From this perspective, the decision of the poultry retailers whether to adopt the frozen poultry line should not be viewed as an adoption of simply another item but from the broader perspective of the development strategy of the retailer. Retailers who are intent on growing through line expansion can be expected to be more willing to adopt the new line than retailers who prefer to follow a limited line—specialization strategy.

More specifically, the sales volume of a poultry store is a function of 1) the average amount spent in the store by a customer and 2) the number of customers patronizing it. In principle, then, the poultry retailer interested in increasing the sales volume of his store can achieve growth by simultaneously effecting these two ends, that is, making his customers spend a larger proportion of their meat and food expenditures in his store and enticing new customers to switch over and patronize his store. However, as is evident from the history of food retailing, different strategies and tools are used in each case. Consequently, small retailers often choose to focus on a single end and each approach results in the development of a distinct retailing philosophy. The first led to the concentration of the retailers' attention on their current customer base and to the addition of more and more product lines in order to capture a larger proportion of these customers' expenditures. Such stores can be expected to be concerned more with the customers residing in the immediate trade area of the store and to be more likely to develop various services to better cater to these consumers. In contrast, in the case of the second approach, the major strategy available to small retailers to entice customers residing in far away areas to their store is that of "specialization." In the meat area specialization involves concentration of few product lines and offering a complete assortment of meat in this area. Also, it involves the development of a reputation for expertness and quality. In the situation that prevailed in Israel in the early 1970s, where poultry meat was sold "fresh," was supplied by a large number of small slaughtering facilities, and then transferred to retailers by small wholesalers often lacking proper cold storage facilities and adequate transportation, the reputation of the retailer was perhaps the most important risk reduction mechanism for consumers and the best guarantee of quality. It was easier for specialized retailers to establish such a reputation and to use it as their main tool to draw to their stores consumers residing in other trade areas.

Based on this theoretical perspective, it can be expected that those poultry butcher retailers who see specialization as the main avenue for success will tend to reject frozen poultry while those that emphasize an assortment expansion and customer service policies will tend to adopt the new line. The specialized poultry butcher is not interested in adding minor lines that will decrease his ability to focus on his major products and also diffuse the specialized and expert image of the store. In addition, the reputation of specialized butchers and their advantage stems from their ability to guarantee quality for consumers purchasing nonstandardized products. No such need exists in the case of frozen poultry, which is a prepackaged, standardized item.

The Study Findings

Both theoretical perspectives discussed above were tested in the study in an effort to understand why some poultry butcher stores did adopt the frozen product while others rejected it. On the basis of these two perspectives, four groups of variables were used to differentiate between the retailers who tried the product and nontriers, and between the adopters and nonadopters.

1) Personal characteristics of retailers: These included age of store owner, education, number of years he owned the store, and the previous occupational history of the owner.

2) Structural characteristics of the store: These included the size of the store, the number of persons employed in it, and the number of product lines carried by the store.

3) Store development policies: Two aspects of the store policy were studied. a) The best assortment policy: retailers were asked to indicate the best assortment policy a poultry retailer should follow in order to succeed in his operation. They were asked to specify their agreement with statements such as, "in order to succeed in a poultry store operation an owner should offer in his store only few meat lines and distinguish himself in these lines" or "in order to succeed in a poultry store operation an owner should offer in his store as many lines of meat and related products as possible." b) The best development policy: retailers were asked to indicate whether the best store development policy is to attempt and sell more to existing customers by adding new products or to concentrate on adding new customers to the store.

4) Area where store is located: since the growth avenues retailers follow may depend on the nature of their trade area (e.g., density of population, income of consumers) information was generated about the location of the store. Especially important in the Israeli context was whether the poultry butcher store was located in the open market—an area of high traffic, or in the residential neighborhoods. It was also noted whether the neighborhoods were composed mainly of high- or low-income families.

The results of the analysis indicated that no statistically significant associations were found between any of the personal characteristic variables of the poultry store owners and any of the two measures of poultry adoption behavior—trying and adopting. In contrast, all store structure factors, the store policy variables, and the nature of the store's location were found to be significantly associated with *trying* the new product. The last two variables and the number of product lines were also found to be significantly related to the *adoption* of the new product. Especially strong is the association found between the number of product lines carried by the poultry stores and each of the two types of adoption behaviors. While the nontriers carried a mean of 2.7 product lines the stores that have tried the new product carried a mean of 4.4 lines. Similarly, while the nonadopting poultry stores carried an average of 3.3 product lines the adopters did carry a mean of 5.4 lines.

The picture emerging is that the innovative poultry stores tend to be stores with an already relatively large assortment of product lines, their owners believe in a strategy of increasing the store's product line assortment and finally, these stores tend to be located in either the higher-middle income residential areas or in the public market area. In contrast, stores that did not try the product carry a smaller number of product lines, their owners believe in operating a store with only few lines and they tend to be located mainly in the lower-income residential areas. These findings clearly indicate that new product line adoption by small food stores can be explained in terms of how the new product fits the overall development strategy and structure of the stores and not in terms of the adoption of innovations perspective. This is an important result, since most efforts in the area of analyzing innovative food stores in developing countries have focused on the characteristics of the retailers.

Limited-Line Vs. Expanded-Line Poultry Butcher Stores

The above analysis clearly shows that the poultry stores studied do not constitute a homogeneous group. They differ considerably in their store structure and policy and these differences were found to be related to the differential adoption behavior of frozen poultry by the stores. Because of the importance of this finding for our understanding of marketing in developing countries, it seems useful to focus on these two groups of stores and further identify the typical characteristics of each.

The sample was divided into two groups. One consists of stores carrying a small number of meat products, while the other is composed of poultry stores carrying a large number of meat and related product lines. The first group was labeled "limited-line" and the second "expanded-line." In this section the differences in store structure, strategy and in the type of customers they cater to are analyzed.

The number of lines carried by the sample stores ranged from one product to eleven. The composition of the product assortments carried by the stores ranged from one product to eleven. The composition of the product assortments carried by the stores varied. In all cases fresh poultry was the main product line. Many stores carried, in addition, fish, cold meats, processed meats, and sausages. Finally, a number of the expanded line stores have even introduced various nonmeat lines, such as delicatessen, canned goods, prepared foods, and take-home foods. It should, however, be emphasized that even the highly expanded line stores had still a very limited product line assortment compared to, say, a grocery store. Only three stores in the sample had an assortment of ten or more product lines (the highest being 11 product lines) and only ten stores derived less than 30 percent of their total sales from "fresh" poultry. In other words, the poultry stores studied still remained stores concentrating mainly on poultry and meat products.

The differences among the two groups of stores are discussed in terms of three issues—the structure of the stores, their development strategy, and the nature of their customer base.

1) The Structure of the Poultry Stores:

The expanded-line stores tended to be larger, both in terms of their physical size and their number of employees. While the mean size of the 27 stores offering only one or two product lines was $19m^2$, the mean size of the 34 stores offering five or more product lines was $24m^2$. Similarly, the first group employed an average of 1.9 employees versus a mean of three in the second group. As can be expected, it was found that the higher the number of lines carried by the store, the smaller is the contribution of the most important product line—"fresh" poultry—to its total sales. Finally, no relation was found between the number of years a store existed and the number of product lines it carried. This indicates that the addition of products is not simply a reflection of the store's age, but a result of policy decisions by store owners.

2) Store Strategy:

Differences in store structure between the limited-line and expanded-line poultry stores are accompanied by major differences in store policies and activities. A number of different aspects of store's activities were used in the analysis. The tendency to regard the best assortment policy as one involving carrying a larger number or product lines was found to increase with the number of product lines a store offers, while the opposite approach was found to be negatively correlated with the number of product lines. Retailers were asked to describe the best development policy a store owner should undertake in order to increase the store's sales volume. The limited-line poultry store owners were found to believe that the best policy is to add new customers, while the expanded-line store owners tended to believe that the most promising avenue is to concentrate on adding new products in order to make current customers spend more of their total expenditures on food in the store. The first approach has led to a heavy emphasis on price and quality as the main promotional tool in the limited-line stores. In contrast, the second group stores developed a high sensitivity to the nature of customers demand. One of the manifestations of this sensitivity is the fact that the expanded-line stores have tended to engage more in new product experimentation during recent years, in order to better serve their customers. Also, they were more service-oriented, as evidenced by a strong tendency to use telephone ordering and home delivery.

3) Nature of Customer Base:

The expanded-line stores were found to tend to cater more to regular customers, to customers who reside near the store, and to customers who emphasize quality over price. Also, they were found to tend to concentrate in higher-income areas.

Implementation

The distribution study identified the existence of two groups of poultry butcher stores. The expanded-line stores were found to be larger in their physical size, to employ more employees, to derive a lower proportion of their sales from "fresh" poultry, to provide a higher level of customer services and to show a tendency to adopt new products. In addition, the owners of these stores were found to regard the policy of offering a larger number of products to an existing customer base as superior to the alternative approach of keeping the existing assortment unchanged while enticing new customers to the store. Finally, the expanded-line stores were found to concentrate in the high- and middle-income neighborhoods and to cater to a more regular customer base, to customers who resided near the store and who tended to emphasize quality as their main patronage motive. The picture emerging is that the expanded-line stores focus on supplying a more limited trade area and a known and regular customer base with a "system" of meat products, while the limited-line stores concentrate on fewer product lines which they offer to a much wider trade-area. While the first group emphasize the quick response to varied consumer's demand, the latter stores emphasize price appeal and product specialization as their main attraction and rely on these to bring consumers to the store from far away areas. Given these findings, the marketing team concluded that the expanded-line stores will be more likely to adopt and regularly carry the new frozen poultry product line. Since the study yielded a clear profile of these likely innovators, the salesmen of the Tnuva organization could easily identify these stores. The results after a year of effort tended to justify the study conclusions and the recommendations for action based on them. The proportion of poultry butcher stores carrying the product has increased in a major way and product accessibility ceased to be a major problem. While no additional distribution study was conducted, the feedback from Tnuva salesmen clearly supported the study conclusions. Most of their approaches to the limited-line, more specialized poultry butcher stores to carry the new product were rebuffed while their level of success with the expanded-line stores was very high.

Summary and Conclusions

The chapter describes how this marketing-based economic development project evolved and discusses the stages involved in conceptualizing, researching, and implementing the marketing reform program. The frozen poultry product faced both consumer and distribution channel rejection. A number of studies were conducted in order to understand the reasons for the slow diffusion of the product. These studies are discussed and the chapter shows how the findings of these studies were used to help formulate policy recommendations and help in their implication.

The case discussed in this chapter should be of interest to researchers in the area of marketing in economic development and comparative marketing for several reasons. First, it is one of the few cases reported in the literature where a marketing-based economic development plan was successfully implemented. Second, marketing scholars have long argued that marketing can serve as an "entry point" for economic development projects.[16] However, with the exception of few cases involving attempted improvements in retailing, wholesaling, and transportation, it seems that this idea was not really tested. In the present situation a comprehensive marketing program involving the development and marketing of a new product was used as a major "entry point" in an economic development project, and has proven to be a viable alternative to production-oriented solutions. Consequently, this case can be also viewed as suggesting the feasibility of using marketing as the key to economic development projects at the level of specific systems. Third, the case demonstrates the usefulness of relying on theoretical conceptualization when carrying out applied projects in developing countries. As demonstrated in this case, the reliance on past research and on theoretical developments in the area of retailing made it possible to identify the potential retail innovators in a much more robust and rich way.

The findings of the distribution study conducted as part of this project also have relevance for theoretical developments in the area of comparative marketing. In spite of their prevalence and importance in the developing countries, relatively little is currently known about the structure and behavior of small specialized food stores. The present study of one type of these stores has made a number of first steps in the direction of increased familiarity with these stores.

Notes

1. J. Abbott, "Marketing Issues in Agricultural Development Planning," in *Markets and Marketing in Developing Economies*, Reed Moyer and Stanley C. Hollander, eds., (Homewood Ill: Richard D. Irwin, 1968), pp: 87–116; Jean J. Boddewyn, "Comparative Marketing: The First Twenty-Five Years," Journal of International Business Studies, 12:6, Spring/Summer 1981, pp: 61–79; and Reed Moyer, *Marketing and Economic Development* (East Lansing: Michigan State University, Institute for International Business Management Studies, 1965).

2. Hiram C. Barksdale and McTier Anderson, "Towards a Conceptual Framework for Comparative Marketing Studies," Fifth Macro Marketing Seminar, University of Rhode Island, August, 1980; Boddewyn, "Comparative Marketing," pp: 61–79; and Marye Tharp Hilger,

"Factors Inhibiting the Development of Comparative Marketing," Seventh Macro Marketing Seminar, University of Colorado, Boulder, August, 1982.

3. Arieh Goldman, "Transfer of a Retailing Technology Into the Less-Developed Countries: The Supermarket Case," *Journal of Retailing*, 57, Summer 1981 pp: 5–29.

4. Dov Izraeil, D. Izraeli, and J. Ziff, *Societal Marketing Boards* (New York: Wiley, 1977).

5. Pinhas Zusman, A. Amiad, and A. Goldman, *Controlling the Poultry Sector*, (Rehovot, Center for Research in Agricultural Economics; (Hebrew), 1975).

6. Abbott, "Marketing Issues," pp: 87–116; and Moyer, "Marketing and Economic", p. 20.

7. Everett M. Rogers, and Floyd Shoemaker, *Communication of Innovations* (New York: The Free Press, 1971).

8. For a discussion of the "fair" or "just" price concept see: Kent B. Monroe, "Buyers' Subjective Perception of Price," *Journal of Marketing Research*, 10, February 1973, pp: 70–80.

9. Everett M. Rogers and Floyd Shoemaker, "Communication of Innovations," and Thomas S. Robertson, *Innovative Behavior and Communication* (New York: Holt, Rinehart and Winston, 1971).

10. Everett M. Rogers, *Modernization Among Peasants: The Impact of Communication* (New York: Holt, Rinehart and Winston, 1969); and E. M. Rogers and F. Shoemaker, "Communication of Innovations."

11. Harold M. Riley and Charles Slater, et al., *Food Marketing in the Economic Development of Puerto Rico* (East Lansing: Michigan State University, Latin American Studies Center, 1970).

12. John K. Galbraith and Richard Holton, *Marketing Efficiency in Puerto Rico* (Cambridge, Mass: Harvard University Press, 1965); and Charles Slater, "Market Channel Coordination and Economic Development," in Louis P. Bucklin, ed., Vertical marketing Systems (Glenview, Ill.: Scott, Foresman and Co., 1970).

13. Arieh Goldman, "Growth of Large Food Stores in Developing Countries," *Journal of Retailing*, 50, Summer 1974, pp: 50–60; "Transfer of a Retailing," pp: 5–29; and Louis P. Bucklin, "Efficiency in Retailing and Wholesaling of Food Products," (F.A.O. Rome: Food and Agricultural Organization).

14. Arieh Goldman, "Stages in the Development of the Supermarket," *Journal of Retailing*, 52, Winter, 1975–1976, pp: 49–64.

15. Goldman, "Growth of Large Food," pp: 50–60.

16. Galbraith and Holton, "Marketing Efficiency" and Slater, "Market Channel Coordination."

5

MARKETING OF EXPORT COMMODITIES: THE CASE OF IVORY COAST

Michael Etgar

A large number of developing countries rely on exports of basic commodities for support of their economies. Commodities like coffee, cocoa, jute, rubber on one hand, and copper, and zinc, on the other, provide a major portion of the foreign exchanges of many Africa, Latin American and Asian developing countries, and contribute to their economic welfare and development.

Design and management of an effective marketing system is crucial for the successful export of such commodities. In many developing countries, building such a marketing system has been the focus of a concerted planning effort by public policymakers and planners, who to a large extent embrace the role of macromanagers in a way not much different from that of marketing managers in large firms in developed economies. They view their role as generating the most favorable exchanges between their country and its markets, as designing proper marketing strategies and policies to influence or affect international demand for their products, and as delivering their products to international markets.

In designing marketing systems for export commodities in developing countries, a major bone of contention has been the role of government as a coordinator and/or active participant in the marketing system. While in some countries and industries, governments do not interfere at all and rely on the private sector to carry out the relevant marketing activities, in other countries and industries, they are active participants in the marketing system, and their agencies are directly involved in the planning and execution of the marketing activities themselves. As a result, diverse systems of marketing commodity exports have been organized in various developing countries.

The purpose of this chapter is to review the issues of governmental involvement in marketing commodity exports through the analysis of the experience of one developed country with two export commodities—coffee and cocoa. The experience of Ivory Coast in developing a marketing system for these two commodities has implications that are relevant not only to that particular country but to other developing countries as well, for several reasons. First, it provides an example of a complex system of regulations and institutions as applied in a developing economy. Second, Ivory Coast has succeeded in becoming a major cocoa and coffee exporter and, as such, it is an object of envy and its model of export and management is viewed with extreme interest by many other developing countries. Finally, the system developed in Ivory Coast is based on the philosophy of limited governmental intervention and greater reliance on the private sector, in contrast to the philosophy embraced by many developing countries.

The chapter starts with a conceptual analysis examining the theory and meaning of an export marketing system for basic commodities. It follows with an exposition of the marketing system that has been developed in the Ivory Coast. It then summarizes the analysis by reviewing the implications of the Ivorian experience.

A Marketing System for Commodity Exports

The point of view undertaken in this chapter is managerial rather than descriptive. First of all, the issues that need to be handled in exporting basic commodities are considered and then the responses provided in Ivory Coast are reviewed. Yet the point of view is also macro- rather than micro-marketing-oriented. The needs of the marketing system as a whole are considered rather than those of particular institutions or agents operating in the marketing system.

Development and expansion of exports of commodities from developing to developed countries requires the established and management of a commodity exporting marketing system. Proper management of such a marketing system involves several stages indicated in Figure 5.1. First, one must identify the pertinent marketing tasks and activities that need to be performed by the marketing system as a whole. Second, various tasks need to be allocated to the specific entities that are to operate within the marketing system and, if necessary, such entities have to be set up. Third, a mechanism needs to be devised to coordinate the various activities performed in the marketing system to achieve maximum impact for its operation. While this

FIGURE 5.1
Management of International Channel

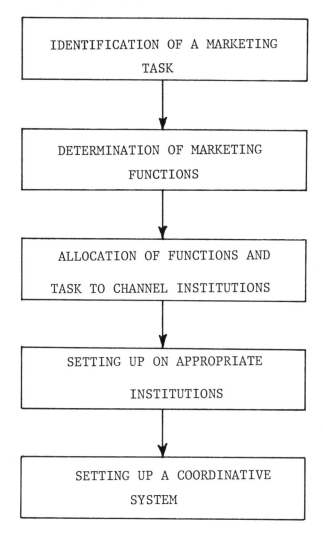

procedure is similar to that used for management of marketing channels for products produced in developed economies, the particular characteristics of exporting basic commodities from developing countries imposes particular requirements on the marketing system and on its management.[1]

These particular characteristics can be better analyzed by reviewing the marketing system for basic commodities not as one whole system but as

FIGURE 5.2

The Marketing System for Commodity Exports

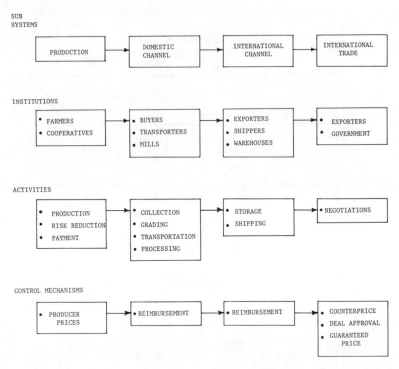

composed of four distinct parts or subsystems. Each of these parts involves different tasks; as a result, different functions need to be performed for each part and, consequently, different institutions need to be set up for the performance of these tasks. Organization of the whole commodity export system involves, therefore, organization of the activities within each part of the system as well as coordination among the various parts. Figure 5.2 presents the four parts of the commodity export management system, the tasks, activities, and institutions involved. The four parts or subsets are respectively the *international trade* subset, the *international channel* subset, the *domestic channel* subset, and the *production* subset. Each of these subsets is discussed in detail below, with application to the cocoa and coffee exports from the Ivory Coast.

International Trade Management Subset

The goal of international trade management for any product is to influence demand through branding, packaging, promotion, and distributive policies designed to achieve superior positioning and higher profits for the supplier. The commodity characteristics of cocoa and coffee have, to a large extent, limited supplier ability to do so. Both products are highly standardized and supplies are easily substitutable and are traded in coffee and cocoa exchanges located in London and New York for immediate and future deliveries in the form of standardized beans according to quality grades. Supplies are offered by marketing boards, private exporters from developing countries, and a range of brokers and other middlemen who buy and sell these commodities. Buyers are food companies, brokers, and speculators.[2]

Due to this structure of the international trade in cocoa and coffee beans, suppliers such as Ivory Coast cannot improve their profits by demand stimulation and the only way that they can affect exchanges is by management of pricing and delivery policies that yield highest returns.

International trade in both commodities is very volatile and price sensitive. Changes in world supplies create extreme reactions that can take place within very short periods. Prices received for coffee and cocoa beans vary from transaction to transaction reflecting international market prices, supply conditions, and the expectations of traders. The extensive price fluctuations for cocoa and coffee present a substantial marketing task for Ivorian export managers. Skilled negotiations and good knowledge of market conditions allows making relatively high profits from selling in favorable market conditions; as a result, international demand management is primarily limited to negotation of transactions on international markets.

International Channel Management

Manufacturers manage their distributive channels to achieve desirable impacts on their ultimate markets. For that purpose, they look to their channels to perform a variety of diverse marketing tasks through which utility is added to the product involved, with regards to such factors as place, time, size, and assortment.[3] The unique characteristics of international markets for cocoa and coffee beans have, however, eliminated the need to design and manage a complex international distribution channel. The operation of international commodity exchanges has limited the role and function of intermediaries and the need and ability of suppliers to control and direct them. Marketing intermediaries are part of the commodity exchanges and constitute the direct buyers for the Ivorian products.

As a result, international channel management tasks for marketing of cocoa and coffee beans for exports are limited to those concerned with management of physical flows of the products from the Ivory Coast to their international destinations. This involves the organization of pertinent shipping arrangements both in the Ivory Coast and abroad to coordinate necessary physical movements of the products with those of ownership changes as arranged in transactions made with the various buyers of the products abroad. As many transactions involve deliveries to be realized at some future date, shipping involves a complex process of organization, loadings, arrival and departure schedules, and warehousing.

Management of the Domestic Production Subsystem

To increase revenues and expand exports, a constant supply of products must be secured. In developing countries, this imposes upon the marketing system the need to design policies and develop *organizations that will motivate farmers to cultivate and deliver the products involved* and often requires that they be motivated to shift from subsistence to cash crop farming. Such a shift imposes several important tasks on the marketing system. When a farmer foregoes subsistence farming and shifts his resources to cash crops, he may gain a higher income in monetary terms; however, such a shift implies a substantial change in his economic operation. He loses the security that subsistence farming provides, and needs to rely on someone else to absorb cash crops and to provide compensation sufficient to enable him to purchase food, seeds, and other farm materials.

Farming for export markets places even greater emphasis on the marketing system. Here, the farmer is completely separated from his ultimate customers with no direct access to or control over them. The geographical, physical, temporal, and cultural differences between producers and ultimate customers requires the development of a complex marketing system to handle physical flows, risk, information, and money. The marketing system and institutions must be able to absorb products provided by farmers, reduce risk of export farming for them, allow them to be paid in an orderly fashion and provide them with information about market preferences.

Under subsistence farming, farmers are insulated from market risks, that is, the risk that demand-supply interactions may affect their revenues, and thus their capacity to purchase food and other necessities. However, once they start cultivating cash crops, farmers become dependent on the money economy and the market forces. The wide fluctuations of prices of commodities such as cocoa and coffee in world markets implies that a substantial risk does exist for these producers. On the average, between 1955 and 1978, the prices of coffee changed by 18 percent annually, both up and down, while the price of cocoa in the world market changed on average by 27 percent, again both up and down.[4]

The shift from subsistence to cash crops imposes another task upon the marketing system. To ensure efficient use of a country's resources, it needs to convey to producers information about conditions in international markets so that producers can direct their resources to the most efficient use. Thus, whenever the international markets indicate a greater need for any of the commodities, the marketing system needs to indicate to producers that they should expand production; on the other hand, whenever the international markets slacken, the system needs to convey information about markets in a form of a set of cues to producers to reduce production.

Management of the Domestic Channel

To deliver cocoa and coffee beans to docks ready for exporting requires that a series of tasks be performed through which the product is collected, graded, processed, shipped, and stored appropriately. It involves development of marketing infrastructure facilities that can perform all the required physical handling as well as of facilitatory marketing institutions that can handle the needed distribution functions.

The particular characteristics of the products involved make the physical handling activities especially important. Thus, coffee and cocoa production is highly decentralized in the Ivory Coast. These products are grown by hundreds of thousands of small- and medium-sized farmers located throughout the southern part of the country. The geographical dispersion is complicated further by the long harvest period of these two products. These two factors have generated a continuous need for collecting the raw products from farmers and bringing them into processing and transportation centers where they are graded.

Another important task that is performed domestically is the processing of the raw cocoa and coffee cherries into beans ready for exports. Till 1974, this task was performed by the farmers themselves; since then, it has been entrusted to specialized mills. The process is somewhat different for the two products but it basically involves drying, cleaning, and extracting the beans.[5]

The larger size of the country and dispersement of production centers over large areas has created also the need for establishment of transportation networks through which raw products are shipped from production points to collection centers, then on to processing mills and finally on to the ports. The long and complicated networks involved implied that a substantial cure had to be given to proper routing and shipping to allow the system to work, and for the products in their raw or processed forms to flow smoothly through the system.

Along the way, products in their raw or processed form are often stored for various periods of time. Both cocoa and coffee can be stored easily with relatively little physical loss. The storage of the two products is usually a result of decisions involving exchange transactions. Because of the vagaries of the world trade, speculative stocks are often maintained as exports and delayed till market prices improve. Transactions thus often involve postponed deliveries that require products be stored from a few weeks up to a year and more.

Coordination of a Marketing System for Exports

Coordination in General

Allocation of marketing tasks performed in a given marketing system to specialized system entities allows the system as a whole to benefit from specialization and the advantages of division of labor. By entrusting performance of diverse marketing and production tasks to specialized units, total system costs can be reduced.[6] However, entrusting economic activities to different economic factors creates a need to combine them again in order to end up with a complete process. Coordination "principally concerns the relationships between tasks and activities that must fit in both form and time into an integrated accomplishment of some overall goal or purpose."[7] Chruch and Alfrod have observed:

> The coordination of effort is an inseparable counterpart of the division of effort. By coordination is meant the prearrangement of a number of separate efforts in such a manner as to produce a definite end. . . . The coordination of administrative effort is the most complex and debatable problem of all. The moment we begin to divide effort, we must also begin to provide for its coordination.[8]

Coordination involves three kinds of processes: *planning, implementation,* and *monitoring*.[9] The first involves deciding what is to be matched in regards to the activities and the actors, and how this matching is to be accomplished. Planning, thus, needs to include determination of the right timing, of performance technologies to be used, modes of transfer of products and information from one actor to another, allocation of responsibility, and monitoring of job performance. The *planning* stage, needs to be followed by *implementation* when the process of adjustment is carried out. This involves performing the relevant activities, transferring outputs between activities and actors, as well as legal negotiations and payment matters. Monitoring involves following up on the performance of the various participants in the transaction and evaluating this performance in light of some preset standards.

Three Approaches to Coordination

Coordination of a marketing system can be achieved by one of three approaches: through reliance on intermediary market mechanisms, through government or state owned enterprises, or by a mixed system. Each of these is discussed below.

a. *Use of the intermediary markets mechanisms.* Under this approach, the role of the government is limited to very broad economic and social policies without having any direct interaction with the marketing system and its mode of operation. Coordination is achieved indirectly by the price mechanism and the forces of competition that direct activities to their most efficient focus of performance; those entities that can perform a given task better than others outbid them and force them to stop performing those activities or even to disappear completely. Thus, each unit performs those tasks for which it is most capable and offers its service to others.

In many developing countries, substantial criticisms were raised against the free market as a mechanism to coordinate commodity exports. One argument is that, under the free market system, exporting firms are allowed to compete against each other in world markets, losing any monopolistic or oligopolistic advantages the country may have as a unit. While this reduces prices for buyers, sellers lose their profits. Another is that, due to their access to information about world markets, exporters tend to accumulate power in the marketing system. Without any government control over their behavior and or over their relationships with farmers, exporters will appropriate the largest share of the system profits, leaving too little for farmers. In some developing countries, the fear of monopolization of profits by exporters has been further enhanced by the desire to get rid of foreigners, who have often controlled international trade. To avoid transfer of national profits to foreign-controlled firms, governments have nationalized the export trade.

Another argument is that in some cases there is a difference in the attitude toward risk between the private and the public sectors. Individual exporters may be too cautious and not willing to invest required investments in infrastructure needed to expand production.[10] While such arguments were for a long time rejected by most economists, a group of economists have recently concluded that, in many cases, when behavioral characteristics of economic actors do not fit the assumptions of the classical economic theory, markets alone cannot coordinate marketing systems most efficiently and other institutional arrangements need to be made to achieve coordination.[11]

One major constraint that is emphasized by these economists is the tendency of economic actors to exhibit "bounded rationality," that is, an inability to calculate the complex and long-term implications of their own decisions. Another constraint is their tendency to behave in an opportunistic way and seek short-term gains through provision of misleading information, taking advantage of unforeseen misfortunes of their trade partners to the disadvantage of the system as a whole.

Both characteristics may deter efficient operation of the system as a whole. Due to bounded rationality, some system members may avoid performing activities that are beneficial in the long run and/or adopt or create necessary changes, because they may not be able to understand the benefits involved. Opportunism may lead, on the other hand, to dysfunctional behavior as system members may on purpose engage in activities which, though beneficial to them individually, are suboptimal or even disturbing to the marketing system as a whole.

b. *Replacement of the market mechanism by government-owned and government-managed entity that performs directly all the required marketing tasks itself.* Under such a system, marketing tasks are entrusted to a government department of a state-owned enterprise, without any or only minor participation of private firms. State-owned enterprises are owned, managed, and financed by the state. Legally, a state-owned enterprise is a separate entity from the government, sometimes incorporated under a general corporation act, sometimes under a specific act. The purpose of these legal forms is to free the enterprise from sales and regulations of the government that may prevent flexibility and reduce operating efficiency and to achieve separation from government activities within state-owned organizations. Marketing tasks are allocated here to subunits through an administrative fiat based on organizational authority. Coordination of activities is carried out by the government officials responsible for the various tasks.

Within such a system, quality of performance of a specific marketing task is not evaluated by any supply-demand response but by bureaucratic procedures. Specific standards are set up to evaluate each task performance and organizational rewards and penalties are used for that purpose.

While extreme reliance on free markets raises substantial reservations, reliance on government-owned enterprises to manage required marketing activities have raised another set of problems.[12] Governmental entities often tend to be bureaucratic, and not business- or profit-oriented, and therefore less capable of operating as traders in world markets. Similarly, substantial reservations are often raised as to the availability in developing countries of managers capable of running a highly complex marketing system and as to the existence of suitable managerial support systems in such economies.

Another criticism raised against state-owned enterprises is that they are expected to direct their operations on the basis of two contradictory orientations. They are supposed to be oriented to the achievement of strict economic goals while at the same time they are expected to pursue various activities in the public interest designed to achieve national goals. The two orientations may, however, create a conflict and even bring destruction to the organization.[13]

As a result, critics of direct government intervention have suggested that replacement of the market system by a vertically integrated government-managed system leads to substantial inefficiencies. Such systems are not very cost-conscious because they have no direct interest in reducing costs; government bureaucrats are not profit-oriented and may therefore be less concerned with maximizing profits for the organization. Instead, they may often strive to achieve political and organizational goals and are ready to sacrifice economic efficiency to these purposes. Finally, the complexity of running large organizational systems with few skilled managers may contribute further to gross inefficiencies.

The disadvantages of both free markets and government organizations suggests that the solution lies in the application of intermediary systems, ones which include a mixture of market- and government-managed systems.

c. In a *mixed system*, some marketing tasks are entrusted to private firms while others are performed by a state-run organization. Coordination of marketing tasks is still explicit through a set of governmental regulations and policies. The government does not intervene, however, into the specifics of performance of the marketing tasks entrusted to the private sector as long as the performance fits the requirements imposed/proposed by the government. Under such a system, the governmental coordinating effort is to a large degree devoted to interorganizational cooperation, and both the market mechanism and administrative standards are used to evaluate and direct performance.

The Ivorian Example

To organize the exporting of coffee and cocoa from the Ivory Coast to the world markets, the Ivory Coast has developed a marketing system characterized by a blend of private enterprise and governmental intervention that offers an example of an interesting mixed mode of organization of a marketing system. The present system has existed with some changes over twenty years in that country and its ability to respond to the challenges posed by the exporting tasks is witnessed by its success in expanding production and exports continuously.

Background

Ivory Coast is located at the West Coast of the African continent. It has a population of about eight million inhabitants, of which about 60 to 65 percent are rural inhabitants who till their land. Yet, few developed or developing countries can match the economic growth record of the Ivory Coast. Its annual growth rate of 7 percent from 1950 till 1975 is unique on the African continent. In 1950, with income per capita of around $70, the Ivory Coast ranked among the poorest nations; at independence in 1960, income had risen to $146 and in 1974 it had reached $450.[14]

Cocoa and coffee have been, and still are, the basis for Ivory Coast's success. Jointly, they contribute over half of the Ivorian exports and have constituted over 20 percent of the Ivory Gross Domestic Product in 1977.[15] Cocoa and coffee were introduced in the country around the turn of the century by the French colonizing authorities as export crops. With ups and downs, production and exports expanded steadily. In 1975, exports of coffee and cocoa were respectively at five and four times the 1950 export volume. Since 1975, production and exports of cocoa have kept on increasing. Exports of cocoa beans grew between 1975 and 1979 by 63 percent, while coffee bean exports have grown more slowly, reaching 270 thousand tons in 1979, an increase of 15 percent of over the 1975 figure. Production area devoted to coffee has grown at the same time by 17 percent.[16] (See Table 5.1)

Though originally grown by African and European planters, after independence coffee and cocoa have become an almost exclusively American owned enterprise, with hundreds of thousands of farmers involved in cultivation. By maintaining attractive producer prices, the government had not only induced farmers to expand production but also had brought purchasing power to substantial numbers of Ivorians.

The Marketing System for Cocoa and Coffee in the Ivory Coast

Figure 5.3 presents the marketing system that has been developed in the Ivory Coast for the exporting of cocoa and coffee. The system is made up by a long channel of diverse institutions involved with the various tasks of export management. Key elements include farmers, buyers-collectors, exporters, processors, shippers, and foreign importers. The long chain of institutions reflects the division of labor that has taken place in the sector.

Farmers occupy a relatively passive role in the marketing system for cocoa and coffee in the Ivory Coast. They are primarily concerned with production, yielding ownership and control over their products at farm's gate. Contractual farming is unknown in this sector and crops are sold on a cash

TABLE 5.1
Annual Production Area and Exports of Coffee and Cocoa from the Ivory Coast

Year	Coffee Production Area (000ha).	Exports (000T)	Cocoa Production Area (000ha)	Exports (000T)
1966	655	177	371	140
1970	652	87	386	178
1973	41	219	440	181
1975	863	233	471	237
1976	901	331	498	226
1977	921	277	527	230
1978	951	235	557	250
1979	1010	270	586	386

SOURCE: Statistiques Agricoles, 1981

FIGURE 5.3

The Marketing Channel for Exporting Coffee and Cocoa Beans

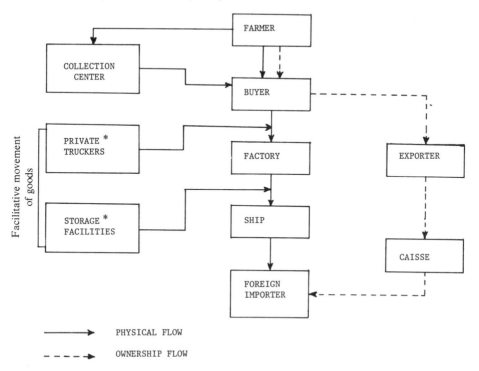

*Private truckers and storage facilities are not part of the marketing channel institutions. They are facilitatory means and as such help the free movement of physical goods.

basis to specialized *collectors-buyers*, owners of small trucks who circulate through the villages and buy raw cocoa and coffee cherries from the farmers. They usually work on a commission basis for exporters, each operating in a particular zone. Produce is then brought to *collection centers* where it is sorted and graded.

From the regional collection centers, products are sent to *mills* which crack the cocoa and coffee cherries, dry the beans and package them for exports. From there, the products are shipped to dock warehouses of exporting houses ready for shipment overseas. In 1979/80, there were 31 licensed exporters, 6 of which controlled, however, 55 percent of total exports. The *exporters* are engaged in shipping the products abroad and responsibile for arranging the physical flows to their final destination with foreign buyers abroad. They also are engaged in arranging the transactions with foreign buyers, under various governmental stipulations discussed below.

Within the country, exporters are responsible for domestic channel management as well. They organize the flows of products from the farm gate to ships, taking ownership of the products either at the farm gate or at collection centers.

Organization of the Marketing System

The approach used by the Ivorian government to coordinate and manage its cocoa and coffee exporting system was to choose the intermediate mode of management, which combines elements of the free market system with governmental control and supervision.[17]

The basic principles of the system management are as follows:

1. The actual performance of almost all marketing activities required is carried out by privately owned firms. The whole chain of activities from farming through processing to exporting is carried out by private Ivorian enterprises. The government does not perform any of these activities itself except for some direct involvement in export transactions, nor is it involved in the specific coordinations among the various system units.

2. Exporters are the actual leaders of the channel. At the beginning of each season, exporters receive from the government quotas that they are not entitled to surpass. They employ the buyers, who collect cherries from farmers, are responsible for arranging the transportation of the produce to the mill, and finance transportation. The exporters also pay the factories for processing. Furthermore, they are also responsible for managing the exports both for the negotiations with international buyers and for delivery of the products to international destinations.

3. The government controls marketing of cocoa and coffee through a *complex system of prices* fixed at the producer and exporter levels by *reimbursements* and by *administrative control* over export transactions. Exporters and other system members need to conform to these regulations, which regulate exports, marketing, and production.

a. *Control over exporting activities.* While exporters are free to negotiate transactions abroad, they have to submit each deal for the authorization of the government. For each sale, the exporter must submit a proosal stating quantity, quality, date of shipment, destination, and price. The government, through its exporting board, has to approve each sale; if it does not, the government exports the specific shipment itself and pays the exporter its own price. In this way, the government does not allow wars among exporters and can maintain a minimum price level for them.

b. *Guaranteed producer prices.* The government fixes each season producer prices to be paid at the farm-gate level for coffee and cocoa in their raw form. Buyers of these products are required to pay farmers these prices throughout the whole country. The prices are announced over the radio, in the press and posted in governmental agencies throughout the country so that farmers usually are well-informed. Producer prices are uniform for all production areas, irrespective of their location; they also do not change throughout the season even if international prices vary substantially. As a result, risk to farmers is minimized.

c. *Fixed reimbursement for marketing activities.* Exporters pay themselves for all production and marketing activities performed in the system. They are, however, compensated for these expenses through a system of fixed export prices. Each year, the government calculates an average export price on a cost-plus basis. This price includes price paid to farmers and estimates of other costs borne by exporters either directly or indirectly. Those include costs of collecting, transporting, processing, storage, and shipping.

These estimates are based on general, country-wide calculations and are not specific to each individual transaction or even an individual exporter. As a result, variations exist between actual expenses or a particular exporter and the calculated prices. Still, the calculated export price constitutes the guaranteed export price to which each exporter is entitled for his transactions.

The guaranteed export price can and often does vary from the actual price achieved in a given transaction. The differences trigger a calculation system between the government and the exporter. If actual export price exceeds the guaranteed price, the exporter has to reimburse the government for the difference. If the price achieved is, however, lower than the guaranteed price, the government reimburses the exporter. The reimbursement system makes the exporter in essence a commissioned sales agent for the government, eliminating the possibility that exporters will accumulate excess profits. At the same time, the system eliminates the risk of operation for them as well.

4. The pricing system so designed gives the government *control over all revenues* accruing from exports of coffee and cocoa. Over half of these revenues have been traditionally retained by the government and not handed over to producers or marketers. Those revenues have been used by the government to finance development projects in agriculture, in infrastructure (roads, land clearance, etc.) and in social projects of education, health, and housing.[18]

5. *Direct intervention in exporting.* The government is also directly involved in export transactions. It employs several brokers abroad who negotiate sales deals on the behalf of the governmental agency involved. The quantities involved come from supplies provided by exporters, who are

compensated for them on the basis of the guaranteed export price without having to sell these quantities abroad themselves.

The governmental policies towards exporting cocoa and coffee is carried out by a state-owned enterprise called the Caisse de Stabilisation et de Soutien des Prix des Produits Agricoles (CSSPPA) or the Fund for Stabilization and Support of Prices of Agricultural Products. The Caisse, as it is known in the country, is a totally independent entity, with a separate budget, personnel, and policies. It reports directly to the government and the president of the republic. Its revenue is based on that part of foreign exchange earned from coffee and cocoa exports that are not transferred to producers and marketers. It has also similar revenues from other agricultural exports.[19] The Caisse is the governmental body directly responsible for setting up, carrying out, and monitoring governmental policies in the coffee and cocoa sector. As such, it sets up prices, executes foreign negotiations, and approves exchange deals.

Implementation

The marketing system established in the Ivory Coast for exporting cocoa and coffee beans has allowed the country to benefit greatly from these exports. The government policies and the pattern of institutional relationships that were set up allowed the system to benefit from many of the advantages embedded in a free market system while avoiding some of its major disadvantages. The major advantages of the system can be summarized as follows:

a. By relying on the private enterprise for performance of the various marketing, production, and processing tasks, the system ensures that the forces of competition are not hampered. This allows the more efficient firms in each subset to thrive and compete successfully with less efficient ones. The latter are forced then to resign, leaving operation to the more efficient ones.

b. Coordination of overall channel activities is carried out through a policy of price systems without direct interference in actual marketing activities. As a result, channel coordination has been achieved with relatively low costs. By leaving channel activities to private enterprises, the excessive bureaucratic costs of running such a channel directly have been avoided. Instead of setting up specific planning and monitoring systems to follow up on performance of marketing tasks, price mechanism was used to control performance.

c. At the same time, governmental intervention has alleviated some of the problems encountered in the private sector. First, by setting up its producer price systems, the government has increased substantially farmers' motivation to shift from subsistence to export crop farming. Farmers are assured now of steady prices, income which can be well predicted, and an easy format of delivery of products. Farmers are thus relieved of many of the risks involved in such a shift in farming.

d. Governmental control over producer prices allows it also to transmit cues to farmers designed to expand or contract production. It can raise prices to encourage expansion over the long run even if short-run conditions differ and vice versa. Such a policy provides the government with a powerful tool without forcing it to be actually involved in production or marketing.

e. Governmental controls over exporters, on the other hand, allows it to eliminate dysfunctional competition among exporters. Through its system of guaranteed prices, the government ensures that none of the exporters will be able to undersell another and thus drive prices of all Ivorian exports down. The policy forces the exporters to relate to the governmental price as a floor price below which none can sell cocoa or coffee exports, and thus in effect, all exporters have to operate as a carte.

At the same time, the guaranteed price system as designed limits substantially the ability of channel intermediaries to reap excessive profits. Through the system of guaranteed prices, the government in effect has eliminated the possibility of monopolistic accumulation by exporters. Even if they succeeded in gaining excessive profits in foreign transactions, these profits have to be transferred to the government and the exporters cannot retain them. The producer-guaranteed price system limits exporters' power as well. It does not allow them to reap excessive profits by reducing prices paid to producers, and forces them to pay the government guaranteed prices. The dual price-guarantee system thus ensures that exporters cannot benefit from their position as channel leaders to accumulate monopolistic profits.

The governmental intervention in the operation of the export marketing system has not been without costs. The major disadvantages that it has brought was the *introduction of political considerations* to decisions concerning the operation of the export marketing system and *dysfunctional effects* on its operation.

By its control over producer and exporter prices, the government in effect could and did tax the whole cocoa and coffee sector, and direct part of these revenues to other uses. While initially planned to be used for infrastructure investments, funds from exports were soon directed to projects with political rather than economic implications. Funds were used to finance large-scale housing projects, and to subsidize rice imports and agricultural projects in the politically unstable northern part of the country. The result of the taxation has been a lower rate of return to the cocoa and coffee sector with a corresponding lower level of incentives for growers, exporters, and others.

Another disadvantage of the governmental policies is that they have reduced the incentive for exporters to seek high-profit transactions. Irrespective of the actual international prices achieved in a particular transaction, exporters are paid on the basis of government-set prices. As a result, exporters may be less concerned with achieving the most profitable deals, with a corresponding loss of foreign exchange for the country as a whole. Again, governmental intervention implies reduced efficiency for the system as a whole and lower revenue for the economic factors involved.

Thirdly, by reimbursing all exporters on a cost-plus basis for their activities, the government may also reduce incentives to perform the various marketing and processing tasks more efficiently. Exporters may be less interested in replacing relatively inefficient technologies, knowing that any resulting profits will be appropriated by the government, and this disinterest would result in a corresponding dysfunctional effect upon the system as a whole.

Yet, in spite of these disadvantages, the benefits of the system developed in the Ivory Coast outweigh so far, these disadvantages. The system has allowed the country to expand production and exports, create a large class of well-to-do farmers, and build a relatively smooth marketing system with few of the bureaucratic snags that often characterize state-owned enterprises in developing countries.

Conclusions

Establishment of the proper procedures in coordinating a marketing system is of crucial importance for success in exporting commodities from developing countries, which do not want to entrust this role to foreign companies and organizations such as multinational firms. Success of an export marketing system requires the performance of a large number of marketing activities through which producers are linked with international markets, and which ensure the proper flow of products, information, and monies in the system. Such activities are tightly linked to each other over large distances and long periods of time, and they are performed by a variety of economic agents. Coordination of decisions, activities, and agents is therefore crucial.

In developing countries, use of free market mechanisms to coordinate export systems has not been well developed. The use of direct government intervention, however, has not been successful, either. This suggests that such countries are better off using an intermediary technology of coordination, an example of which can be found in the coffee and cocoa export system in the Ivory Coast. While the system so developed has several disadvantages, it has succeeded to avoid most of the pitfalls of an administrative, government-controlled system while avoiding the excess and costs of the free market system.

Notes

1. Louis W. Stern and Adel El-Ansary, *Marketing Channels*, 2nd ed., (Englewood Cliffs, N.J.: Prentice Hall, 1981).

2. I.B.R.D., *Price Prospects for Major Primary Commodities*, Report No. 814/80. Washington, D.C., The World Bank, 1980

3. L. Bucklin, *A Theory of Distribution Channel Structure* (Berkeley, California: Institute of Business and Economic Research, University of California, 1966); and Louis W. Stern and A. El-Ansary, *Marketing Channels*."

4. I.B.R.D., *Price Prospects*.

5. Guy Delaport, "La Caissee de stablisation et de Soutien des prix de production agricoles", *Marches Tropicaux*, April 9, 1976, pp: 950–78; and Ministry of Planning, *The Five-Year Plan 1980–1985* (Adhidjan, Ivory Coast, Ministry of Planning, 1981).

6. Bucklin, "A Theory of Distribution."

7. Joseph A. Litterer, *The Analysis of Organization* (New York: John Wiley and Sons, 1965); and Ministry of Agriculture, *Le Prix de Produits Agricoles* (Ahidjan, Ivory Coast, Ministry of Agriculture, 1981).

8. A. A. Church and L. Afford, "The Principles of Management," in H. Merril, ed., *Classics in Management* (New York; American Marketing Association, 1960), p. 204.

9. Ian F. Wilkinson, "Coordinating Economies and the Economies of Coordination in Marketing Channels: Towards a Theory of Channel Structure," *Working Paper*, School of Business Administration, University of California at Berkeley, 1982.

10. Yair Aharoni, *Markets, Planning and Economic Development*, Cambridge, Mass.: Ballinger, 1977; and Albert Waterson, *Development Planning: Lessons of Experience* (Baltimore, Md.: The Johns Hopkins Press, 1965).

11. Victor P. Goldberg, "Toward an Expanded Economic Theory of Contract," *Virginia Law Review*, 67, September 1976, pp: 1089–1150; Michael Etgar, "The Effects of Administrative Controls on the Efficiency of Vertical Marketing Systems," *Journal of Marketing Research*, February 1976, pp: 12–34; Oliver Williamson, *Markets and Hierachies: Analysis of Antitrust Implications* (New York: Free Press, 1975); and "Transaction Cost Economics: The Governance of Contractual Relationships," *Journal of Law and Economics*, 22:3, 1981; pp: 548–77; and "The Economics of Organization: The Transaction Cost Approach," *American Journal of Sociology*, 87:3, 1981, pp: 548–77.

12. Aharoni, *Markets, Planning and Economic Development*,

13. *Ibid.*; and Michael Etgar, "Vertical Integration in Food Distribution in Developing Countries: The Failure of the Governmental Solution," forthcoming *Journal of Macromarketing*, 1982.

14. Van Tuiden, *Ivory Coast* (Baltimore, Md.: Johns Hopkins Press, 1977).

15. Van Tuiden, *Ivory Coast*; and Ministry of Agriculture, *Statistiques Agricoles* (Ahidjan, Ivory Coast: Ministry of Agriculture, 1981).

16. I.C.O. *Coffee in the Ivory Coast* (London: International Coffee Organization); and Ministry of Agriculture, *Le Prix de Produits Agricolee* (Ahidjan, Ivory Coast; Ministry of Agriculture, 1981).

17. Delaport, "La Caisse de Stabilisation," pp: 950–78; Ministry of Agriculture, "Le Prix de Produits"; and Ministry of Planning, *The Five-Year Plan*.

18. Ministry of Planning, *The Five-Year Plan*.

19. Van Tuiden, *Ivory Coast*.

IV

COMPARATIVE BUYER BEHAVIOR AND RESEARCH METHODOLOGIES

In this part, the first chapter by Douglas and Craig try to identify the various types of nonequivalence that may arise in comparative consumer research, and to suggest ways of dealing with these in the research design. Four key areas in comparative research design where equivalence needs to be established are examined. These are: 1) the definition of the constructs to be studied in different countries and sociocultural contexts; 2) the instruments used to measure these constructs; 3) the samples to whom instruments are administered; and 4) the ways these are administered in each country. The chapter by Cavusgil and Kaynak examines sources of consumer dissatisfaction in various environments, including developing economies. What are the causes of consumer dissatisfaction in developing nations? How do the sources of consumer dissatisfaction vary among nations? How responsive is the marketplace to the needs, wants, and purchasing power of consumers in different environments? Answers to these and similar questions cannot be given until adequate conceptualizations of consumer discontent are developed and their relevance is assessed for multiple environments.

In the final chapter of this part, Szabo examines the role and relevance of marketing and marketing research in the socialist countries and uses Hungary as a case in point. The author tries to find answers to questions such as how can marketing be reconciled with a centrally planned economy and what degree of efficiency can one attain with the help of marketing in a centrally planned economy.

6

ESTABLISHING EQUIVALENCE IN COMPARATIVE CONSUMER RESEARCH

Susan P. Douglas and C. Samuel Craig

Introduction

The comparative method is used extensively throughout the behavioral sciences. Comparative sociology,[1] comparative political science,[2] and cross-cultural psychology[3] are all well-established disciplines in their own right, applying methodologies adapted to the specific issues of interest and related problems. Yet, while studies of consumer behavior often rely heavily on concepts and methodologies borrowed from their parent disciplines, i.e., sociology and psychology, little attention has been paid to the findings and methodologies used by their comparative offshoots.

The purpose of the present chapter is both to identify the various types of non-equivalence that may arise in comparative consumer research, and to suggest ways of dealing with these in the research design. Four key areas of research design where equivalence needs to be established are examined, namely, in the: 1) definition of the constructs to be studied in different countries and sociocultural contexts; 2) instruments used to measure these constructs; 3) samples to whom instruments are administered; and 4) way these are administered in each country. Potential sources of non-equivalence that may occur in each of these areas are discussed, and some ways of examining non-equivalence, and avoiding errors of misinterpretation due to non-equivalence, are suggested. Finally, some recommendations are made concerning the design of future research, which is hoped may lead to improved contributions from the application of the comparative method.

Areas of Data Equivalence

In conducting comparative consumer research, a key concern is the equivalence of the data collected in different countries. This is important in that unless the equivalence of data collected in different cultural or national contexts is established, inappropriate inferences about comparisons between countries may be made, which reflect differences in research methodology and procedures, rather than actual differences between countries or socio-cultural contexts.

Issues of data equivalence may arise in four areas of research design. These are outlined in Table 6.1. In the first place, equivalence has to be established in terms of the constructs that are studied. Here, it is necessary to assess whether a given concept or behavior has the same role or function in society from one country to another, i.e., its functional equivalence. The interpretations and meaning due to differences in familiarity with different conceptual equivalence, has also to be considered. In addition, the equivalence of different categories studied from one country to another, as for example, of product classes or occupational categories, has also to be examined.

The next area in which equivalence needs to be considered, is in the development of operational measures of these constructs. Here, equivalence in the calibration of the measurement instrument needs to be considered, as for example whether the measurement units, i.e., points on a scale, use of metric vs. other measuring systems etc.—or in the case of nonverbal stimuli, colors and images—are comparable. Similarly, where verbal stimuli are utilized, the equivalence of the translation and translation procedures should be established. Furthermore, equivalence in terms of how responses are scored needs to be evaluated. Positions on a scale may have different interpretations and meaning due to differences in familiarity with different scales, and different response biases from one country to another.

Once an appropriate measurement instrument has been designed, the next step is to establish comparability with regard to samples drawn from different countries. Here, a basic dilemma arises, since samples that are representative of the country or cultural context are unlikely to be comparable with regard to other characteristics, e.g., education or income. This may create a problem if these factors are related to the problem studied, since the comparison may reflect the impact of these factors rather than the country or sociocultural factors. In like manner, whether or not similar respondents, i.e., husbands, wives, or children, should be sampled in different countries has to be considered, since different family members are respons-

TABLE 6.1

Areas of Data Equivalence in Comparative Consumer Research

A. Construct Equivalence
   1. Functional Equivalence
   2. Conceptual Equivalence
   3. Category Equivalence

B. Measure Equivalence
   1. Calibration Equivalence
   2. Translation Equivalence
   3. Metric Equivalence

C. Sample Equivalence
   1. Respondent Equivalence
   2. Composition of Sample
   3. Frame Equivalence
   4. Sample Selection Equivalence

D. Instrument Administration Equivalence
   1. Data Collection Procedures
   2. Contextual Equivalence
   3. Temporal Equivalence

ible for various tasks in different countries. Differences in the availability and reliability of sampling frames such as census or telephone books may also create obstacles to sample equivalence. Often, therefore, interviewers are used to generate samples, via, for example, block or random walk sampling.

Finally, issues of equivalence can arise with regard to how the instrument is administered in different countries. Equivalence of results generated by the use of the same or similar data collection procedures as, for example, mail, telephone, or interviewer, has to be examined due to differences in error and reliability from one country to another. Related to this are differences arising as a result of the context in which the research is conducted, as, for example, in the nature of the interviewer/interviewee interaction. Here, specific response biases in a given sociocultural context may materially affect interaction. Differences in the time at which research is conducted may also need to be evaluated. If, for example, research is conducted six months later in one country, differences in the time lapse may account for at least part of the observed variation. Equivalence in seasonality may also be a factor if research is conducted in different hemispheres.

Each of the elements that may affect equivalence of data from one country or socio-cultural context to another is next examined in more detail. Procedures for examining comparability are discussed relative to each type of equivalence, and some suggestions are made regarding the design of research so as to reduce error arising from non-equivalence.

Equivalence Issues in Comparative Data

Construct Equivalence

The first issue to be examined in considering the equivalences of comparative data is that of construct equivalence. This has three distinct aspects. First, the researcher must assess whether a given concept or behavior serves the same function or role from country to country, i.e., its *functional* equivalence. Secondly, he must determine whether the same concepts or behavior occur in different countries, and whether their meaning is the same and the way in which they are expressed is similar, i.e, their *conceptual* equivalence. Thirdly, he must examine whether the same classification scheme of objects can be used across countries, or, in other words, the degree of *category* equivalence. In essence, this amounts to assessing whether the market structure and relevant parameters, including, for example, objects, use of objects, habit patterns, attitudes, and value standards, are the same or equivalent, from one country to another, as well as factors which condition these such as, for example, the distribution structure and the degree of competition. Each of these types of equivalence is next considered in more detail.

Functional Equivalence

First of all, it is important to remember that the concepts, objects, or behaviors studied may not necessarily be *functionally* equivalent, i.e., have the same role or function in all countries studied.[4] Thus, for example, while bicycles are predominantly used for recreation in the U.S.A., in the Far East they are often a basic mode of transportation. This implies that the relevant competing product set must be defined differently. In the U.S.A., it will include other recreational products while, in the Far East, alternative modes of transportation may be considered.

Apparently similar activities may also have different functions. In, some countries such as the U.S.A., for example, adult education courses may be regarded primarily as a leisure activity designed to provide broader cultural awareness. In other countries, such as Japan, adult education is geared primarily to improving work performance. Similarly, while for many U.S.A. families grocery shopping is a chore and a work activity to be accomplished as efficiently and conveniently as possible, in other countries it plays an important social function. Interaction with local shopkeepers and vendors, and with other neighbors and acquaintances in stores or in the marketplace, is thus an integral part of day-to-day living.

Conceptual Equivalence

While functional equivalence is concerned with the role of objects and behavior in society from a macro-cultural level, conceptual equivalence is concerned with the interpretation that individuals place on objects, stimuli, or behavior, and whether these exist or are expressed in similar ways in different countries and cultures. Thus, while the same object or behavior may occur in two different countries, it may not have the same interpretation or significance in different countries or cultures or may be manifested in different types of behavior. Similarly, an attitude, behavior, or object may be unique to a specific country, or occur in some countries but not in others.

Personality traits such as aggressiveness, authoritarianism, alienation, or affiliation needs may not be relevant in all countries and cultures, or may be expressed in different types of behavior, hence requiring different measures. Some attitudes or behavior may be unique to a specific country. The concept of *philotimo*, or behaving in the ways members of one's "in" group expect, for example, is unique to the Greek culture.[5] This includes meeting obligations and sacrificing self to help group members such as family, friends, or guests.

Even where the same concept or construct is identified, it may be expressed by different types of behavior in different cultural settings. Innovativeness, for example, may be a relevant concept in both the U.S.A. and France. In the U.S.A., this is reflected not only in the purchase and trial of new products, but also in conversations and in providing information to friends and neighbors about new products and brands. In France, however, to be innovative is not socially valued, and consequently, those who purchase new products will rarely discuss these problems with others.[6]

Similarly, a physical, male-oriented life-style may be defined in the U.S.A. in terms of attitude such as wanting to be a professional football player, liking war stories, and by behavior such as reading *Playboy* or the sports page in the daily paper.[7] In Canada, it is defined not only in terms of liking war stories, but also in liking hunting and fishing; and in Mexico it is expressed in terms of wanting to be a soccer star, liking sports events, liking to go to bull-fights and fiestas and admitting to being a girl-watcher.

Category Equivalence

A third type of construct equivalence relates to the category in which objects or other stimuli are placed. Relevant product class definitions may, for example, differ from one country to another. In the soft drink and alcoholic beverage market, for example, forms of soft drinks such as carbonated sodas, fruit juices, and powdered and liquid concentrates vary significantly from one culture to another and, hence, how these are defined and delineated differ. In Mediterranean cultures, for example, beer is considered to be a soft drink.[8] Similarly, in the dessert market, items that are included will vary substantially, ranging from apple pie, jellies, and ice cream to baklava, rice pudding, and zabaglione. In some societies, cakes or cookies are included as desserts, while in China sweet items do not form part of the meal. This implies that what is included in the relevant competing product set will vary. Careful attention to such factors is thus an important consideration when developing product-related measures. In addition, the characteristics or attributes perceived by consumers as relevant in evaluating a product class may differ from one country to another. In France, for example, the hot-cold continuum is a key attribute in characterizing consumer's perceptions of fragrances. In the U.S.A. and the U.K., however, this is not an attribute that is perceived as relevant by consumers.

Differences in background or sociodemographic characteristics have also to be considered. In the case of marital status, for example, in various African countries it is not uncommon for a male to have several wives, and, in some cases, women may have several husbands. Occupational categories also do not always have strict equivalence in all countries. The counterpart of the U.S. lawyer, the English barrister, or the Japanese subway packer may be difficult to find. Occupations may also differ in status from one country or society to another. Being a priest, religious minister, or teacher is, for example, often more prestigious in less-developed than in the more literate industrialized nations. Similary, the social prestige attached to government administrative positions or to being a lawyer varies from society to society.

Examining Construct Equivalence in Comparative Data

The difficulties that may arise in establishing comparability of the constructs examined in different countries or sociocultural contexts, suggest that rather than attempting to develop pan-cultural or "culture free" measure of concepts, a hybrid approach allowing for identification of both pan-cultural and also culture-specific measures should be adopted.[9] First, country or cultural measures are developed. These are then compared, combined, or modified, and where possible common "pan-cultural" concepts that do not have a specific cultural bias are identified. Where no equivalence is found, country-idiosyncratic measures are used. The comparison is thus made based on both common, i.e., pan-cultural and country-specific measures.

For example, in comparing life-styles in different countries, certain elements such as attitudes toward a woman's role, degree of home orientation, or conservatism may be common to all countries, and may be tapped by similar attitudinal variables. Others such as innovation or sociability may best be measured in terms of different yet equivalent variables.[10] Yet others, for example, the Oriental notion of "saving face," are unique to the culture and, hence, country-specific measures will need to be developed.

Where life-styles are being examined and, hence, are the dependent variable, the interrelationships among different aspects of life-styles can first be examined within each country or culture. These interrelationships can then be compared across countries, examining, for example, whether there is any apparent similarity in the patterning and whether similar factors appear to be interrelated. Where similar factors are identified in two countries, how uniquely defined factors relate to these can be studied.

Where life-style is used as an independent or explanatory variable, not only can the interrelationships of different aspects of life-style be compared across countries, but also their relation to a dependent variable such as product purchases or media habits. Again, whether the same aspects of life-style appear to be related in the same way to the dependent variable can be examined, as well as the strength of the relationship relative to uniquely or differently defined variables.

Such comparisons not only provide substantive information with regard to similarities and differences between countries, but can also be viewed as a further test of the validity of the measures used and of their equivalence. This assessment is based on the extent to which similar relationships are found among the various independent variables, and also among independent and dependent variables.

Measure Equivalence

Once construct equivalence has been examined, the next step is to consider measure equivalence. Construct and measure equivalence are highly interrelated insofar as the measure operationalizes the conceptual definition of the construct. It is, nonetheless, useful to separate the conceptual definition from the actual measurement procedure insofar as the conceptual definition indicates what the researcher aims to measure, while the measure is the instrument used to tap that construct. Here equivalence with regard to three aspects has to be considered: 1) the calibration system used in measurement; 2) the translation of the research instrument; and 3) the metric or scalar equivalence of the instrument.

Calibration Equivalence

In the first place, in developing a research instrument, equivalence has to be established with regard to the calibration system used in measurement. This includes not only equivalence with regard to monetary units and measures of weight, distance, and volume, but also other perceptual cues, such as color, shape, or form, which are used to interpret visual stimuli.

The need to establish equivalence with regard to monetary and physical measurement units is clearly apparent. Standard procedures or tables for conversion are readily available. Comparability with regard to measurement standards and procedures needs, however, also to be considered, as they may vary from one context to another. For example, comparability with regard to standards such as product grading, or product quality and safety regulations, should be investigated, since these are not uniform from one country to another.

More subtle differences in instrument calibration, which are particularly relevant in the case of nonverbal instruments, relate to perceptual cues such as color, form, or shape. Studies in cognitive and cross-cultural psychology suggest that a substantial degree of commonality exists with regard to the manifestations of these in different countries and cultures.[11] However, ability to differentiate and to develop gradations in these schema appears to differ.

Studies in color in different cultures have shown the existence of an identical color spectrum throughout cultures,[12] but the ability of cultures to differentiate between different points on the color spectrum varies. They claim that there are never more than eleven basic color classes but there may be less. Western subjects, for example, typically have more color classes than African subjects, and some primitive people have only a two-term color language.[13] The Bantu of South Africa, for example, do not distinguish between blue and green. Consequently, they do not discriminate between objects or symbols in these colors. Awareness of such nuances is thus an important consideration in instrument design and development, especially in relation to visual stimuli.

Translation Equivalence

A second aspect of measure equivalence concerns translation of the instrument so that it is understood by respondents in different countries and has equivalent meaning in each research context. The need for translation of questionnaires and other verbal stimuli where research is conducted in countries with different languages is readily apparent. The need to translate nonverbal stimuli to ensure that they evoke the desired image and to avoid problems of miscommunication is less widely recognized.

Translation equivalence is a central issue in the establishment of construct validity in survey research, since this is the stage in the research design at which the construct is defined in operational terms. The translation procedure, thus, frequently helps to pinpoint problems with regard to whether a concept can be measured by using the same or similar questions in each cultural context, and whether a question has the same meaning in different research contexts. If different questions are used, then issues arise with regard to the minimal level of equivalence necessary for two questions to be considered the same, and what criteria for equivalence can be established.

Translation of nonverbal stimuli require attention to how perceptual cues are interpreted in each research context. Misunderstanding may arise because the respondent is not familiar with a product or other stimulus, for example, an electrical appliance, or the way in which it is depicted. Alternatively, respondents may misinterpret stimuli because the associations evoked by the stimuli, as, for example, those associated with color or shape, differ from one country or culture to another.

Interpretation of meaning attached to colors, may, for example, vary from one culture or cultural context to another. White, for example, is a color of mourning in Japan, while in Chinese culture, red is a symbol of happiness and plays a focal role in weddings, from invitations being printed in red, monetary gifts given in red envelopes, to the red dresses worn by the bride. Green, in Malaysia, symbolizes the jungle, and hence has connotations of danger. Translation of verbal and nonverbal stimuli thus plays a key role in the establishment of equivalence. Often it proves a focal point both for uncovering and for making pragmatic decisions as to how to resolve construct equivalence issues.

Metric Equivalence

A final concern is metric equivalence. This is the scoring or scalar equivalence of the measure used. Two aspects have to be considered in determining metric equivalence; the first concerns the specific scale or scoring procedure used to establish the measure, the second, the equivalence of response to a given measure in different countries. The greater the emphasis placed on quantitative measurement and data interpretation, the more important the establishment of metric equivalence becomes. It is, thus, an integral part of decisions relating to data analysis, especially where attitudinal scaling or multivariate procedures are entailed.

Metric equivalence in scale and scoring procedures is of particular relevance insofar as the most effective gradation of scales or scoring procedures may vary from one country or culture to another. This depends essentially on the type of scales and scaling procedures most commonly used in a country or culture. While in the U.S.A., use of 5- or 7-point scales is common, in other countries 20-point or 10-point scales may be more typical. Similarly, use of nonverbal response such as latency measures, i.e., speed of response, requires consideration of the implications of the results obtained in each country and culture.

A second aspect of metric equivalence concerns the response to a score obtained on a measure. Here, the question arises as to whether a score obtained in one research context has the same meaning and interpretation in another context. For example, on an intentions-to-purchase scale, do the top two boxes, commonly used to predict the proportion of likely buyers, indicate a similar likelihood of purchase from one country to another, or does a position on a Likert scale have the same meaning in all cultures?

Examining Measure Equivalence in Comparative Data

As in the case of construct equivalence, it is important to include procedures for examining measure equivalence in the research design. In contrast to construct equivalence, measure equivalence can be only examined once the data have been collected. Prior experience or examination of similar types of measures in the relevant country or culture may provide some guidelines as to appropriate scales and typical response patterns. This may also suggest the types of data analysis and statistical procedures which will be required to test for measure equivalence and are appropriate in view of typical response patterns.

Another more systematic and comprehensive approach is to develop multiple measures of each construct. Since different measures may have different biases in different countries or cultures, the results obtained from using different measurement methods can be compared in order to assess their equivalence.[14] In examining product preferences in different countries, for example, one method commonly used is to conduct paired product tests. Respondents are thus asked to indicate their preferences for one or the other product or whether they have no preference. One problem that can bias cross-cultural comparisons of such measures are differences in yea-saying or nay-saying bias, or in extreme response bias. Respondents in some countries or cultures may tend to be particularly enthusiastic; for example, Chinese and Irish give highly favorable ratings to stimuli that they like. Other respondents, particularly those with lower educational levels, may tend to make greater use of extreme points on a scale. Consequently, comparisons of average responses may be misleading as they reflect these biases, rather than "true" responses.

This may be tested by including, in addition to the paired product test, a unipolar or unbalanced scale, e.g., a scale from one to ten, and a scale rating an object of neutral affect.[15] A comparison of the ratings on the different scales can thus be made. If, for example, there are greater differences between samples from two countries on the unipolar or unbalanced scale than on the balanced five-point scale, one may suspect that extreme or yea-saying bias may be greater in one country than the other. This may be checked against the ratings on the neutral scale. If ratings on this scale are substantially higher in one country than in another, this suggests a greater degree of yea-saying in that country than in the other. The ratings will, therefore, need to be adjusted accordingly to reflect "true" response.

Various procedures may be utilized to adjust scales. They may, for example, be standardized or normalized. If scales are standardized, the mean for each subject is made equal to zero, and deviation expressed in terms of standard deviation around that point. In normalization, the individual differences are expressed in terms of deviation from a group (i.e., country) mean. Another alternative procedure is ipsatization.[16] This is similar to normalization in that an individual's score is adjusted for the group (or country) mean.

Sampling Equivalence

The third form of equivalence concerns the comparability of samples drawn from different countries. Here, in addition to lack of comparability due to standard sampling errors, a number of issues that may affect sample comparability need to be examined. The first concerns the relevant respondent, i.e., individual(s) within the household, to be sampled. The second is the comparability of the composition and representativity of the sample. A third issue is the equivalence of the frames from which the samples are drawn, while a fourth relates to the equivalence resulting from the sample selection procedure. Each of these issues is next examined in more detail.

Respondent Equivalence

In determining the appropriate sample to be used in comparative consumer research, an important consideration is whether these respondents should be the same in all countries. Differences may, for example, occur in terms of whether one or several family members are involved in purchase decisions. In some cases, a single individual is responsible for purchase decisions as in relation to certain food or convenience items or purchases of personal items such as clothing and toiletries. In others, several individuals may be involved, when, for example, husbands accompany wives on grocery-shopping trips or all family members participate in an automobile purchase decision. Even when a single individual is responsible for making the purchase, others may, nonetheless, play a role, as when husbands set a budgetary limit on the purchase of a household appliance or indicate their preference for a type of food or a particular brand. Thus, it is important to consider differences in the roles played by various family members from one country or sociocultural context to another.

In addition, the relevant household members to be considered may vary from one country to another. In the U.S.A., it is not uncommon for children to exercise substantial influence in purchases of cereal, toys, desserts, and other items. In other countries, where families are less child-oriented, they have much less influence. Similarly, with the increasing proportion of working wives in many Western nations, husbands participate to an increased extent in grocery shopping activities and, hence, influence brand choice. The *Reader's Digest* has, for example, sponsored a number of surveys of husband-wife interactions in purchase decisions in various European countries which reveal substantial husband influence and participation in a wide range of products. In Oriental nations, continuance of the extended family relationship implies that several families may continue to live together, and, hence, only senior family members are responsible for many purchase decisions. Similarly, in some Oriental, Latin America, and white non-Afrikans, South African families of upper socioeconomic status, a maid or *amah* is frequently responsible for purchasing food and groceries, and often for menu-planning.

Sample Composition and Representativeness

A second issue to be considered in sampling is the extent to which samples are comparable and also representative of the population of interest from one country to another. Here, a basic dilemma arises. Probability samples of the population of a country, although representative, are unlikely to be comparable with regard to their composition on characteristics, such as income, education, or other sociocultural factors. If, on the other hand, samples are matched so as to ensure comparability on relevant characteristics, other confounding effects may be introduced, and representativeness is lost.

Use of probability sampling in comparative consumer research can thus generate problems that result in samples that are not comparable with regard to key characteristics influencing consumer response. For example, if, in a comparison of innovativeness in different countries, probability samples are drawn, they may not be comparable with regard to characteristics such as income, education, or other factors likely to affect innovativeness. Mistaken inferences may thus be drawn about "cross-national" differences and similarities, when these in fact reflect the impact of differences in sample composition rather than "true" national differences.

If on the other hand, samples are "matched" based on characteristics thought likely to affect results, other problems of influence and interpretation may arise.[17] The preselection of respondents on the "matching" criteria may introduce other confounding effects due to the association of the "matching" criteria with other variables related to the behavior studied.

Frame Equivalence

A third issue concerns the equivalence of sampling frames used in different countries or sociocultural contexts, and whether or not these will generate comparable samples. While in the U.S.A., in many cases, telephone directories provide adequate sampling frames, in other countries telephone directories may not be available or telephone ownership so low that only a small segment would be reached.

Especially in the developing countries, considerable difficulties may arise in reaching the rural low-income illiterate population due to lack of sampling frames. Thus, use of a procedure such as quota, cluster, or stratified sampling may generate a more representative sample. For example, major towns or villages are identified and a random walk procedure used. A number of starting points are identified, and the interviewer is instructed to visit every nth dwelling, e.g., one in five, until his quota is filled. In some cases, a somewhat creative approach may be required in drawing the sample. For example, when sampling the river population in Peru, one company identified a number of points along the river, and every fourth boat or raft from each point was sampled.[18]

Noncomparability arising from non-equivalent frames can be further compounded by differences in nonresponse rates from one country to another. Evidence exists to indicate differences in rates of response to surveys and to interviewing, as well as to specific types of questions.[19] This arises as a result of factors such as fatigue with interviewing, suspiciousness of the intent of the survey or the interviewer, differences in social sensitivity to various topics, willingness to be interviewed or to respond to surveys or simply in the efficiency of data collection procedures used in different countries.

Thus, it is not safe to assume that if the same sampling procedures are used in each country with known biases, the results will automatically be comparable.[20] Different procedures are subject to different types of bias, and these vary from one country or culture to another.[21] A sampling procedure underestimating commercial travelers might have a different effect in various countries due to a different incidence of commercial travelers. Thus, the results would not be comparable.

Sample Selection Equivalence

Noncomparability can also arise as a result of the sample selection procedure, i.e., the way in which the sample is selected from the frame. This is particularly likely to occur where nonprobability sampling is used and where interviewers are used to generate the sample. If, for example, respondents are picked in the marketplace or in a shopping mall, or to fill quotas in a given category, they may have certain specific characteristics and, hence, not be representative of the overall population. Shoppers in suburban or out-of-town malls may, for example, tend to be more mobile than the average, and are less likely to be working. Furthermore, such differences may vary from country to country.

Similarly, when interviewers are required to fill certain quotas, they are likely to select respondents who are easily accessible. They may, for example, select respondents from among their friends and acquaintances, or from those who are close to their home. This may generate some bias since, again, such people are likely to have certain specific characteristics, coming from a particular social background or having certain affinities. Consequently, the sample may have certain particularities, which account for findings of similarities and differences when a comparison is made with a sample from another country or culture.

Examining Sample Equivalence to Comparative Data

Various procedures may be utilized to detect sample equivalence to comparative data. These range from the use of different sampling procedures in various countries to statistical analysis. Use of different sampling procedures representing different potential biases in different countries has been advocated.[22] Thus, if similar findings occur in each country, these are likely to be substantive, rather than reflecting bias due to the use of a specific sampling procedure. This procedure was used in one multi-country industrial survey.[23] A consistent pattern was found on one of the main variables studied, namely, the percentage of firms in each size category owning the test product. Since different sampling procedures were used in each country, it was clear that this result was not an artifact of a specific sampling procedure. It is, however, important to note where this procedure is used that if differences are observed, it is not clear whether these are in fact substantive, or reflect biases of the different sampling procedure. Prior experience with the various sampling techniques in the countries may, however, aid in interpreting results.

An alternative procedure is to use statistical analysis. This requires prior specification of the variables generating non-equivalence between the samples. If, for example, a comparison of media habits such as a T.V.-viewing behavior in several countries is to be made, factors such as age, income, education, or whether the wife works, as well as cultural values and attitudes and life-style patterns, may all be expected to influence these habits. If, however, samples are drawn that are nationally representative, it is unlikely that they will be comparable in composition with regard to such variables, since countries will differ in terms of distribution on these. Consequently, observed differences or similarities may reflect the impact of these factors, rather than country differences.

This issue can be examined by statistical procedures such as univariate or multivariate analysis of covariance. In this case, the country samples are treated as units in an experimental design,and variables thought likely to affect the behavior studied entered as covariates in order to examine their impact.[24] In comparing media habits, for example, background characteristics such as income, occupation, sex, age, etc., or the attitudinal/ behavioral variables can be entered as covariates. This procedure enables, first of all, examination of the impact of these characteristics (i.e., the covariates) on differences or similarities in response. Secondly, data (i.e, national means) can be adjusted for differences in the covariates, so that the impact of these characteristics is removed from the analysis. The size of this adjustment can also be examined. Finally, the significance of the relationship between specific characteristics or covariates, and the behavior studied, i.e., the dependent variable, can be examined based on the F statistics associated with each covariate.

Covariance analysis is thus useful in examining the impact of sample characteristics on differences and similarities observed between national samples. Often when this procedure is applied, differences that appear initially may diminish. This further underscores the need to pay attention to the critical importance of sampling and its impact on multi-country comparisons.

Instrument Administration Equivalence

The fourth and final type of equivalence to be considered relates to the way or conditions under which the research instrument is administered. Here, three aspects of the administration process need to be considered. First, the biases associated with different instrument administration procedures i.e., by telephone, mail, or personal interview, may affect equivalence. Finally, the timing, particularly whether data are collected sequentially or at different times in various countries, may give rise to problems of non-equivalence.

Data Collection Equivalence

In comparative consumer research, three types of data collection procedures may be utilized: telephone, mail or personal interview. These differ, however, from country to country in terms of their potential biases and reliability due to factors such as the communications infrastructure, the degree of literacy and the limited availability and adequacy of sampling frames. Consequently, it is not clear that use of the same procedure will necessarily generate equivalent or comparable results.

In the U.S.A., telephone surveys enable coverage of a broadly distributed sample as well as facilitating control over interviewers. Telephone ownership is widespread, and hence telephone directories or listings provide reasonably accurate sampling frames. In other countries, however, low levels of telephone ownership and poor communications limit the coverage provided by telephone surveys. In addition, telephone costs are often high, and volume rates may not be available. Telephone directories also may not be available or accurate listings, from which to draw a sample. Consequently, a telephone survey may not provide an appropriate method of generating equivalent samples, unless relatively upscale or affluent socio-economic segments are to be sampled.

Similarly, while the U.S.A. mail surveys provide a low-cost means of reaching a broad sample without necessitating a field staff, in other countries they may not be as effective. Particularly in developing countries, use of mail surveys may give rise to some problems. Mailing lists comparable to those in the domestic market may not be available, or not sold, and sources such as telephone directories may not provide adequate coverage. Lists that are available, i.e., magazine subscription lists or membership association lists, may be skewed to better educated segments of the population. In addition, in some countries, the effectiveness of mail surveys is limited not only by low levels of literacy, but also the reluctance of respondents to respond to mail surveys. In Asian and African markets, for example, levels of literacy are often less than 50 percent, thus limiting the population that can be reached by mail.

Consequently, as in the case of telephone surveys, mail surveys may only generate equivalent results where comparisons are being made between appropriate industrialized countries in which levels of literacy are high and mailing lists comparable. In other countries, they may only generate equivalent results if it is desired to study relatively up-scale and well-educated segments of the population. If, on the other hand, a study focuses on comparisons of attitudes or behavior of the overall population, mail surveys are unlikely to be appropriate in developing or middle-income countries.

The problems encountered with the use of both telephone and mail surveys in developing countries implies that, in this context, data may be more equivalent if the instrument is administered by interviewers. In any event, this may be desirable, since field staff may be needed to draw the sample. This does, however, require the availability of trained interviewers who are fluent in the relevant language. Furthermore, differences in factors affecting the interviewer/interviewee interaction from one country or cultural context to another may tend to affect the equivalence of the data collected. These factors are next discussed in more detail.

Contextual Equivalence

In the case of surveys administered by telephone or personal interview, the interviewer/respondent interaction may affect the comparability or equivalence of the data. While in the U.S.A. consumers are accustomed to the notion of being interviewed, in other countries suspiciousness about the interviewer's motivations and feelings that interviewing constitutes an invasion of privacy, as well as negative attitudes towards questioning by strangers, may exist. This affects the willingness of respondents to participate or cooperate in both industrial and consumer surveys and also the extent to which respondents will deliberately conceal information or give false answers.

The ease with which cooperation of respondents can be obtained thus varies from one country or culture to another. In Latin American countries, and particularly in the Middle East, interviewers are regarded with considerable suspicion. In Latin American countries, where tax evasion is a national pastime, interviewers are often suspected of being tax inspectors, and hence interviewees may tend to give a biased response. In the Middle East, where interviewers are invariably male, interviews with housewives often have to be conducted in the evenings when husbands are at home. Similarly, in a country such as Italy, it may be difficult to interview the housewife without her family being present. In both cases, the presence of others may affect responses, and these may not always be the same as if the housewife were interviewed alone.

Similarly, respondents in various countries differ in the extent to which they may desire to be socially acquiescent, to provide the socially acceptable response, for their responses to specific items in the questionnaire. The desire to be socially acquiescent and to provide the response that may be felt to be desired by the interviewer is particularly prevalent in certain countries and certain cultures, especially in Asia.[25] Here, cultural values imply that it is an obligation for the respondent to see that the interviewer is not distressed, disappointed, or offended in any way. Replies may not only be intended to please the interviewer, but also to reflect the "done" thing in his culture.[26] For example, a respondent may say that he purchases a product regularly, whether or not this is the case. This bias is particularly marked among better educated urban respondents who will tend to give answers reflecting their greater sophistication and knowledge as to what they *should* answer, rather than their genuine beliefs. Willingness to respond to questions such as income, or topics such as sex or alcoholism, also varies from one country or culture to another. In the Scandinavian countries, for example, respondents are considerably more willing to admit to overdrinking than in Latin countries.[27] In India, sex tends to be a taboo topic.

Yet, another factor affecting the equivalence of data from one country to another is the tendency for certain dominant cultural traits to affect the nature of the response. The Japanese are, for example, more humble, which leads them to undervalue assets or property, while the Middle Eastern respondent is more prone to exaggerate.[28] Similarly, to the extent that the Irish are more ebullient than the English, one might expect them to tend to give more affirmative responses.

Willingness to respond to different types of questions, such as questions relating to income or age, has also been found to vary from country to country. A recent study of nonresponse to different items in a public opinion survey in eight European countries found nonresponse to questions on income to be higher in the U.K. and Ireland than in other E.E.C. countries.[29] Sensitivity, and hence willingness to respond to political questions, appeared to be highest in Germany and Italy. All these factors can thus influence results and generate data that are not strictly comparable from one country to another.

Temporal Equivalence

A third and final source of non-equivalence can result from differences in the time at which studies are conducted from one country to another. If studies are not conducted simultaneously in all countries or contexts, differences or similarities in data may occur due to the passage of time. Thus, for example, if a study of attitudes towards a woman's role or of teenagers consumption of toiletries is conducted in one country one year, and in another country another year, the comparison may be affected by the evolution of dominant cultural values and behavior patterns or changes in the retail infrastructure.

Yet, simultaneous conduct of studies does not necessarily imply equivalence of results from one country to another. Depending on their geographic latitude, countries have different seasons and climatic conditions. Consequently, studies relating to purchase of soft drinks, food products, or clothing would need to take such factors into consideration. It may, therefore, be more appropriate to conduct the study at different times, when the seasons are comparable. Similarly, external events such as political elections and consumerist campaigns may influence consumer behavior and lead to noncomparable results.

Procedures for Examining Equivalence in Instrument Administration

In contrast to the examination of equivalence in concepts, measures, and samples, there are no clear-cut procedures to be followed in research design to examine equivalence in instrument administration. This stems in part from the different potential biases associated with different methods of instrument administration and the fact that these may vary from one country to another. Furthermore, this stage of the research is concerned with the actual fieldwork in implementation of the design. Consequently, there are a number of factors external to the design, as for example, the research infrastructure, which may affect equivalence from one country to another.

In theory, following similar principles to those suggested in relation to earlier aspects of research design, the equivalence of different methods might be tested by using multiple methods in each country in a given study. In practice, however, this is likely to be unfeasible due to the high costs associated with such a procedure, as this would require resampling the same respondents using different procedures, in order to provide a reliable test.

As noted previously, use of the same method of instrument administration does not necessarily ensure equivalence of results. Understanding of the factors which may bias results in a given country or cultural context and generate non-equivalence is thus essential. In many cases, use of different methods which did not on the surface appear to be equivalent may generate equivalent results.

Accumulated experience from previous research may thus in many cases be helpful in providing indications of different sources of bias. The impact of such factors is rarely likely to be studied systematically, i.e., using different methods to study the same constructs. Findings from previous studies may, nonetheless, provide insights as to the biases associated with different procedures. Furthermore, knowledge of the research infrastructure, i.e., the level of telephone ownership, the reliability of the mail service, the level of literacy and willingness and ability of respondents to respond to different instruments, as well as the availability of trained interviewers in a given country or culture, may also suggest which procedures are likely to be most effective and generate equivalent results in different countries and socio-cultural contexts.

Conclusion

One of the more crucial issues in comparative consumer research is the equivalence of the data collected in different countries or sociocultural contexts. Even in cases where truly equivalent data cannot be collected, the extent of non-equivalence needs to be determined. Unless attention is paid to such issues, it is difficult to tell whether observed differences or similarities are in fact real or purely specious.

Equivalence needs to be examined first in terms of the concepts studied and in the operational measures of these concepts. Then it should be considered in terms of the samples from which data are collected, and finally in the procedures for instrument administration. At each stage, the research design should incorporate explicit procedures for examining equivalence and attempt to develop data that are as comparable as possible.

Adopting a longer-term perspective, a tradition of comparative consumer research based on sound research methodology needs to be established. In the first place, this can furnish insights into substantive issues and the extent to which different concepts and findings can be generalized from one country or sociocultural context to another. In addition, it can provide a body of experience in research methodology, which can help in the development of improved conceptual and operational definitions, instrument design, and administration and sampling procedures.

In establishing this tradition it is, however, of paramount importance to ensure the validity of the comparison made between countries both in terms of the concepts examined and in their measurement. Following the logic of the Campbell-Fiske multi-trait multi-method approach, research design might thus center on the use of multiple organizations and multiple methods in each country and cultural context to examine convergent and discriminant validity, and to identify sources of bias in the use of various measures and measurement procedures. If this approach is adopted, it should lead to significant improvements in research design and a greater contribution to consumer research from comparative studies.

Notes

1. Joseph W. Elder, "Comparative Cross-National Methodology," *Annual Review in Sociology*, 1976, Palo Alto, California and R. M. Marsh, *Comparative Sociology: A Modification of Cross-Societal Analysis*, New York: Harcourt, Brace and World, 1967.

2. Robert T. Holt and John M. Richardson, "Competing Paradigiums in Comparative Politics," in *The Methodology and Comparative Research*, Robert T. Holt and John E. Turner, eds., (New York: Free Press, 1970), pp: 21–71; and A. Preworski and M. Tuene, *The Logic of Comparative Social Inquiry* (New York: Wiley Interscience, 1970).

3. R. Brislin, Walter J. Lonner, and Robert M. Thorndike, *Cross-Cultural Research Methods* (New York: Wiley, 1973; and Harry C. Triandis and Roy S. Malpass and Andrew R. Davidson, "Psychology and Culture," *Annual Review of Psychology*, 1973, 24, pp: 355–78.

4. J. W. Berry, "On Cross-Cultural Comparability," *International Journal of Psychology*, 4, 1969, pp: 119–28.

5. Harry Triandis and C. Vassilou, "A Comparative Analysis of Subjective Culture," in Harry C. Triandis, *The Analysis of Subjective Culture* (New York: John Wiley, 1972).

6. Robert Green and Eric Langard, "A Cross-National Comparison of Consumer Habits and Innovator Characteristics," *Journal of Marketing*, 49, July 1975, pp: 34–41.

7. Joseph Plummer, "Consumer Focus in Cross-National Research," *Journal of Advertising*, 6:2, Spring 1977, pp: 5–15.

8. Paul-Howard Berent, "International Research is Different," in Edward M. Mazze, ed., *Marketing in Turbulent Times and Marketing: The Challenges and the Opportunities— Combined Proceedings* (Chicago: American Marketing Association, 1975, pp: 293–97).

9. Yoram Wind and S. P. Douglas, "Comparative Consumer Research."

10. Susan P. Douglas and Christine Urban, "Life-style Analysis to Profile Women in International Markets," *Journal of Marketing*, 41, July 1976, pp: 46–54.

11. Jan B. Deregowski, "Perception," in Harry C. Triandis and Walter Lonner, eds., *A Handbook of Cross-Cultural Psychology*, 3 (Basic Processes, Boston): Allyn and Bacon, 1980, pp: 21–117; and Anne D. Pick, "Cognition: Psychological Perspectives," in Harry C. Triandis and Walter Lonner, ed., *A Handbook of Cross-Cultural Psychology*, 3 (Basic Processes, Boston: Allyn and Bacon, 1980, pp: 117–54).

12. B. Berlin and P. Kay, *Basic Color Terms: Their Universality and Evolution* (Berkeley: University California Press), 1969.

13. Edward T. Hall, *Beyond Culture* (New York: Anchor Press-Doubleday, 1976).

14. Donald T. Campbell and Donald W. Fiske, "Convergent and Discriminant Validation by the Multi-trait Multi-method Matrix," *Psychological Bulletin*, 56, March 1959, pp: 81–105.

15. Richard W. Crosby, "Attitude Measurement in a Bilingual Culture," *Journal of Marketing Research*, 6, November 1969, pp: 416–21.

16. Murray A. Straus, "Phenomenal Identity and Conceptual Equivalence of Measurement in Cross-national Comparative Research," *Journal of Marriage, and the Family*, 31, May 1969, pp: 233–39; and William H. Cunningham, Isabella Cunningham, Robert T. Green, "The Ipsative Process to Reduce Response Set Bias," *Public Opinion Quarterly*, 41, Fall 1977, pp: 379–94.

17. D. T. Campbell and J. Stanley, *Experimental and Quasi-Experimental Designs for Research*, Chicago, Ill: Rand-McNally, 1966.

18. William J. Wilson, "Pitfalls in International Research," *Marketing Review*, 37, December/January, 1982.

19. G. Almond and S. Berba, *The Civic Culture: Political Attitudes and Democracy in the Nations* (Princeton: Princeton University Press, 1963.

20. Robert T. Holt and John E. Turner, eds., *The Methodology and Comparative Research* (New York: Free Press,) 1970.

21. Lucy Webster, "Comparability in Multi-Country Surveys," *Journal of Advertising Research*, 6, December 1966, pp: 14–18.

22. Oscar Werner and Donald T. Campbell, "Translating Working through Interpreters and the Problems of Decentering," in *A Handbook of Method in Cultural Anthropology*, Raoul Naroll and Ronald Cohen, eds., (New York: Columbia University Press, 1967, pp: 398–420).

23. *Ibid.*

24. Susan P. Douglas and Robert Shoemaker, "Item Non-Response in Cross-National Surveys," *European Research*, August 1981.

25. Donald T. Campbell and D. W. Fiske, "Convergent and Discriminant," pp: 81–105.

7

CRITICAL ISSUES IN THE CROSS-CULTURAL MEASUREMENT OF CONSUMER DISSATISFACTION: DEVELOPED VERSUS LDC PRACTICES

S. Tamer Cavusgil and Erdener Kaynak

In recent years the topic of consumer satisfaction/dissatisfaction (CS/D) and complaining behavior has received considerable attention, mainly in the industrialized developed nations. As these nations move toward becoming more affluent societies, the balance in the marketplace is increasingly shifting in favor of the consumers. As the consumer movement gains momentum and becomes better organized, government agencies and business firms alike have become more sensitive to demands of consumers. It may also be noted that more legislation has been enacted during the past 15 years to protect the rights of buyers/consumers than was passed during the previous 189 years.[1] Because of the increased activity, a number of scholars, not necessarily confined to marketing, have focused their attention on the sources and measurement of consumer satisfaction/dissatisfaction. A recent monograph by Hunt listed some 73 entries.[2] Most of these were published in the last several years. They all attempt to advance and integrate underlying concepts of CS/D and share insights leading to more valid and widely accepted measurement methodologies.[3]

The need for adequate conceptualization and measurement of consumer satisfaction/dissatisfaction has been recognized by legislators, public policy staff, and consumer behavior theorists, in addition to consumerists themselves, businesses, and nonprofit organizations.[4] Legislators need more than an elementary theory of what leads to and detracts from consumer satisfaction for enacting legislation as well as determining whether the enactment had its intended effect. Public policy makers need to rely on dissatisfaction measures as a social indicator, for determining whether the marketplace is functioning and whether any intervention in the consumers' interest is needed. Business and nonprofit organizations need to evaluate how well products and services are meeting customer needs and wants. Customer dissatisfaction measures could be used to alert firms and industries to situations where all is not well and corrective action is in order.

Over the past decade, a series of studies have been conducted to monitor public attitudes toward marketing, consumerism, and government regulation.[5] At least five national surveys have been completed in the United States that record public opinion on a variety of topics related to the infrastructure of the consumer movement.[6] Unfortunately, relatively few researchers have focused on measurement of consumer dissatisfaction in different environments, including developing economies. What are the causes of consumer dissatisfaction in developing nations? How do the sources of dissatisfaction vary among nations? How responsive is the marketplace to the needs, wants, and varying purchasing power of consumers in different environments? Answers to these and similar questions cannot be given until adequate conceptualizations of consumer discontent is developed and their relevance is assessed for multiple environments. This chapter addresses these issues. Specifically, a conceptualization of the sources of consumer dissatisfaction is offered, and special problems of measuring consumer dissatisfaction across nations are discussed.

Definitions and Consumer Dissatisfaction

If we attribute the existence of economic activities to the needs of the consumer sector, the importance of effectively fulfilling these needs and wants will become apparent. A chief concern for consumers in any society is to obtain desired goods and services in sufficient quantities, at desirable locations and times, and at reasonable prices. As postulated by the microeconomic theory, the consumer is in a constant struggle in order to find an optimal balance between the utilities derived from goods and services and the scarce resources to be sacrificed. The consumer is satisfied or dissatisfied with an exchange to the extent that he/she perceives an equitable balance is established between the expended resources and derived utilities. A definition of consumer dissatisfaction should stress the relative character of dissatisfaction, and the discrepancy between expectations and performance. Beyond these general remarks, definitions of consumer dissatisfaction that have been offered exhibit substantial variety. Consider the following comments:

> (Satisfaction) is a stepping away from the experience and evaluating whether it was as good as it was expected to be. Satisfaction is not the pleasurableness of the experience, but the evaluation that the experience was as pleasurable as it was supposed to be or expected to be.[7]

> Consumer satisfaction results from the interaction levels of a) expectations about anticipated performance and b) evaluations of perceived performance.[8]

> Consumer satisfaction is an attitude in the sense that it is an evaluative orientation which can be measured. It is a special kind of attitude because by definition it cannot exist prior to the purchase or consumption of the attitude objective. In structural terms, the attitude is based on actual purchase/consumption experience. Perceptions of that experience are compared with the motivations which underly the action, the expectations previously formed concerning the outcome of the experience, and further modified by standards concerning desirable and normative outcomes.[9]

> We define consumer dissatisfaction as the gap or distance between the consumer's "ideal" attribute combination of this product or service and the attribute combination of this product or service offered in the marketplace which comes closest to this ideal. Consumers have no choice but to purchase that product-attribute combination available in the marketplace which most nearly matches their ideal attribute combination. Thus, this concept of consumer satisfaction, in effect, measures the perceived extent to which product and service alternatives desired by consumer are not incorporated into any specific choice in the marketplace. It focuses on market performance rather than consumer's satisfaction with different brands within a product line.[10]

Although these conceptualizations vary in nature, perhaps a common thread among them refers to confirmation of prepurchase expectations. If we assume that the consumer enters into a marketplace transaction with some expectations concerning the performance of the product or service, he/she will be satisfied with the choice to the extent that these expectations are confirmed. Dissatisfaction will result to the extent that postpurchase evaluations are not in agreement with prepurchase expectations. But, then, this may be a vary narrow conceptualization of consumer dissatisfaction, as it is tied to a single marketplace transaction. As will be argued later in this chapter, there is a "macro" as well as a "micro" dimension of consumer dissatisfaction. The macro dimension of consumer dissatisfaction—which arises from the general state of the economy—should not be ignored, especially in the developing country settings.[11]

Dissatisfaction with a product or service may be reflected in varying forms, ranging from a slight disappointment to a feeling of frustration one experiences when charged an unreasonable price, for example. Various consequences of dissatisfaction are illustrated in Figure 7.1. Substantial research suggests that much dissatisfaction goes unreported. A recent study, for example, indicated that only about four percent of dissatisfied customers complained to a manufacturer.[12] Instead, they usually stopped buying the product and also bad-mouthed it to nine or ten other people. A study conducted by Day on grocery products revealed that in 45 percent of the instances where people found a defect in their grocery product they did not do anything about it.[13] Doing something about it included stopping buying the brand or saying something to their peers. Many consumers appear to keep their dissatisfaction to themselves, partially as a result of not knowing what to do about it or not believing that their efforts will product worthwhile results.

There is also considerable evidence that those consumers who do complain have different personality and socioeconomic backgrounds.[14] One study suggested that these consumers are better educated, earn higher incomes, are in higher social classes, are more active in formal organizations, and are more politically committed and liberal than other groups.[15] Another study by Wall, Dickey, and Talarzyk[16], on the other hand, found that product characteristics (clothing) interact with such consumer variables as age and experience in predicting consumer satisfaction/dissatisfaction.[16]

Despite the variations in the conceptualizations of CS/D construct, there is a widespread agreement that the satisfaction of consumer needs is a basic goal for any marketing economy. This does not necessarily mean that all types of demands are to be fulfilled. Societal values, resource scarcities, and conflicts of interest often impose limitations on consumer demands. Certain goods or services may be banned in some countries, or conflicts may arise among certain groups in a society. In other cases, consumers may be forced to use some products, such as safety belts and lead-free gas in automobiles. Unlimited, unrestrained satisfaction of wants and needs is hardly the issue.

It would also be inappropriate to limit the discussion of consumer dissatisfaction to basic first-level needs of food, clothing, and shelter. Beyond these essential items difficulties may be encountered in obtaining other goods and services. Communication, utilities, transportation, and education-related needs are examples. This implies that consumer dissatisfaction may arise not only out of private sector offerings but also public sector offerings and programs that have economic consequences for consumers. State Economic Enterprises are especially active in developing countries. In short, consumer dissatisfaction emerges from difficulties encountered by the consumer in all phases of living, in the process of striving to achieve a better quality of life.

A Typology of Consumer Dissatisfaction in Developed Versus Developing Countries

An adequate understanding of the sources of consumer dissatisfaction in various economies is a prerequisite for successful measurement. A conceptualization of the many sources of consumer dissatisfaction is offered in Figure 7.1. Similar conceptualizations are offered by Renoux[17] and Straver.[18] Various causes of consumer discontent are first classified into micro and macro sources in Table 7.1. Those that can be directly traced to the practices of an individual producer or reseller are labeled micro sources of consumer dissatisfaction. Exorbitant prices, illegally high interest rates on installment sales, and products of inferior quality are examples. In other cases, the nature of the discontent is much broader, and better attributable to the prevailing social, economic, and political condition of the system in general. High rates of price increases, unresponsive political institutions, and lack of opportunities for seeking redress are examples of the macro sources of consumer dissatisfaction. This dichotomy is offered as a simplifying assumption; the difference between the micro and macro sources may not always be apparent. In general, micro-level sources appear to lead, over time, to a diffuse, latent discontent with the state of the marketplace; that is, to macro-level dissatisfaction. Unsatisfactory experiences with specific products and services seem to be reflected in a disillusionment with all institutions of the society.

The sources of consumer dissatisfaction listed comprehensive enough to apply equally well to both developed and developing economies, still focus on primary needs of food, shelter, clothing, and protection from illness. Food-related concerns are especially notable. Surveys taken in such countries reveal that more than 40 percent of disposable income is spent for food. Poorest households typically spend more than half of their income on food.[19] Displeasure in developed economies, however, involves a broader group of goods and services, including recreation, education, and ecological concerns. Another difference is that product availability, level and consistency of product quality, after sales service, are more of a problem in developing economies, whereas product variety, style, and differentiation may constitute concerns for developed country consumers. Many other differences can be found by contrasting the environmental circumstances that face consumers in both types of economies. For insights into the nature of food retailing systems in developed and developing nations, the reader is referred to Kaynak and Cavusgil.[20]

Consider the distribution of milk in developing nations, for example. In Istanbul, approximately 60 percent of milk and other dairy products are sold by street peddlers, some of whom still use horses to take their merchandise to different neighborhoods of the city. The raw milk sold by the street peddlers

FIGURE 7.1
Manufacturer/Reseller-Consumer Interface

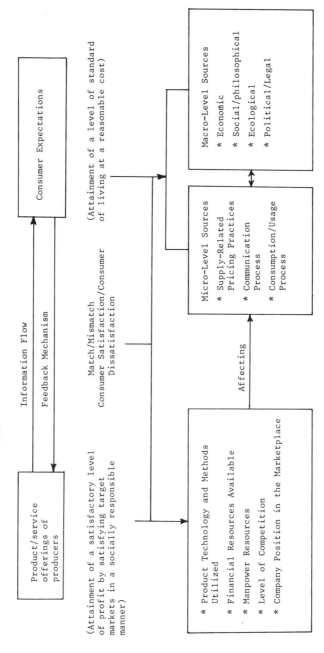

TABLE 7.1

A Conceptualization of the Sources of Consumer Dissatisfaction

MICRO-LEVEL SOURCES	MACRO-LEVEL SOURCES
Supply-Related/Pricing Practices:	*Economic:*
Deliberately holding the supply of goods low	Inflation and high cost of living
Hoarding by resellers in the expectation of price increases	Low income; unequal distribution of income
Exorbitant, unreasonable prices	Sellers' market prevails
	Monopoly; lack of competition from within and abroad
Communications Process:	High margin-low turnover commercial philosophy
False, deceptive misleading advertising	Inefficient channels of distribution
Lack of informative, factual advertising	Low productivity of producers
Appeals that rely on fantasy and emotions	Import-dependent production system
Creating expectations that the product cannot meet	
	Social/Philosophical:
	Uneducated consumers
Shopping Process:	Skepticism of business
Variable prices—lack of fixed prices	Anxiety over manipulation by advertising
Haggling and resulting psychological fears	Excessive materialism
Waiting lines/lists and queues	
	Ecological:
Consumption/Usage Process:	Environmental pollution
Unsafe, unsanitary products	Depletion of scarce resources
Shoddy, inferior, malfunctioning products	
Lack of durable or high-performance products	*Political/Legal:*
Misuse due to lack of adequate use directions	Unresponsive political institutions
Inappropriate, deceitful packaging and labeling	Inability to seek convenient remedy.
Inadequate and unsatisfactory warranty and servicing	Lack of opportunities for seeking redress
Unsatisfactory return and exchange opportunities	

Source: S. T. Cavusgil and Erdener Kaynak, "A Framework for Cross-Cultural Measurement of Consumer Dissatisfaction," in R. L. Day and H. K. Hunt eds., *New Findings on Consumer Satisfaction and Complaining*, St. Louis, Missouri, November 6–8, 1980. P. 81.

is not pasteurized and it is generally sold in large metal containers. Most street vendors do not adequately wash and sterilize their milk cans. Covers over the milk containers are usually in poor condition. The milk itself is of low nutritious value due to adulteration and lack of sanitation. One study estimated that the raw milk sold in urban areas is often adulterated with water by more than ten percent.[21] Consider also the marketing of bread. Even in the largest cities in Turkey, none of the bakeries sell prewrapped bread. A survey was conducted several years ago on the feasibility of prewrapped bread production that found that the wrapping cost would add an additional 20 percent to the retail price of bread. The attitude of the consumers toward buying prewrapped bread was also uncertain. Turkish consumers are accustomed to buying their bread daily from a bakery or a corner grocery store. As a result, the project was dropped.[22]

Inflation is a major macro-level source of consumer dissatisfaction in developing economies. Annual price level increases of 50 percent or higher are steadily eroding the purchasing power of many developing-country consumers. The majority are unable to maintain their real incomes. High prices of food items and high rents, in particular, constitute a serious problem for residents of urban areas. Rising prices develop into one of the most sensitive political issues at times. A major reason for excessive inflation in developing economies is the outmoded nature of the distribution sector. Products pass through a large number of intermediaries whose margins contribute to unnecessarily high levels of retail prices. At the retail level, the faults are attributed to the large numbers of traditional food stores that are too small to be efficient. With their low sales volume, these enterprises need to rely on relatively high margins to survive. Producers, on the other hand, tend to be small-scale, relatively inefficient, and import-dependent enterprises.

It should be noted that the relatively high prices paid for products and services reflect only a part of the cost of the consumer. In addition to the "monetary" cost reflected by the dollar price, there are some "nonmonetary" costs. The latter costs stem from the general hassle of obtaining goods/services in developing countries. Long waiting periods, queues, inconvenient locations of some retailers, haggling over price, fear of being exploited by the sellers, and other frustrations are among the realities the consumer has to put up with in developing economies. It is not unusual, for example, for a consumer to wait as many as ten years before a request for a telephone number is processed.

In developed economies, branding, quality control, and stringent government regulation of good purity and labeling permit the consumer to buy food products "off-the-shelf" with minimum inspection. In developing economies, however, these protections are not well developed, and the shopper must rely much more on her buying skills. She must do a good deal of inspection. Personal relationships with vendors often prove advantageous. Usually, food shoppers get to know how far they can trust a food retailer, and can negotiate prices and other terms.

Factors That Exacerbate Consumer Dissatisfaction

Not appearing in Table 7.1 are a number of circumstances that tend to exacerbate consumer discontent, especially in developing economies. These factors cannot be considered the causes of consumer dissatisfaction; but they facilitate the emergence of dissatisfaction. These factors are summarized as follows:

1. The prevailing challenge of technological change for the consumer. Indeed, the marketplace is becoming increasingly complex for the consumer in developing economies due to the proliferation of products as well as their technical intricacy. Products and services are growing varied and complex and increasingly difficult to understand in terms of the way they function and what they can do for consumers. The demands on the consumer in terms of the amount of information to be acquired for intelligent decisions are becoming greater. Consequently, the opportunities are greater for the consumer to experience displeasing marketplace transactions.

2. The effect of the partial industrialization process and its resultant repercussions on urbanization in developing economies. These developments tend to remove previously existed face-to-face relationships between the buyer and the seller. As the physical and functional distance between the buyer and seller increase, the opportunity for the consumer to seek immediate, and somewhat convenient remedy to his/her dissatisfaction is eliminated.

3. Rising expectations of consumers in developing economies is changing product-consumer relationships drastically. Truly, a revolution is taking place in consumer aspirations in these countries. This is created and fostered largely by the mass media as well as the increased educational attainment of consumers. Radios and even television have made their way into the living rooms of households in the most remote areas of developing nations. Consumers are now better informed and aware of the level of development elsewhere in the world. Recognizing the standards of living possessed by the more "fortunate" citizens of another country, they raise their expectations. Hence, the "deficit" between what they actually experience and the norm is now even greater. A special case in point is provided by the Turkish "guestworkers" in West Germany and other Western European countries. Currently, there are over a million semi-skilled Turkish workers in West Germany. These workers return periodically in

order to visit their relatives. Over the years, it has been customary for each returning worker to bring back, among many other consumer luxury goods, a Mercedes Benz automobile. The influx of such modern consumer goods and the exposure of a such large segment of the population to modern European life-styles have simply revolutionized the indigenous Turkish life-styles, creating a tremendous increase in expectations. Interestingly, some recent statistics indicate that the per capita ownership of Mercedes Benz cars in Turkey may be higher than in anywhere else, including West Germany, the automobile's home country.

4. In most developing countries, producer and reseller groups have been better able to organize and protect their interests collectively than consumers. It would be quite unrealistic to expect that consumers can organize and exert similar influences on the political and legislative systems in these nations. As a result, producers and sellers often constitute a stronger pressure group in these countries and have an unfair advantage over consumers.

Difficulties in Cross-Cultural Measurement

Many difficulties stand in the way of the researcher who is interested in measuring and contrasting consumer dissatisfaction in multiple environments.[23] Various issues need to be satisfactorily resolved before further work can be done in this direction. A discussion of these issues will now be attempted in an effort to lay the ground-work for further research in the area.

Satisfaction or Dissatisfaction?

Leavitt has suggested that satisfaction and dissatisfaction do not represent the opposite ends of the same continuum.[24] If one accepts the view that they represent different dimensions, a choice has to be made as to what dimension—satisfaction or dissatisfaction—should be measured. Even if they are considered on the same dimension, the researcher has to pull out the satisfied end of the scale through one or more levels. As Hunt points out, the distribution is usually highly skewed toward being highly satisfied.[25] Theoretically, satisfaction is a more difficult psychological construct to define and measure than dissatisfaction. In addition, Andreasen remarks that maximizing satisfaction is an elusive goal.[26] Consumer aspirations are constantly changing and it is difficult to conceive of ever making all people fully satisfied. Thus, in light of the theoretical and practical considerations, measurement of dissatisfaction rather than satisfaction should be attempted.

Micro or Macro Dissatisfaction?

As has been argued in this chapter, consumer dissatisfaction is a comlex phenomenon that emerges both at the individual product/supplier level and at the societal level. Furthermore, dissatisfaction at each level has various facets. Micro-level dissatisfaction, for example, may arise from price, performance or safety-related concerns. It has been also noted that the relevance of each source of consumer dissatisfaction will vary from one economy to another. Micro-level sources are likely to dominate in developing economies, and macro-level sources may be more of a concern in developed nations. In cross-cultural comparisons of consumer dissatisfaction, the researcher should ideally develop measures for both types of causes and then contrast the findings among nations.

Objective or Subjective Measures?

Up until now, investigations of consumer dissatisfaction have employed two types of measures of dissatisfaction. Subjective measures involve asking people how well they feel they were satisfied with a given purchase.[27] Objective measures, on the other hand, are largely uninfluenced by personal idiosyncracies. Examples of both types of measures for consumer dissatisfaction are given in Table 7.2 along with the names of the researchers who utilized them. Andreasen favors the use of objective measures, as he notes several problems with subjective measures.[28] These are: 1) subjective measures are psychological constructs and there is great potential for measurement and response bias; 2) subjective measures may be unreliable under the influence of situational variables; and 3) there are significant aggregation problems: what one customer means by "somewhat satisfied" may not be the same as what another means by the same term.

One may agree with the limitations of subjective measures as pointed out by Andreasen, but objective measures have their shortcomings, too— e.g.: "frequency of complaints." For, as research indicates, only a small fraction of consumer dissatisfaction tends to be reported, and such a measure would significantly underestimate the true extent of dissatisfactions. Also, it is questionable whether such measures could really determine the "subjective, evaluative, or perceived" nature of consumer dissatisfaction.

Compared to What?

Withey and others have commented that most judgments tend to be relative.[29] Consumers can be asked to make at least three types of comparisons. An individual can make comparisons with his/her past experience (temporal comparison), with conditions in other areas (cross-

TABLE 7.2

A Typology of the Measurements of Consumer Dissatisfaction

	MICRO	MACRO

OBJECTIVE	Frequency of complaints
	Frequency of warranty claims
	Repeat purchasing
	Brand switching
	
	Best and Andreasen[36]
	McNeal[40]
		Level and distribution of income
		Extent of consumerism activities
		Extent of consumer protection
		   legislation
		Public expenditure on consumer research
		   and education
		Related spending by firms, industry, and
		   trade associations
		Straver[18]
		Cavusgil and Kaynak[41]

SUBJECTIVE	Direct assessments from consumer Opinions of salesmen and middlemen Intentions to repurchase Intentions to recommend to a friend Best and Andreasen[36] Handy and Pfaff[37] Thorelli, Becker, and Engledow[39]	Perceived life quality Alienation from the marketplace Consumer discontent scale Index of consumer satisfaction Attitudes toward business and advertising Allison[32] Andrews and Withey[35] Lundstrom and Lamont[33] Pfaff[38] Thorelli, Becker, and Engledow[39]

Source: S. T. Cavusgil and Erdener Kaynak, "A Framework for Cross-Cultural Measurement of Consumer Dissatisfaction" in R. L. Day and H. K. Hunt eds., *New Findings on Consumer Satisfaction and Complaining*, St. Louis, Missouri, November 6–8, 1980, p. 83.

quality), and with conditions experienced by others (social comparisons). The last type of comparison may be best for cross-cultural studies, as it is more revealing in terms of the individual's position in the society. A related issue is determining the base against which consumers compare their positions or feelings. In many cases, the dissatisfaction consumers report refers to the discrepancy between the actual experience *and* the expected one or some norm. Expectations and norms are not necessarily the same; hence, the need to determine which one to use as a base for comparisons. Using norms as a base for comparisons would especially be problematic for cross-cultural research since the norms vary from one society to another. As for using expectations for comparisons, there are problems, too. As Miller points out, there are different types of expectations; the ideal; the expected, the minimum tolerable, and the deserved.[30] This issue remains to be resolved.

Sampling of Products and Services

Measurement of consumer dissatisfaction at the micro level can especially be burdensome in cross-cultural research. For some measurements, one has to gather a list of products and services that meet certain specifications. To ensure reliable comparisons, these products and services should have existed in respective societies for similar periods and should enjoy comparable popularity. The uses and benefits should also be similar. Furthermore, decision-making processes for purchasing these products and services should also be comparable. The use of evaluative criteria and their relative importance for the consumers of developed and developing nations are expected to differ, which again makes the task of measurement more cumbersome.

Sampling of Respondents

Past research clearly suggests that satisfaction is a function of the individual's level of awareness and information. Substantial shifts can occur in satisfaction as a result of increasing the information an individual possesses about product and service alternatives. Since consumers are expected to be different in terms of the marketplace information they possess, the researcher has to pick respondents who are similarly informed. This would ensure that differences in satisfaction are not the result of differences in understanding. It would also be desirable that the respondents come from comparable socioeconomic backgrounds both within nations and across nations.

Difficulties of Gathering Data

It is well known that relevant data is less readily available and that collecting new data is a challenging task in developing nations. If one intends to use subjective measures of CS/D, various problems will be encountered, including reluctance of respondents and their inability to articulate their dissatisfaction to the extent that it is the result of being less educated and sophisticated buyers. If, on the other hand, one intends to use objective measures of CS/D, useful data is rarely available. Most of the consumer-related studies undertaken in developing environments are of exploratory and descriptive natures and as such they do not offer analytical insights. For an elaboration of the difficulties in undertaking marketing research in developing country environments, the reader can be referred to Kaynak.[31]

Conclusions

While the measurement of the sources of consumer dissatisfaction in developed and developing economies and contrasting the findings are deemed desirable, the task is not an easy one. This chapter addressed itself to some of the difficulties researchers may encounter in measuring CS/D across cultures. The researchers must have an adequate understanding of how consumer dissatisfaction emerges and evolves in both types of economies before an attempt can be made to measure it. It has been noted that there are several decisions that face researchers in the process of measurement. The choices between the micro-macro measures and objective-subjective measures are especially important. It seems that the measurement of macro-level dissatisfaction can be achieved with less difficulty than that of micro-level dissatisfaction. Cross-country comparisons are likely to be easier as well. Also, as noted before, micro-level dissatisfaction tends to be reflected in macro-level dissatisfaction over time. Thus, an attempt to measure macro-level dissatisfaction should carry a higher priority. One can use, for this purpose, the battery of statements developed by Allison[32] or those developed by Lundstrom and Lamont.[33] Alternatively, one can use his own methodology for deriving more suitable statements.

Given the differences in the nature or sources of consumer dissatisfaction in developed and developing countries, future studies may design ways of measuring consumer satisfaction in developing countries. In addition to this, experience gained with such techniques in developed countries can be transferred to different socioeconomic and cultural environments of developing countries. As such, the development of operational measures of consumer satisfaction in these countries is needed. However, consumer dissatisfaction cannot easily be used as a social indicator in developing countries due to the relative character and the difficulty of cross-cultural comparisons.[34]

It is clear that more research should be conducted into the nature of consumer dissatisfaction in developing countries. Given the relatively disadvantageous position of developing-country consumers, it would be unrealistic to expect much initiative in this regard from the consumers themselves. It is imperative that the governments and public agencies in these countries take the lead in establishing a research agenda for consumer dissatisfaction, fund such research projects, and attempt to implement any recommendations that may follow from the research.

Notes

1. H. C. Barksdale and W. D. Perreault, "Can Consumers be Satisfied?" *MSU Business Topics*, 2, Spring 1980, pp: 19–20.

2. H. K. Hunt, "Consumer Satisfaction/Dissatisfaction: Overview and Future Research Directions," in H. K. Hunt, ed., *Conceptualization and Measurement of Consumer Satisfaction and Dissatisfaction* (Cambridge, Mass.: Marketing Science Institute, 1977).

3. R. L. Day, "Toward a Process Model of Consumer Satisfaction," in Hunt, ed., *Conceptualization and Measurement*, 1977, pp: 153–86.

4. A. R. Andreasen, "A Taxonomy of Consumer Satisfaction/Dissatisfaction Measures," *The Journal of Consumer Affairs*, Winter 1977, pp: 11–24.

5. William D. Perrault and H. F. Rodner, "Consumer Attitudes Toward Marketing and Consumerism in the United States and Venezuela: A Cross-Cultural Comparison," in George Fisk and R. W. Nason, eds., *Macro-Marketing: New Steps on the Learning Curve*, Proceedings of the Third Macro-Marketing Seminar, August 13–16, 1978, p: 382; Hans B. Thorelli and S. Thorelli, *Consumer Information Systems and Consumer Policy*, Ballinger, 1977; and Jagdish N. Sheth, *Cross-Cultural Influences on Buyer-Seller Interaction/ Negotiation Process*, University of Illinois at Urbana-Champaign Faculty Working Papers, September 1980, p. 3.

6. Stephen A. Greyser, *Consumer at Crossroads*, A National Opinion Research Survey conducted by the Marketing Science Institute, 1977; and Hiram C. Barksdale, W. D. Perreault, and J. Arndt, "A Cross-National Survey of Consumerism and Government Regulations," *Columbia Journal of World Business*, 17:2, Summer 1982, pp: 71–86.

7. H. K. Hunt, "Consumer Satisfaction and Dissatisfaction: A Developing Methodology," in *AMA Business Proceedings*, 1978, pp: 241–44.

8. J. A. Miller, "Studying Satisfaction, Modifying Models, Eliciting Expectations, Posing Problems, and Making Meaningful Measurements," in Hunt, ed., *Conceptualization and Measurement*, 1977, pp: 72–91.

9. J. A. Czepiel and L. J. Rosenberg, "The Study of Consumer Satisfaction: Addressing the "So What" Question," in Hunt, ed., *Conceptualization and Measurement*, 1977, pp: 92–119.

10. C. R. Handy, "Monitoring Consumer Satisfaction with Food Products," in Hunt, ed., *Conceptualization and Measurement*, 1977, pp: 215–39.

11. For an interesting discussion on this topic see: Marya T. Hilger, "Consumer Perceptions of a Public Marketer in Mexico," *Columbia Journal of World Business*, 15:3, Fall 1980, pp: 75–82, and "Decision Making in a Public Marketing Enterprise: Conasupo in Mexico," *Journal of Inter-American Studies*, 22:4, November 1980, pp: 47–494.

12. *Wall Street Journal*, "More Firms Use 800 Numbers to Keep Consumers Satisfied," April 7, 1983, p. 27.

13. Day, "Toward a Process Model."

14. E. L. Landon,"Consumer Complaints: A Marketing Opportunity," in *AMA Business Proceedings*, 1978, pp: 245–50.

15. Rex H. Warland, Robert O. Herrmann and Jane Willits, "Dissatisfied Consumers: Who Gets Upset and Who Takes Action?" *Journal of Consumer Affairs*, Winter 1975, pp: 148–62.

16. Marjorie Wall, Lois Dickey, and Wayne Talarzyk, "Correlates of Satisfaction and Dissatisfaction with Clothing Performance," *Journal of Consumer Affairs*, Summer, 1979, pp: 104–115.

17. Y. Renoux, "Consumer Dissatisfaction and Public Policy," in F. C. Allvine, ed., *Public Policy and Marketing Practices*, American Marketing Association, 1973, pp: 53–65.

18. W. E. Straver, "The International Consumerist Movement," *European Journal of Marketing*, 11:2, 1977, pp: 92–117.

19. Erdener Kaynak, "Changes in the Food Retailing Institutions of Urban Turkey-The Istanbul Experience," *Studies in Development*, 18, Winter 1978, pp: 53–71; and "Food Distribution Systems: Evolution in Latin America and the Middle East," *Food Policy*, 6:2, May 1981, pp: 78–90.

20. Erdener Kaynak and S. Tamer Cavusgil, "The Evolution of Food Retailing Systems: Contrasting the Experience of Developed and Developing Countries," *Journal of the Academy of Marketing Science*, 10, Summer 1982, pp: 249–69.

21. Erdener Kaynak, "Consumerism: A Social Phenomenon," *Adana I.T.I.A. Journal*, No. 2, May 1978, pp: 123–28.

22. Erdener Kaynak and R. Culpan, "Consumer Protection Movement in a Developing Economy: The Case of Turkey," *Hacettepe University Bulletin of Administrative Sciences*, 1:1, June 1978, pp: 128–46.

23. For a more detailed examination of the relevant methodological literature in cross-cultural psychology see: Harry C. Triandis, *The Analysis of Subjective Culture* (New York: John Wiley and Sons, 1972); H. C. Triandis and John W. Berry, eds., *The Handbook of Cross-Cultural Psychology*, Vol. 2, Methodology, Allyn and Bacon, Inc. Boston, 1980; Robert Green and P. White, "Methodological Considerations in Cross-National Consumer Research," *Journal of International Business Research*, 7, Fall/Winter 1976, pp: 81–87 and Charles Mayer, "The Lesson of Multinational Marketing Research," *Business Horizons*, 2:6, December 1978, pp: 12–14.

24. C. Leavitt, "Consumer Satisfaction and Dissatisfaction: Bipolar or Independent," in Hunt, ed., *Conceptualization and Measurement*, 1977, p: 132–52.

25. Hunt, "Consumer Satisfaction and Dissatisfaction", pp. 241–244.

26. Andreasen, "A Taxonomy of Consumer", pp. 11–24.

27. *Ibid.*

28. *Ibid.*

29. S. B. Withey, "Integrating Some Models About Consumer Satisfaction," in Hunt, ed., *Conceptualization and Measurement*, 1977, pp: 120–31.

30. Miller, "Studying Satisfaction", pp. 72–91.

31. Erdener Kaynak, "Difficulties of Undertaking Marketing Research in Developing Countries," *European Research*, 6, November 1978, pp: 251–59.

32. N. K. Allison, "A Psychometric Development of a Test for Consumer Alienation from the Marketplace," *Journal of Marketing Research*, November 1977, pp: 565–75.

33. W. J. Lundstrom and L. M. Lamont, "The Development of a Scale to Measure Consumer Discontent," *Journal of Marketing Research*, November 1976, pp: 373–81.

34. Folka Olander, "Can Consumer Dissatisfaction and Complaints Guide Public Consumer Policy?" *Journal of Consumer Policy*, 1:2, 1977, pp: 124–37.

35. F. M. Andrews and S. B. Withey, "Developing Measures of Perceived Life Quality: Results from Several National Surveys," *Social Indicators Research*, 1, 1974, pp: 1–26.

36. A. Best and A. R. Andreasen, *Talking Back to Business: Voiced and Unvoiced Consumer Complaints*, Washington, D.C., Center for Study of Responsive Law, 1976.

37. C. R. Handy and M. Pfaff, *Consumer Satisfaction with Food Products and Marketing Services*, United States Department of Agriculture, Agricultural Economics Report. No. 281, 1975.

38. A. B. Pfaff, "An Index of Consumer Satisfaction," in M. Venkatesan, ed., *Proceedings of 3rd Annual Conference*, 1972, Association for Consumer Research, 1972, pp: 713–37.

39. H. B. Thorelli, H. H. Becker, and J. Engledow, *The Information Seekers—An International Study of Consumer Information and Advertising Image* (Cambridge, Mass.: Ballinger, 1975).

40. J. U. McNeal, "Consumer Satisfaction: The Measure of Marketing Effectiveness," *MSU Business Topics*, Summer 1969, pp: 31–36.

41. S. Tamer Cavusgil and Erdener Kaynak, "A Framework for Cross-Cultural Measurement of Consumer Dissatisfaction, in R. L. Day and H. K. Hunt, eds., *New Findings on Consumer Satisfaction and Complaining*, St. Louis, Missouri, November 6–8, 1980, pp: 80–84.

8

MARKETING AND MARKETING RESEARCH IN THE SOCIALIST COUNTRIES

Laszlo Szabo

Marketing is fast becoming an indispensible function of the market-economy countries of Eastern Europe. In spite of this fact, nowadays like their counterparts in the developed Western European and North American countries, a great number of producers and traders in these countries have yet to be convinced of the importance of producer and consumer relationship as a device in influencing market efficiency. Under these circumstances, it seems strange that in Central and East European countries, with centrally planned economies, the role of marketing and its use by organizations is becoming more visible. An independent marketing system has been operating in recent years in Yugoslavia, Romania, and Poland. In addition, independent, efficiently operating marketing committees of the chambers of commerce in the Soviet Union, Hungary, and Bulgaria are at the disposal of their member companies. There are independent marketing institutions in the German Democratic Republic, the Soviet Union, Yugoslavia, and Hungary. In the latter two countries, a marketing periodical has been published for the last 15 years and with fairly wide circulation. With the help of postgraduate courses, conferences, and executive training programs, the role and importance of marketing for economic development and for profitability of enterprises has been demonstrated to public policy makers.

In all this, it might well be asked, how can marketing be reconciled with a centrally planned economy and what degree of efficiency can be attained among East European companies with the help of marketing methods in an extremely regulated and controlled market? Prior to responding, let us outline more specifically the features of a controlled market.

Characteristics of the Controlled Market

Market regulation is a system of economic undertaking through which government influences and, in a way, determines market conditions, and, as a result, has substantial impact on the course as well as the level of overall production. There is a huge difference in the extent of market regulation in the two basic economic systems—that is, in a market economy and in a centrally planned economy. In addition, one can observe discernable differences among the individual countries within a given economic system.

With regard to market regulation, countries having a centrally planned economy might be placed in two groups: those with direct management and those with indirect management. The main characteristics of these two systems are summarized in Table 8.1. The differences between direct and indirect management often result in distinct forms of marketing operations. Of paramount importance to marketing in the indirectly managed, centrally planned economy is foreign trade. Although achievements in domestic marketing are very much limited, indirect management does provide a relatively wide horizon for efficient marketing planning and implementation both in the domestic market and abroad.

Basic Conditions of Marketing in Hungary

In 1968, Hungary shifted from direct to indirect control of its planned economic system. The use of marketing has started only recently. As part of the centrally planned economy it has, as might be expected, both strong and weak aspects. There are four factors worthy of mention here: 1) company independence; 2) company profit orientation; 3) commodity supply conditions; and 4) degree of market freedom.

Company Independence

The majority of medium-sized companies and all of large-sized companies operating in different parts of the national economy are either owned by the state or by the cooperative sector. More recently, many private companies and labor societies have been established. Their size is limited and they are exclusively small ventures. Supervision of the state-owned companies is conducted by various ministries. The latter organizations provide the enactment clauses of National Acts adapted to individual sectors. They also appoint directors of companies and supervise their

TABLE 8.1
Main Characteristics of Countries Having a Centrally Planned Economy under Direct and Indirect Management

Characteristics of Management and Marketing Strategy Variables	Characteristics of Markets Under Direct Management	Characteristics of Markets Under Indirect Management
Price and Price Conditions	Uniformly set fixed prices for the whole country relevant to industrial products and foodstuffs with the exception of vegetables, fruits, and some animal products, as well as services. Prices are modified through enacted clauses implemented nationally.	Fixed prices are set for high-technology basis foodstuffs and a few industrial products and services. Price modifications for these products are centrally implemented. A free pricing system is accepted for the majority of commodities.
Competition	There is no competition among producers, service, and trading companies.	There is competition among producers and trading companies as well as service companies: it is gradually increasing.
Foreign Trade	There is state monopoly. Exclusive operation of specialized foreign trade companies.	Besides specialized foreign-trade companies, more and more producers and domestic trading companies obtain rights for direct export and import of commodities.
Company Management	Only ministries regulating operations of specific economic sectors can establish and close companies.	Besides running its own organization, any firm involved in producing "economic goods" can establish an affiliate or a small company. The latter may be in private ownership.

(continued next page)

133

TABLE 8.1 (*continued*)
Main Characteristics of Countries Having a Centrally Planned Economy Under Direct and Indirect Management

Characteristics of Management and Marketing Strategy Variables	*Characteristics of Markets Under Direct Management*	*Characteristics of Markets Under Indirect Management*
Private Sector	Approved only in agribusiness and in some service sectors. Percentage is very limited.	In the fields of agriculture, production services, and trading, but within given limits; there is a ceiling set on the number of employees utilized.
Distribution	It is carried out through predetermined, geographically set, and limited distribution channels.	Except in the case of some products, distribution is not limited. There is complete freedom.
Interest on Borrowed Capital	Very Limited	Gradually Increasing

economic activity. In addition to this, adherence to state regulations is supervised regularly and randomly by the Ministry of Finance. Other organizations whose operations are managed by the ministry include customs and excise offices, and banks.

Generally those companies managed by their appointed directors are operated virtually independently. Large companies, however, have separate supervisory committees for facilitating their directors' tasks. The supervisory committees in most cases supervise companies' economic activities and try to make it sure that they conform with the National Acts. This means that the companies themselves determine production scheduling and programs, volume and structure of sales, and set the price of their products. They also make their own decisions on development of marketing programs, and extension or reduction of their product lines or service ranges but leave supervision of their activities to the specific committees.

Consistency between the company plans and the sketchy national economic plans with regard to market fluctuations is assured by the government with the help of indirect factors such as credit policy, investment policy, tax policy, and export incentives.

Company Profit Orientation

The main goal of company operation, in all but nonprofit public organizations, is to make the highest profit possible. Both employees and managers have a direct interest in attaining a high profit level. Attained profit after taxation—which is strongly progressive—is allocated according to the character of the companies' own reserve (guarantee) funds which are shared among company employees in accordance with labor contracts signed by employees and employers. Different rates of taxation also have an important impact on profit allocation.

Directors of companies, besides their salary and profit share, receive a bonus, dependent on company's economic performance. This bonus for directors is approved by the ministry supervising their operations. Management is also penalized for poor performance. The maximum reduction in salary of a company director in case of loss is 25 percent.

It should be added that a company involved in production, servicing, and/or trading does not receive subsidy from the government except under very special cases. As a rule companies showing deficit or losses will be liquidated and their productive forces will be incorporated in other profitable companies.

Commodity Supply Conditions

When judging the market situation, the important question is, what is the relationship between commodity supply and demand? To be more exact, to what extent is consumer demand satisfied? The current commodity supply in the Hungarian market has made a good impression on local citizens as well as foreigners. However, the situation varies for given commodity groups. Supply is positive for a wide range of foodstuffs and pharmaceuticals. In spite of the large supplies of home-furnishing items, durable consumer goods, and garments, at times there are assortment problems creating discrepancies between assortments offered by companies and assortments demanded by consumers. There are some commodities for which consumers have to wait a short time; for others they must wait longer. For instance, customers have to wait years for certain brands of cars, but only several months for storage heaters. The quantity and assortment of commodities imported from the countries of Western Europe is rather small and poor. The reason for this is that Hungary's hard currency supply is limited. Besides these items, however, many other articles produced locally under the licenses from Western European countries are available on the market.

Degree of Market Freedom

Each of the producers decides independently how to distribute his commodities to the final consumer. Use of distribution channels is compulsory only for the products of the state monopoly, for instance, tobacco, alcohol, sugar, and some imported raw materials of high value. Distribution is thus diversified. Producers are not only forwarding their commodities to consumers through different intermediaries like wholesalers or retailers, but also are directly selling to consumers. This is the reason that more and more showrooms belonging to producers, as well as other marketing middlemen, have recently emerged. Emergence of new forms of marketing techniques has generally increased competition among all types of firms and has increased the marketing competence of companies. As a result of increasing competence, the number of new products introduced to the market has substantially increased; the major areas are foodstuffs, cosmetics, garments, housewares, and different kinds of items relating to higher order needs e.g. recreation goods, entertainment and educational products.

However, foreign-trade activity is still limited compared to that in the newly freed-up domestic markets. Foreign-trade activities are basically managed by foreign-trade companies. Recently, however, more and more manufacturers have the right to export, and "demigross"* companies, whose number is around 150, have the right to import.

---

*Demigross is a large type of Hungarian corporation entitled to import products from overseas countries.

Justification of Marketing in Hungary

At present, the Hungarian market, despite its regulated state, possesses the appropriate characteristics to allow for the implementation of marketing in the work of industrial and trading firms. The current market situation is the result of a decade's socioeconomic development process. Hungary's New Economic Mechanism (NEM), implemented in 1968, provided the means for the fundamentals of the country's free decision making and profit interest. It will be some time, however, before company management in Hungary can make the most of these opportunities.

A cutback in the course of economic development has resulted from the world oil crisis. This, in turn, has increased competition among firms for scarce market opportunities. This situation, however, has stimulated the majority of Hungarian firms to continue the race for markets through more rationalized production and more thorough trade objectives—that is, through more efficient marketing programs. In the future, this tendency can only be expected to grow.

As a precondition of marketing implementation, company independence, profit interest, balance of demand and supply, and freedom of market activity are all indispensable. If even one of these factors is missing, marketing may not be efficiently implemented or applied. It has already been emphasized that market situation varies on the basis of different commodity groups. Thus, where demand is satisfied and there is competition in the market, or anywhere a strong need to influence the market exists, marketing can become of ongoing importance in the activities of a company. However, in cases when consumer goods can easily be marketed in the local market because of extreme demand, companies do not care much about marketing. In recent years the situation in Hungary has changed rapidly due to new production capacity and dwindling marketing possibilities in foreign markets. Companies who are unprepared to implement marketing concepts and techniques find themselves in a rather difficult situation.

Some of the instruments of marketing in use in countries having market-economy systems are product policy, distribution, price policy, packaging policy, advertisement, and market research. These marketing variables are already widely accepted and implemented by competing companies in Hungary. The emergence of the fundamentals of marketing and their rapid development have rationalized organization of commodity routes and the application of up-to-date market influencing methods. When studying the Hungarian domestic market from this point of view, one can see noteworthy improvements despite certain shortcomings. Some of the characteristics of the current marketing system of Hungary are as follows:

1. In recent years, there has been extraordinary improvement in the product policy of companies. Due to this, improvement of the assortment of

supplies in certain commodity groups has become very satisfactory from all aspects. Prior to new product introduction to the market, most companies undertake consumer research to assess market opportunities as well as the intensity of demand. In recent years, foodstuffs, household detergents, housewares, plastics, glass, and chinaware have been at the top of the list. It is expected that this trend will continue in the future.

2. Organizational structure of companies presently operating in the market is more diversified. Manufacturers, wholesalers, and retailers were strictly separated from each other in the 1960s and now are not easily distinguished. As stated previously, more and more producers engage in direct marketing to consumers. Wholesalers set up factories, establish producing associations, get themselves involved in retail business, and open shops. There is a move toward backward as well as horizontal integration in company operations. Retailers in many cases undertake to fulfill functions of wholesalers or bypass wholesalers and buy directly from producers.

3. According to estimates, annual advertising expenditures in Hungary is about two billion forints.* Advertisement accounts for 0.3 percent of the national income. However, the extent of this spending in marketing-economy countries is four times more. Today, advertising is used by Hungarian companies as a decision-making tool to create primary as well as selective demand for the goods these companies are offering to their customers. As a result, in recent years, there is an increase in the percentage of successful TV, radio, and newspaper advertisements used in Hungary. More recently the role of direct mail has substantially increased. This medium is mainly used for promoting nonconsumer goods.

The State of Marketing Research in Hungary

With the exception of a small number of large industrial firms that were able to benefit from market opportunities and whose operations were dynamic and efficient from the very start, manufacturing companies in the first years of large-scale freedom were just "tasting" marketing. As export and import business is in the hands of specialized foreign-trade companies, firms involved in production are expected to obtain foreign market-related economic and technical information from them. Although obtaining market information is a very important and indispensable activity in foreign trade, the foreign-trade companies, who are marketing many thousands of items, at times, are unable to supply market information to their industrial partners. This is the reason why producers who are interested in exporting and who have no standing orders on a long-term basis have tried to establish their own research facilities and rely more on the information provided by outside

---

*One Hungarian Forint is equal to 2.4 U.S. cents

TABLE 8.2

Marketing Activities Considered to Be Most Important by Hungarian Managers (On the Basis of Surveying 129 Producing Firms)

| | Percentage of responses in relation to the total number interviewed | | |
| | Companies with rights of foreign | Companies without rights of foreign | |
Marketing Activities	trade	trade	Total
Market Research	64.3	79.1	77.5
Product Development	50	65.2	63.6
Forecasting	50	34.8	36.4
Sales Promotion	21.4	25.2	24.8
Customer Service	71.4	15.7	21.7
Public Relations	21.4	17.4	17.8
Diversification	7.1	19.1	17.8
Advertisements	7.1	17.4	16.3
Publicity (fairs, exhibitions)	7	12.2	11.6

SOURCE: Laszlo Szabo, *Company Marketing Situations* (A vallanlati marketing helyzete, Marketing-Piackutatas, 1977), pp. 4 and 480.

market research agencies. In relation to the domestic market, the need for market research in this period emerged only in cases when supply and demand were balanced or when the supply exceeded the demand. According to an estimate during the first years of the New Economic Mechanism, more manufacturing firms were interested in market research, and increasingly so. Those companies who had their own market-research expertise accounted for about 20 percent of the total number of industrial firms in Hungary. The ratio, due to market development, has increased substantially during the 1970s. This fact is well supported by a 1977 survey. (See Table 8.2.) Among the different marketing functions performed by Hungarian companies, the first place is taken by marketing research. The fact is that companies not having the right to import or export directly have a greater demand for foreign-market information than foreign-trade companies who are directly involved in international trade.

Market research in Hungary is utilized differently than in North American and West European companies. To assess this, we need to answer two interrelated questions: What do companies mean when they talk about market research, and what market research expertise do they have. Generally, Hungarian managers have an immediate self-interest in market research. On the other hand, the managers of industrial firms not having the right to direct export but keen to export have a more roundabout approach to it. They take business trips to foreign countries and obtain first-hand information about the market and its characteristics. They visit foreign fairs and exhibitions to exchange ideas and information on recent developments. These fairs are an important source of new product ideas; sample respondents receive market information on an ad hoc basis from their foreign-trade partners. They regularly study trade and professional journals. In those areas where there is not sufficient in-house expertise, they refer to outside market research agencies for expert advice.

According to the results of the survey, 40 percent of companies that consider market research significant and have their own expertise are conducting market research on a regular basis, 34 percent of them on an occasional basis, and the remaining 26 percent of them on an ad hoc basis. Past experiences of companies have proved that the so-called complex market research in the traditional sense is only conducted by companies where this activity is a regular task.

The newest and most dynamic phase in the development of market research started at the beginning of the 1980s. This was the time when the government announced an offensive strategy to counterbalance the deterioration in the country's terms of trade and opened an ever wider horizon for market competence. As a result, demands for market research relevant to both exports and domestic trade has increased substantially.

As methods of applied market research in a socialist environment, exploratory (desk) research and empirical (field) research are both important. Public policy makers and business firms alike are good sources of valid secondary source of information within the country. There is also a reliable statistical reporting system, which means that all manufacturing, service and retailing companies have to compile statistical documentation on a monthly basis. Unfortunately, these reports do not provide all the details that are in most cases required for comprehensive market research studies. Besides these reports, there are "data bases" at various state planning organizations, e.g., the National Planning Bureau, the Bureau of Standards, the National Committee for Technical Development, the Hungarian Chamber of Commerce, and information bureaus at ministries as well as different types of data banks sponsored by either public or quasi-public agencies. Access to secondary sources of information on foreign markets required for market research is easily assured by being in close contact with foreign data banks, information centers, marketing research institutes, and statistics offices.

Primary (empirical) research is used by Hungarian companies on a regular basis as well as experiments supported by field surveys. Other methods like group-focus interviews, simulation, motivation research, and taste tests are widely conducted. As the importance of consumer economy increases in Hungary and competition intensifies, more and more companies will use market research to be able to find out what consumers want and how they can satisfy their needs in a profitable and socially responsible manner.

There are several market research institutes in Hungary. Most important of these is the Hungarian Institute for Market Research. Operations at this institute exemplify the current status of marketing research in Hungary. Established 15 years ago, the institute has a large expert staff of specialists that carries out market research on behalf of the Hungarian firms and organizations as well as foreign corporations, some of them Western European. The institute conducts about 120 complex market research studies yearly. Sixty percent of this research is related to consumer goods, and the remainder is concerned with industrial commodities.

This research not only focuses on an analysis of the domestic market but explores export marketing, cooperation and procurement possibilities afforded by other countries in Western Europe and overseas, including well-developed and developing economies. Surveys of representative samples of respondents is completed with the help of specially trained interviewers. Mail surveys as well as personal interview techniques are utilized. Interviewers are applying the same methods used in any one of the developed Western countries. For mail surveys, however, the efficient panel system developed 15 years ago is still being applied. As a result, the Hungarian Institute for Market Research is in regular contact with some 22,000 households. Considering an average of two to three members per household, this means the involvement of about 70,400 inhabitants, which accounts for .7 percent of the total population of the country. At least some of the members of each household are interviewed six to eight times a year. Depending on the survey topic, 1,500 to 2,500 households are involved in a specific panel. Response rate to questionnaires is very satisfactory. On an average, between 72 and 75 percent of the interviewed families respond to questionnaires. Out of these returned questionnaires, representative samples of appropriate size can be developed, taking into account the unequal response rate of the individual segments.

When organizing a panel system, people to be interviewed are randomly selected, with the help of name and address list used in the population census. In the first letter (mail survey) forwarded, addressees are asked to participate in the public opinion research of the institute, provided they are interested. Their only obligation is to fill in the questionnaires systematically and to return them to the institute. Although the number interviewed initially runs around 20 percent, this number dwindles to between 10 and 12 percent following trial interviews. In panels involving 1,500 to 2,500 households, this means interviewing some 15,000 to 25,000 households. It also means that 350,000 households had to be surveyed initially for the different panels involving some 22,000 actual households. However, the real number is double this sum. There is a 20 percent replacement need because of panel effect and possible panel attrition. In a period of six to seven years, panels have to be replaced completely. Consequently, operating a panel requires continuous organization job in which the strict rules and adherence to random sampling is required. The role of panel members is voluntary.

The institute is in close cooperation with market research institutes and organizations operating in West Germany, England, France, Austria, Switzerland, the Soviet Union, and Cyprus. Cooperative market research projects are conducted with the institutes in other countries.

The old proverb says: "A prophet has no honor in his own country." It is the opinion of the author that the opposite of this is true for market research. The market features of a specific country and the demand for a specific product/commodity are determined most efficiently by market researchers of that country. This is of course true for Hungary as well. Accordingly, Hungarian market research organizations are at the disposal of any foreign organizations interested in exploring the Hungarian market.

Marketing-Strategy Alternatives for Foreign Companies Operating in the Socialist Countries

The importance of foreign trade provides vast opportunities for market research conducted by foreign firms in the individual socialist countries. For this, the Hungarian Institute for Market Research has a so-called multi-phase survey system, which may be adapted.* There are certain steps involved in this process worthy of mention here:

Phase 1: Foreign party describes in detail its marketing and cooperation intentions. The market research organization makes a scanning survey and decides whether the surveyed product has a chance or not to be introduced to the Hungarian market at that specific time or whether it should be introduced later. If the prospects are negative Hungarian marketing research organizations generally do not charge their customers.

Phase 2.: In cases of a positive response to the query, a *pilot study* is developed. This study incorporates the most important features of the market and gives the names of business partners, industrial firms, and end consumers.

Phase 3.: Representatives of the foreign firm meet at a so-called round-table conference with their would-be business partners. At the same time, if necessary or otherwise deemed worthwhile, products analyzed in the survey are demonstrated to participants at the conference.

---

*In some socialist countries, for instance in Czechoslovakia, Romania, Bulgaria, such surveys are conducted by advertising agencies, in other countries by the trading centers, e.g. SOVINCENTR in the Soviet Union.

Phase 4.: In the period following this conference, associates of the marketing institute inform the client of the possible volume of demand for their products and the conditions of sales. They do this by interviewing a sample of potential buyers.

Phase 5.: Test marketing and a public product show follow. On the basis of observed experiences at the show, the market-research institute will work out a proposal for the most efficient applicant.

Phase 6.: Finishing action. A comprehensive market-research program is developed from which an outline of client company turnover and a profit forecast are developed.

Despite many positive signs, however, one cannot conclude that marketing and marketing research is yet conducted with a high level of sophistication and efficiency by Hungarian companies. The initial results are promising, but a very thorough updating remains to be done. More testing and evaluation are necessary before marketing can become a truly vital part of Hungary's economic life.

V

COMPARATIVE DISTRIBUTION SYSTEMS

One of the most serious problems faced by the multi-national retailer is the estimation of the structure of retail markets in the many countries that he might want to enter. While marketing scholars have developed methods for assessing market potentials and for evaluating economic and political conditions, they have not been as successful in solving the market-entry problem as it relates to the development of retailing. In the first chapter, Savitt suggests that one approach that might help the difficulties of market entry is to apply historical research methods to the problem of understanding change. These methods, by their very nature, embody the elements of comparative analysis and offer the added advantage of dealing with specific firms and events rather than concentrating on more aggregate categories. There are a large number of models of retail change that can be applied to the process; however, they generally fall short of management desires. In the first place, these models are often based on untested hypotheses of retail change in the North American market; in the second place, few of them have been evaluated with respect to any wider context. Finally, these models are not comparative and their use in comparative analysis would suffer from the absence of acceptable categories and data.

One type of retail institution—the hypermarket that has developed during the "retail revolution,"—is the subject of the second chapter. According to Dawson, the hypermarket has diffused through many countries and promises to be a potent retail form through the 1980s and beyond. The chapter also considers the origins, evolution, and diffusion of the institution as well as the public policy response to the conflicts created by it. The Stock and Lambert chapter focuses on the role of physical distribution in international marketing planning; it explores examples of how such distribution is handled in several countries. Finally, Hazard tries to apply a comparative approach to transportation systems. The rapid growth of international trade, the expansion of international investment and multinational business, and improvements in transportation and communication have played a major role in making interchange systems more compatible. As a result of these developments there has been a greater integration of transport systems, with more to be learned by comparing the experiences of participating countries. Despite the promise of such an approach, relatively few formal studies employing it have emerged.

9

AN HISTORICAL APPROACH TO COMPARATIVE RETAILING

Ronald Savitt

The Setting for Comparative Retailing

Given the ever-increasing push for expansion in international trade, multinational retailers are confronted with the problems of assessing foreign-market opportunities. The processes for evaluating and reconciling differences in consumer behavior, and cultural, socioeconomic, and political conditions are well-known. However, an understanding of retail change and evolution in multiple environments is not fully developed. This chapter advocates a methodology to be used in the comparative study of retail change and development. The discussion directs the manager and the marketing scholar to the types of issues which must be confronted and solved if we are to be capable of better comparative analyses about the state of retail development. "Given the magnitude and rapidity of the changes, *the importance of predicting* future institutional developments in retailing needs recognition."[1]

The comparison of retail institutions in North America and the European Economic Community, in Britain and France, or even in markets within a single country depends upon the correct choice of comparative elements and the establishment of proper evaluative criteria. What is meant by elements is the set of structural and behavioral factors to be considered in the decision process. There is a long list of items which, except for their rank or emphasis, can be generally agreed upon. Among these factors are culture, income levels and distribution, communications infrastructure, and the political structure. These elements and their subcomponents are exceedingly helpful in the task of assessing the potential of a new market. Such principles are commonly accepted and applied.

How the criteria should be evaluated is a more difficult problem since there is need for great subjectivity. The answer is really found in the use to which the manager is putting them to. Clearly, a manufacturer of heavy equipment will focus on a set of criteria and will be able to evaluate the state of that industry's structure with great ease. Technology is well-known and direct comparison between one foundry and another can be easily made. The potential retail element does not enjoy the same luxury. The items for comparison may be identifiable, but their evaluation will be difficult. For example, items such as social class differ between and among countries and regions. The retailer must rely upon surrogates.

A manufacturer of consumer goods can use income, education, housing, and durable ownership as surrogates for assessing market potential. From any combination of these, conclusions can be drawn about the structure of a country. These can then be compared to similar items in the host country or other countries where the firm has been successful. The retail entrant can adopt much the same elements, without, however, enjoying the advantages of such analysis. Paying attention to the retail institutions present in any country hides more than it discloses, in so far as physical institutional forms reveal not much more than the transportability of retail forms. It is easy, for example, to build the physical entity of a supermarket in a developing country, but difficult to operate it as it should be in the developed economy.

A critical element that is often not fully recognized or included in the use of surrogates is the state of retail development. When this factor is ignored or given only a partial role to play in the decision-making process, problems arise. What happens, as in the case of human transplants, is that the retail institution does not "take." As an institutional type it may be too new for the circumstances or too old. The entry of Mothercare Ltd. into the U.S. market is an example of a case where management had difficulty in assessing the development retail structure and, hence, was not successful in adapting to it. Mothercare, as a result of the miscalculation, had to make adjustments to the new conditions that went beyond those that might be considered "learning how to operate in the market." More detailed historical analysis of the nature of retail change might have made the entry much easier and more successful.

The State of Comparative Retailing in Regards to Retail Change

The question is, how do we make comparisons of differing retail structure among economies? The accepted approach has been to make direct comparisons of the retail structure between countries or to use economic and social indices as the basis of comparison. In the first case, the analysis uses the traditional industrial organization definitions of market structure to describe wholesale and retail trade. There is a substantial literature that reports on the "state of" retailing and wholesaling in Great Britain, France, Italy, and Spain.[2] Comparisons are then made among the specific situations without regard to the differences in classification systems, the age and validity of the data, and, more importantly, the process of retail change, a process that differs from economy to economy. Another approach is to use the various economic and social indicators as the basis of establishing differences in the retail structures in different economies.[3]

Both of these approaches fail to adequately deal with the specific differences among the environment they also fail to analyze the conditions of retail change. States of development and change in retail institutions are inferred from indirect variables rather than measured directly. Further, these approaches implicitly suggest that there is a single model of retail change valid for all countries, with as little regard to the pace and variety of retailing existing in any two markets, say Britain and Finland; and there is almost no acknowledgment of the process of retail change going on regionally within countries.

In order to complement these approaches to market entry, another dimension must be added. That dimension must focus on the historical development of retailing within a given setting. Historical research provides a description of the change as well as the means for understanding the process of change. Historical research can be applied to a wide variety of marketing problems.[4] More importantly, historical research is broad and flexible enough to meet the general criteria for comparative marketing. Namely, historical methods cover the various levels of analysis, such as society, the firm, and the ultimate consumer; they can be applied to marketing systems in a variety of environments and in a variety of periods; and, the process can comprehend the additional subconnections of marketing that are necessary to do justice to the study of that which is, after all, a very complex institution.[5]

A Review of Retail-Change Theories

The purpose of theories of retail change is to describe patterns of retail development. They have as a second-order purpose a predictive function, namely, to suggest the direction in which future change might go. The predictive power of such theories would be an important source of information for retailers operating wholly within one or more economies. If valid, such theories would, when carefully tested and applied, make entry decisions much better informed than is presently possible.[6] They, in themselves, would be the vehicles by which comparison could take place.

Unfortunately, they offer more in potential than in reality. Before evaluating the current theories of retail change, it is necessary to outline them.

There are three general types of retail-change theories: stage theories, cycle theories, and dialectic theories. Stage theories are characterized by linear or curvilinear chronological progression. Retail institutions are hypothesized to have a historical trend toward an increase in complexity of functions and offerings. Cycle theories emphasize a dynamic movement in which change leads from simple to complex and then back to simple or a dynamic movement based on some predetermined biological pattern. Dialectic theories are based on arguments that one type of institution in an almost biological sense produces its opposite.

There are two basic stage theories. W. J. Regan's theory argues that retail change is characterized by an increase in the complexity of retail offerings. There are three stages, "simplex," "multiplex," and "omniplex," which represent the numbers and types of combinations of store service level and the levels of merchandise quality.[7] The second stage theory has been put forward by Goldman. This theory is based on the principle of "trading-up." Each stage is characterized by a set of variables, including the number and nature of product lines, the organizational characteristics of the store, the price strategy, the nature of the store's trading area, and the size of the establishment.[8]

Cycle theories have a more varied pattern of development than that found in stage theories. There are distinct patterns that retail change is thought to follow. Hollander has described the "retail accordion." It emphasizes the movement from general to specialized product assortments and the movement back to general assortments.[9] Dreesman premised his theory on biological analogies; in it he isolated patterns similar to the sequence of birth to death. They differ from the Hegelian-based dialectic theories, which accept an unending process,[10] only in terms of the ends produced. Dawson, more recently, has applied the product life-cycle concept to retail change. His innovation has been to combine life cycle with the theories of diffusion of innovation.[11]

The best-known cycle theory is the "wheel of retailing" proposed by McNair.[12] It states that the new retail institutions begin with crude facilities, little prestige, and a reputation for cutting prices and margins. As they proceed through time, they often acquire more expensive buildings, provide more extensive and elaborate services, increase margins and prices, and then become vulnerable to new competition.[13]

How valuable are these theories for approaching the problem of intermarket comparisons? Unfortunately, they have limited value in solving the problems of international market entry. There have been only a few attempts to make the definitions operational, the absence of these definitions and the subsequent measurements have thwarted empirical studies.[14] Those studies that are available for scrutiny focus on events in single countries;[15] others fall back on social and cultural indices;[16] and others still concentrate on differences in economic development. Furthermore, most of these students introduce a strong North American bias into the analysis; the studies are based on the theories of retail change that come from that environment. While these studies provide important insights into retail change, they cannot be regarded as a coherent body of theory for making comparison let alone decision rules for multinational retail managers.

Finally, these studies fail to deal with specific marketing elements because of the models used and the data applied. Retail-change theories themselves are concepts that have been borrowed from economics and sociology. They are often at arm's length from the actual events. The hypotheses are tested with available data, much of which is secondary. These studies often represent "case histories" without the systematic rigor necessary.

Historical Research and Comparative Retail Change

How can our understanding of comparative retail change be improved? Historical research is one approach. It is appropriate because historical methodology is aimed at defining, measuring, and understanding change. Its limitations stem from the fact that historians are generally reluctant to predict future events—although they do engage in a form of prediction called "retrodiction"—and from the fact that few people in retailing have undertaken extensive historical analysis. It is an attempt to work out what might have happened.

Historical studies are not deterministic in the terms of general equilibrium analysis of economic theory; they focus on issues of probable cause, rather than deterministic cause. They are not intended to contain the axiomatic development of mathematical theory.[18] In spite of the absence of a predictive stance, however, historical studies do provide the means for understanding the ways in which change takes place—hence the managerial function of making statements about the future can be made easier. After all, predictions about the future and the risks therein are the prime function of management.[19]

Historical analysis has a different starting point than traditional approaches employed in the social sciences and in marketing. Historical research begins with the description of a specific event, continues with the narration of the sequence of events, moves on to analysis or explanation of the relationships between and among, and concludes with synthesis or interpretation. It is a process that seeks generalized statements, but does so without the loss of individual events. This is, of course, in great contrast to much marketing research, in which the individual events are aggregated in such a way that reference back to a specific event is virtually impossible.

The historical approach goes beyond the case method because it is based on systematic evaluation of events in time and in space. The case method can be historical to the extent that it provides a more or less continual narration of events; however, it does not contain the comparative element, nor is there the specified set of activities found in the historical method. These activities include: 1) The definition of the perceptual experience of the researcher with regard to the problem; 2) The comparison of the perceptions of the real world as compared with the relevant literature; 3) The development of hypotheses for verification; 4) The definition of the research design; 5) The collection of data; 6) The verification or testing of the hypotheses; and 7) The construction of explanatory statements.[20]

In order to test or verify historical hypotheses, specific events are described in detail. Unlike marketing research in which the emphasis is on aggregation, historical research requires that attention be paid to the origin, development, and change of specific events. Instead of accepting the "wheel of retailing," for example, as a starting point for historical study, the historian would want to examine a specific innovation such as the hypermarche in the context of a specific country. He would want to know why this originated and what factors affected it. Because the historian is continually assessing developmental patterns among a variety of environmental elements, he or she would be more able to explain major transitions in structure. A research undertaking historical analysis would more easily explain the quantum change in French retailing from a structure of small-food retailers to hypermarches.

Historical Research and Comparative Studies

Historical research methodology employs comparative methods. Indeed, it requires that intertemporal and/or interspatial comparisons be made. The meaning of the events of one period take form and value as they are compared with the events of another period. Traditionally, historical comparisons are always thought of as a chronological progression from earlier to later periods. But this is not true in so far as historical periods and institutional developments take place at different times in different environments. Hence, it is possible to see different historical events at the same time. For example, the hypermarket is in a different historical setting from the supermarket at the present time. A historical study of hypermarkets in 1983 in Canada, France, Great Britain, and The Netherlands is possible. Such a study would be comparative and historical because recognition is given to the differences in developments among the economies chosen for the study. Not all comparative studies necessarily include time, but all historical studies do. What this acknowledges in the context of the example is that "time passes" at different rates so that the process of change for a hypermarket will be different. The measurement of these rates would be one result of the analysis. A full discussion of the concept of time is beyond the limits of the present discussion.[21]

The goal of historical research is reaching, "as closely as possible," an observation of events as they took place. Explanation of change is based on the factors that influence the specific event; it develops through an examination of the effects of the event. In order to understand the impact on retail trade of the opening of a superstore near a major high street in Edinburgh, more than general patterns must be observed and measured. Critical to an understanding of the effects is a knowledge of its specific external causes. All too many studies of retail change do not properly account for external factors on a direct basis. Historical studies must account for such; hence, in the case of retailing it is important to directly account for the impact of retail planning in each of the economies. Since retail planning takes different forms, there are different outcomes on the patterns of development of retailers. For example, the process of retail planning in Great Britain has led to a different locational pattern of malls there than in France or the United States.[22]

Historical methodology forces direct comparisons of institutions and factors since the center of the analysis is the individual retailer and the specific factors that affect it. A Woolworth store in the United States will be treated differently than one in England. Instead of assuming that both are "variety stores," no assumption is made at the initial point of examination. Comparisons and contrasts of similarities and differences come before the establishment of generalities.

Some Questions About the Historical Perspective

How do the theories of retail change fit the historical perspective? They provide milestones and observation points from which historical studies can start. They are the antithesis of historical research because they are based on generalization, and while good generalization should be encouraged, more is needed at a more specific level. We know some things about the birth and evolution of the supermarket as a group, but we know very little about specific institutions. Theories of change, especially when they are to be applied to several markets, must be based on the elements which make the markets differ. The theories of change should be the end points of comparative analysis, not the beginning.

Should all marketers become historians? The answer is no; in the same way that they should not all be statisticians. On the other hand, correctly applied historical research can illuminate factors for decision makers that often are ignored in the search for generalizations. To the extent that decisions are "item-specific," historical studies can provide data of that type.

Will such research help us to better predict retail change across economic and national boundaries? The answer is yes, to the extent that contemplation about the past makes us think more seriously about the future. Like other tools, it is a means of framing problems. Management, faced with multi-market entry, must look to the future; this task of "creative guessing" can be improved with the understanding of how others have previously dealt with the same issues.

Notes

1. A. Goldman, 'An Updated 'Wheel of Retailing' Theory," in Woodside, Sims, Lewison, and Wilkinson, eds. *Foundations of Marketing Channels*, Lone Star Publishers, 1978, p. 189.

2. For example, see: M. S. Sommers, and J. B. Kernan, eds., *Comparative Marketing Systems: A Cultural Approach*, Appleton-Century-Crofts, 1969.

3. J. Arndt, "Temporal Lags in Comparative Retailing," *Journal of Marketing*, 40, April 1972, pp: 40–45.

4. R. Savitt, "Historical Research in Marketing," *Journal of Marketing*, 44, Fall 1980, pp: 52–58.

5. J. Boddewyn, "A Construct for Comparative Marketing Research, *Journal of Marketing Research*, 3, May 1966, pp: 149–53.

6. E. Kaynak, "A Refined Approach to the Wheel of Retailing," *European Journal of Marketing*, 13, 1979, pp: 237–45.

7. W. J. Regan, "The Stages of Retail Development," in Cox, Alderson, and Shapiro, eds., *Theory in Marketing*, American Marketing Association, Second Series, Richard D. Irwin, 1964, pp: 139–53.

8. A. Goldman, "Stages in the Development of the Supermarket," *Journal of Retailing*, 51, Winter 1975–1976, pp: 49–64.

9. S. C. Hollander, "Notes on the Retail Accordion," *Journal of Retailing*, 42, Summer 1966, pp: 29–40, 54.

10. A. C. R. Dreesman, "Patterns of Evolution in Retailing, "*Journal of Retailing*, 44, Spring 1969, pp: 64–81. Gist has a dialectic theory based on evolution and the Hegelian notion of "thesis," "antithesis," and "synthesis." A retail institution will produce another type of institution that is its opposite; the two types then produce newer types. R. Gist, *Retailing Concepts and Decisions*, John Wiley, 1968, pp: 106–09.

11. J. A. Dawson, *The Marketing Environment*, Croom Helm, 1979, p. 185.

12. M. P. McNair, "Significant Trends and Developments in the Postwar Period," in A. B. Smith, ed., *Competitive Distribution in a Free High-Level Economy and Its Implications for the University* (University of Pittsburgh Press, 1958), p. 17.

13. S. C. Hollander,"Measuring the Cost and Value of Marketing," *Business Topics*, Summer 1961, pp: 17–27.

14. O. Neilsen, "Developments in Retailing,"in M. Kjaere-Hansen, ed., *Readings in Danish Theory of Marketing*, North Holland, 1966, pp: 101–15.

15. R. Savitt, " 'The Wheel of Retailing' and Retail Product Management," *European Journal of Marketing*, 18, (forthcoming).

16. Arndt, "Temporal Lags."

17. E. W. Cundiff, "Concepts in Comparative Retailing," *Journal of Marketing*, 29, October 1972, pp: 59–63.

18. D. Harvey, *Explanation in Geography*, Edward Arnold, 1969, p. 232.

19. W. Alderson, *Dynamic Marketing Behavior* (Richard D. Irwin, Chicago, Illinois, 1965), pp: 60–64.

20. Savitt, "Historical Research."

21. G. J. Whitrow, *The Nature of Time*, Penguin Books, London, 1975.

22. J. Beaujeu-Garnier and A. Delobez, *Geography of Marketing* (Longman Group, 1979), pp: 10–63.

10

STRUCTURAL-SPATIAL RELATIONSHIPS IN THE SPREAD OF HYPERMARKET RETAILING

John A. Dawson

The considerable structural changes in the retail trades over the last few decades have been accompanied and complemented by spatial changes in the organization of retailing. In North America, the changes in the business structure have a longer history than in Western Europe, where effective and massive changes have taken place only since the early 1960s. Even in Europe, however, it is possible to see the precursors in the 1950s to the changes of the 1960s and 1970s. These early trends towards new business structures, new sales techniques, and new operational environments were spasmodic, piecemeal, and effective for only a small proportion of both European retailers and European consumers. Since the early 1960s, change has been more rapid and widespread and has been accompanied by structural change elsewhere in the economy and by far-reaching social changes that many social scientists see as signaling the emergence of postindustrial society. This transformation of the structural and spatial processes in distribution has been considered elsewhere in general terms, but many of the individual components of change have not received much detailed attention.[1]

The aim of this chapter is to consider, in a comparative manner, one retail institution, the hypermarket, which has developed during the "retail revolution," and has prospered, evolved, diffused through many countries, and promises to be a potent retail technique through the 1980s. Sections of this chapter consider the origins, evolution, and diffusion of the institution, as well as the public policy response to the conflicts created by it. First it is necessary to define hypermarkets both as merchandising concept and as a form of retailing.

What Is a Hypermarket?

Definitions formulated by individual national agencies vary slightly, but all attempt to characterize hypermarkets in essentially the same way. The definition of the International Chamber of Commerce is, "A retail establishment of a minimum sales area of 2,500 m²* selling mainly in self-service and at very competitive prices a wide range of food and nonfood products with adequate parking facilities available."[2] Whilst this definition distills the essence of the hypermarket, the hypermarket concept is more than just a large unit with a mix of foods and nonfoods. Whilst not all the following characteristics are present in all hypermarkets, the mix of features commonly present includes:

1) A *retail* establishment usually operated by a *horizontally integrated* chain organization. Stores are operated as part of corporate, cooperative, and contractual chains. Stores may also be part of a vertically integrated distribution system but this is only true of a minority. Horizontal integration is much more common. Out of the 466 hypermarkets operating in France in January 1982, only three did not belong to either a corporate, contractual, or cooperative horizontally integrated chain. Typical of an operating chain is *Casino* in France, which had in 1981 a shop mix as shown in Table 10.1. Hypermarkets in this group constitute one store format in a chain of over 2,000 units.

2) A *sales area* of at least 2,500 m². In the United Kingdom, stores with a sales area of 2,500 to 5,000 m² are sometimes termed superstores, with the name hypermarket limited to units over 5,000 m². Elsewhere in Europe the term superstore is used to denote large supermarkets of over 1,000 m² sales space but having a limited range of nonfood items on sale. In the U.S.A., the term superstore is used to describe supermarkets of at least 2,780 m² (30,000 ft.²) gross floorspace with an expanded nonfood section, and the term *combination store* is used to describe units similar to hypermarkets. Large hypermarkets have sales areas in excess of 20,000 m².

3) The *merchandise mix* results in at least 35 percent of sales area and often more than 50 percent given over to nonfood items. Combination stores in the U.S.A. are defined as having 40 percent of floorspace in nonfoods. Comparison of British and French surveys show, respectively, 50 percent and 55 percent of sales space in nonfoods.

---

*One square meter is equal to 1.2 square yards

TABLE 10.1

Store Formats of the *Casino* Chain in France in 1981.

	Number	Sales space m²	% of sales space	% of group sales
Standard self-service units	2,014	107,865	31.7	26.5
Supermarkets	75	76,851	22.6	32.7
Hypermarkets	18	124,308	36.5	38.5
Nonfood stores	13	31,336	9.2	1.8
Restaurants in stores	72	—	—	0.5
TOTAL	2,120	340,360	100	100

4) *Gross floor space* ranges from more than twice the sales area to about 20 percent more than sales area. A survey of British hypermarkets by Jones showed for a sample of 53 stores that sales space as a percentage of gross floorspace was 62 percent and that this proportion increased with store size.[3] German data, shown in Table 10.2, suggests sales space accounting for a higher proportion of gross floor area.

5) The *product range* involves a wide assortment but shallow range of lines with relatively few brands, colours, and sizes of any one item. Statistics on the U.S.A. from the Food Marketing Institute show the average number of regular items carried in combination stores of 3,500 m² gross floorspace as 22,500 but in European hypermarkets the number of regular lines is fewer.

TABLE 10.2

Floorspace and Product Range in West German Hypermarkets—January 1982

Sales space m²	Percentage floorspace in		Percentage of gross area in sales space	Number of lines	
	Foods	Nonfoods		Food	Nonfood
2,500–3,999	45	55	79	7,100	13,400
4,000–4,999	39	61	80	8,300	19,100
5,000–6,999	36	64	82	8,700	23,200
7,000–9,999	32	68	79	11,400	26,900
10,000 and over	24	76	80	10,600	36,100

SOURCE: Institut für Selbstbedienung und Warenwirtschaft (1982) These figures are not directly comparable but are certainly indicative of the scale of food/nonfood space ratios. Although accounting for 55 percent of floorspace on average in France, nonfoods generate only 38 percent of sales volume. Generally the proportion of space and of sales in nonfoods increases with size of unit.

TABLE 10.3
Percentage Gross Margins in Stores of Different Types—France 1980

	Hypermarket	Supermarket	Department stores	Variety stores
Groceries	4.76	11.83	18.16	15.24
Fresh food	17.22	18.18		20.45
Clothing/textiles	22.01	24.63	37.71	31.05
Other nonfoods	17.52	22.92	34	29.60

The Mammout chain in France, for example, carried in its stores approximately 2,000 food lines, 1,200 toiletries and cosmetics, and 13,000 nonfood lines, but additionally there are approximately 9,000 extra-seasonal lines. Carrefour, again in France, is somewhat exceptional, with, in its large stores of over 15,000 m², more than 40,000 lines of nonfoods 4,000 food, as well as cosmetics items. As with other definitional variables, product range increases with store size. The American combination store would seem to have greater depth with more food lines and more variety of household hardware but fewer clothing items. This difference in product mix between hypermarkets and American combination stores makes it difficult to consider the two store formats as entirely synonymous.

6) The *merchandising policy* is one of mass, scrambled merchandising with relatively low margins and high sales volumes. Table 10.3 shows for France the relatively low margins in hypermarkets, particularly on food items. The higher margins on nonfoods offset the lower sales per m² in the nonfood sector.

7) *Prices* are relatively low, reflecting low gross margins. Price surveys show hypermarket prices 8 to 10 percent less than average price levels for most products. Several studies in France using different shopping baskets of goods reveal hypermarkets to have consistently the lowest prices of a full range of store formats.[4] Even when one company operates a range of store formats it is usual for corporate price policy to place hypermarket prices around 10 percent below those of the other stores in the group.

8) The store *sales technique* is one of customer self-service, with the customer checking out all purchases at a single front-end station. Sales space per checkout is approximately 140 m² in smaller stores rising to 250 m² in the very large units with an average of about 180 m².

9) Stores generally have *extended opening hours* in the evenings and at weekends.

10) *Associated operations* integral to the main store typically consist in a cafeteria, an auto center including petrol and tire sales, a garden center, and, in some cases, other operations such as timber sales. These operations

are separately accounted from the main store. Larger stores may have *concessions* within them, but these are usually located off the main sales floor. Typical are the four concessions in the Sava-centre at Reading in England, where a newsagent/magazine stall, photographic/electronics store, fruit and nut kiosk, and a building society branch are located inside the main store building.

11) The level of *automation* in the store operation is high, with scanning systems in operation and a widespread use of pallets, including manufacturer-packaged caged pallets. A survey in France in 1977 showed that the investment cost of store equipment and fitments in a new 8,000 m^2 hypermarket was 34 percent higher than in a 800 m^2 traditional supermarket, and this investment-cost represented 34 percent of total capital cost in hypermarkets compared with 29 percent in the supermarket case.[5]

12) The *supply channels* for the store involve a high proportion of goods obtained, in large lots, directly from the manufacturer. Typically a hypermarket chain has a central-buying department. A director of a British operation reports "Hard on the heels of the creation of central-buying services, we were then able to request total direct deliveries to our stores, thus saving central warehouse and distribution costs."[6] Store management often has executive-buying responsibility for perishable lines, but again direct purchasing is usual.

13) *Car parking* space is provided close to or at the store site. Parking space for over 1,000 cars is not uncommon, with parking ratios seldom less than 10 places per hundred m^2 sales space, and in large units the parking ratio rises to over 20. Average values for parking ratios derived from surveys of operating characteristics are 15 in the United Kingdom, 19 in France, 12 in Belgium, and 18 in Spain, whilst reports on individual combination stores in the U.S.A. suggest a figure of eight to ten as a typical parking ratio per hundred m^2 selling space.

14) *Development* of the hypermarket site and property is frequently initiated by the retail operation rather than by a property developer. Recent trends towards the incorporation of hypermarkets within shopping centers has introduced established property developers into hypermarket development, but it still remains common for the whole hypermarket-based shopping center to be developed by the retailer. In Britain, the ASDA company, principally a hypermarket operator, is close to the top ten of shopping center developers, having developed by mid-1982 over 100,000 m^2.

15) Early schemes favored *locations* in out-of-town or edge-of-town positions, but more recently hypermarkets have been operated in all types of locations including inner cities, within various types of shopping centers, and in small towns. The edge-of-town locations for early stores appears to have been simply the result of land-cost differentials. Carrefour, the large French firm operating over 50 hypermarkets, gave their rationale, in 1970, for

peripheral development in terms of the differentials in land cost—amongst central Paris at £1,100/m^2, residential Paris at £250/m^2, suburban communities at £20/m^2, and out-of-town at £2.5 m^2. The land requirement for a 10,000 m^2 is about 50,000 m^2.[7] The major locational criterion would appear to be a catchment population of at least 30,000 people within ten minutes travel time. A report on a combination store in Sacramento, California quotes the operator, "Combination stores can be successful in both developing suburbs and smaller cities. But there must be at least 35,000 customers within the store's trade area."[8]

16) Hypermarket *design* stresses functionalism. Stores have few architectural frills, use low-cost construction techniques and are built to minimize operating costs, in energy use for example. The French survey of investment costs referred to earlier showed the construction cost of hypermarkets to be 34 percent of total investment compared with 43 percent for supermarkets, with construction cost per square meter of sales space 5.5 percent lower in hypermarkets than in supermarkets.

17) Store *management* structure varies by organization but generally is more decentralized than in other store types. Local management has a relatively high level of executive responsibility over the main aspects of store operation.

All of the above characteristics are not present in all hypermarkets, as inevitably there is variability within any one type of store format, but the mix of characteristics typifies what is usually considered as hypermarket retailing. Defined in this way, hypermarkets are now widespread through Europe, increasingly common in middle income, less-developed countries, and emerging in Eastern Europe. Table 10.4 shows the worldwide extent of hypermarket retailing in 1980. Since then hypermarkets have become operational in Greece, New Zealand, Mexico, Argentina, and Saudi Arabia. Furthermore, stores very similar to hypermarkets and using many of the trading concepts seen in Western hypermarkets have been opened in Hungary and Yugoslavia. Data for the U.S.A. are difficult to obtain. Bates is one of the few American researchers to differentiate between combination stores and hypermarkets, doing so on the basis of size more than any other measure.[9] He argues that hypermarkets have at least 10,000 m^2 sales space whilst combination stores more typically are 3000 to 6,000 m^2. This is a rather narrow view of hypermarkets and one which would not be widely accepted in Europe. He characterizes hypermarkets as one branch of warehouse retailing suggesting that they are "a warehouse-oriented combination of the supermarket and the discount department store."[10] Other American reports also tend to overestimate the size of European hypermarkets,[11] seeing as typical "60 checkstands operating full-tilt at one time."[12] There are, in the U.S.A., a limited number—probably fewer than 100—of discount department stores selling a full range of food and also

TABLE 10.4

Estimates of the Number, Sales Space, and Market Penetration of Hypermarkets in 1980

	Number	Sales space '000 m²	m² per '000 population	Share of retail trade
W. Germany	821	4,950	80.6	10.0
Belgium	78	605	61.3	8.9
France	408	2,473	46.4	10.8
Sweden	39	347	41.8	4.1
Switzerland	42	250	39.4	4.4
Finland	35	153	32.2	4.4
Austria	41	210	28.0	3.2
Denmark	11	128	25.0	3.0
U.K.	275	1,040	18.7	3.9
Netherlands	39	181	12.9	2.1
Spain	32	214	5.8	*
Norway	2	9	2.2	*
Italy	16	108	1.9	*
Australia	20	62	4.6	*
Brazil	14	85	0.6	*
South Africa	12	40	1.6	*
Gabon	1	3	5.4	*
Ivory Coast	1	9	1.1	*
Japan	45	189	1.7	*
U.S.A. (1)	80	375	1.6	*
U.S.A. (2)	470	2,500	11.0	1.3
Canada	10	42	1.8	*
Israel	4	15	4.1	*

*Less than one percent
(1) European type hypermarkets
(2) Combination stores.
SOURCE: National survey reports and International Association of Department Stores (1982).

meeting the criteria suggested above to typify hypermarkets. There are, however, over 500 combination stores, most of which have opened since 1975. Even including combination stores in the total, hypermarket density remains low in the U.S.A. and the reason for the techniques' lack of spread in the U.S.A. is usually given as the intensity of competition existing in the supermarket and nonfood discount store sectors.

Origins and Innovation Phase

In achieving the spread penetration, and sophistication it has today, the hypermarket has evolved considerably since its origin in Belgium in 1961. The first hypermarket opened with 3,300 m² sales area in Bruges, Belgium in August 1961.

The guiding light behind this innovation was Maurice Cauwe, who made several visits to the U.S.A. during the 1950s, while he was a director of the retail corporate chain Grand Bazar (GB). On these visits he saw the structural changes underway in U.S. distribution, the economies of scale obtainable in supermarketing, and the successful growth of self-service department stores such as *K Mart, Two Guys,* and *Atlantic Mills.* He took part also in the National Cash Register seminars organized by Bernard Trujillo. These seminars, in 1957, and particularly in 1960, when large groups of European executives attended, were important sources of new ideas about distribution, and particularly about retailing.[13] A Belgian group including Cauwe and sponsored by the government's Bureau for Productivity Improvement attended these seminars. Cauwe was greatly impressed by the dynamism of U.S. retailing and the willingness of U.S. retailers to take risks and pursue innovations. Convinced of the economic potential of mass-scrambled merchandising from large units, Cauwe decided to launch such stores in Belgium, building on the British experience of supermarketing developed in the late 1950s and on his own experiences of U.S. retailing, particularly self-service department stores. In October 1960, the decision was made by GB to build, under the name Superbazar, "stores of 5,000 to 15,000 m², which will be constructed at low cost, located at the periphery of towns, with large areas of free parking; we will sell there in self-service all convenience goods and all food goods; these stores will be open from 9 to 21.00 hours."[14] A joint company was launched with Bon Marché of Brussels and Jewel Tea Company of Chicago to devlop these stores, which were in effect the first European-style hypermarkets. The first opened at Bruges (3,300 m²) in August 1961 and a month later stores at Auderghem (10,000 m²) and Anderlecht (8,000 m²) in suburban Brussels were opened.

In France, Marcel Fournier and Louis Defforey also were disciples of Bernard Trujillo, and like Maurice Cauwe became aware of the possibilities of discounting and mass merchandising through large units. Fournier operated a 1,000 m² nonfood store in Annecy, a town of 60,000 people, and Defforey was a food wholesaler in a small town near Lyon. In 1959 they agreed to cooperate and form a company, Carrefour, to operate supermarkets but using the discounting methods they had seen in the Leclerc stores then in operation in France. These stores retailed food items at very low prices with operating margins cut to a minimum. Although heavily criticized by other retailers, French consumers were attracted by the low prices in the Leclerc stores. Operating through supermarkets, the Carrefour company opened a store in Annecy in 1960; the store was relatively small (650 m²) but differed from existing French supermarkets in being built at the edge of town, having a relatively large car park (80 cars), and operating a discount-price policy. The success of this store, in addition a visit to North America in 1962, where they met Trujillo, and an awareness of the innovations of Cauwe all convinced Carrefour's directors that hypermarkets could be operated successfully in France. In June 1963, almost two years after the Superbazar in Bruges, the first hypermarket in France was opened at Ste. Genevieve-des-Bois. At 2,500 m², and with parking for 450 cars, it was small by current standards, but was located on the periphery of a small town in outer suburban Paris. The store was very similar to discount department stores in the U.S.A., but consolidation of sales through a single checkout system was soon introduced. From 1963 on the Carrefour company opened stores steadily, and in February 1982 they opened their fiftieth hypermarket. The innovation of hypermarkets in France may be traced to the vision of two entrepreneurs aware of developments not only in their own country but elsewhere in Europe and the U.S.A.—an awareness of the value of comparative marketing. The hypermarket concept resulted from the borrowing and adaptation of existing retail techniques together with the willingness of individuals to take a calculated commercial risk and be innovators.

Elsewhere in Europe in the early 1960s there was a limited interest in hypermarket type operations. In Sweden the consumer cooperative movement was an important innovator in introducing the concept to Swedish consumers. In December 1963 executives of the Stockholm Cooperative Society opened their 10,600 m² (sales space) Obs! store in the southern Stockholm suburb of Varby. A few months later a second hypermarket opened at Stenby Garde on the edge of the city of Vaseras. These two stores rapidly proved successful and served as forerunners for extensive investment by consumer cooperative societies during the late 1960s. In Britain, the Gem store of 8,000 m² gross area opened in 1964 in suburban Nottingham, and a smaller unit was built in Leeds. Very much a copy of American discount department stores, with the operating company 65 percent American-owned, these stores did not achieve their full potential in early years largely because they aped, too closely, American developments.[15]

By 1964 hypermarkets with innovative features were established in Belgium, France, Sweden, and England. In the first two cases, growth was the result of individuals' efforts to create new companies to develop hypermarkets. In Sweden, once the influence of a small group of people was very important, but the development occurred within an established retail organization. In other European countries, there were moves towards hypermarkets but they did not result in the established institutions of Belgium, France, and Sweden. In Britain, an attempt was made to bring in

FIGURE 10.1
Growth in Numbers of Hypermarkets in Several Countries

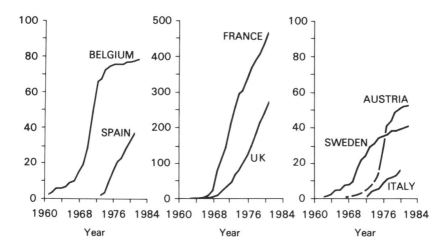

the original American model from which hypermarkets evolved, while in Denmark and West Germany there were attempts to diversify the product mix in supermarkets and variety stores, thus making them more like hypermarkets. The process of adaptation speeded up considerably in the late 1960s as hypermarkets were developed, *ab initio*, alongside the adapting supermarkets and variety stores. The period of origins of hypermarkets is from 1961 to 1964, after which date there occurred a period of mass diffusion.

Diffusion and Establishment Phase

Since 1964 several features in the organizational evolution, technical adaptation, and spatial diffusion of hypermarkets may be discerned. The bibliography of Burt, Dawson, and Sparks lists many papers describing specific stores and their operations and also papers concerned with hypermarket operations with specific towns.[16] The years immediately following innovation may be seen as a period of establishment of the concept. Figure 10.1 shows the growth of hypermarkets in several European countries. In France, a six-year period of rapid growth is apparent since mid-1968. In Belgium, the growth period was in the early 1970s. It should be pointed out that the data in Figure 10.1 refer to openings. As planning and construction may take a year, the dates of the start of the period of rapid growth are rather earlier than appears from this figure. In other countries, the innovation period is followed similarly by an establishment period and then a phase of rapid growth.

The lag between initial innovation, ending in 1964–1965, and the period of rapid growth is accounted for by the time required by companies other than the innovators to accept the concept and design, and then construct and open stores. It was almost five years after opening their initial store that Carrefour had any competition from other operators in France. During these five years, Carrefour opened six stores and had a further six planned for opening in 1969; by 1969, however, several other companies were opening stores, and the preeminence of market share enjoyed by Carrefour had started to decline. By the end of 1969, 73 hypermarkets were in operation, with close to 400,000 m² floorspace. Table 10.5 shows the changing pattern of operations in French hypermarkets. The Carrefour group rapidly became a specialized operator of hypermarkets, but growth potential was such that by 1969 it was operating as a franchiser of Carrefour hypermarkets, which were in turn operated by established corporate chains wishing to enter the market rapidly. With the increase in scale of hypermarket operations, other enterprises specializing in hypermarkets were formed. By 1970, the market was split between specialist operators and a few existing chain-store groups, and only later, as the period of rapid growth got underway, other forms of organization and a larger number of chain-store groups became involved.

The postinnovation period is characterized by similar features elsewhere in Europe. In Belgium, development was dominated by the GB Company, with only three or four stores operated by other groups—mainly contractual chains—in 1970. GB effectively maintained its stranglehold on the market throughout the period of rapid growth during the 1970s, and other companies and operators have never seriously challenged GB Centres, the descendents of Superbazar. In Britain, the limited success of the Gem stores led to their sale in 1966 to ASDA stores, a subsidiary of Associated Dairies based in Northern England. The existing fresh food retail company formed ASDA stores in 1965 through involvement with Peter Asquith, who operated two discount supermarkets. To develop their hypermarkets, the company, in the first five years, bought and adapted existing premises for use as hyper-markets. Former industrial premises were purchased and converted to hypermarkets. Experience was gained in their operation and an organiza-tional base established for expansion in the 1970s. Other supermarket operations, such as Tesco, were becoming hypermarkets through the addition of increasing proportions of nonfood goods in their large—often over 1,500 m²—markets. The Woolworth Corporation, through Woolco, was moving in the opposite direction, introducing foods into their large discount and variety store operations. In this postorigin, establishment phase, in Britain, large established corporate chain companies dominated hypermarket develop-ment, with only an occasional attempt to enter the market being made by

TABLE 10.5

Hypermarket Numbers by Form of Organization of Operator—France, January 1, Each Year

	1965	1969	1973	1977	1981
Independent inc. voluntary chains		1	31	59	79
Retail corporate chains		12	79	115	128
Consumer cooperatives			11	28	39
Department stores		2	10	16	17
Enterprises specializing in hypermarkets	2	13	76	122	170
TOTAL	2	28	207	340	433

independent traders and consumer cooperatives. By 1970 20 or so hypermarket operations were trading in Britain and almost all were operated by one of three companies.

The establishment phase was also characterized by a notable increase in store size. Figure 10.2 shows the average size of new hypermarkets opened in France and Belgium and the difference in size between markets in the early 1960s and late 1960s is clearly indicated. The increase in size of new units reflects the operators' attempts to increase sales volume in individual stores. Given the small number of stores, there was little interstore competition, and returns to sale could be achieved through even larger units. Additionally, as experience was gained in day-to-day store operations, with the necessarily new buying techniques and in large-store management, operators became more confident and again store size was increased. A similar pattern is apparent elsewhere. In the ASDA group in Britain, increasingly larger units resulted from the conversion of existing buildings and, eventually, from the development of larger purpose-build structures when the trading concept had become established and operational experience had been gained. The cooperative societies in Sweden also opened steadily larger units. The innovative Stockholm Society's second store was 10 percent larger than its first. The store of the Vasteras Society, opened in 1964, was almost doubled in size, to 10,200 m^2 sales space, in 1967. The trading area constraints imposed on a cooperative society based in a single town result in increases in size of individual hypermarkets rather than growth by building additional stores.

In the larger store units, associated operations were introduced into hypermarket schemes during the establishment phase. Cafeterias and motor fuel and tire bays became standard features of the new larger units and in some cases garden centers were added. A second and more fundamental

FIGURE 10.2
Size of New Hypermarkets in France and Belgium

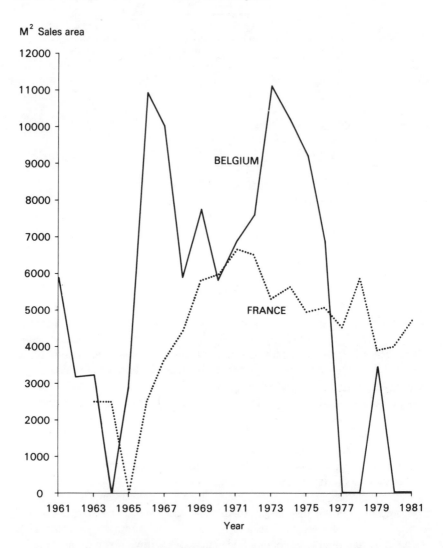

structural change in operating techniques may be seen to be starting during this postorigin, establishment phase. Some operators began to see hypermarkets as anchor tenants for suburban and out-of-town shopping centers. The concept was for a small gallery of specialist shops and services to be provided within the hypermarket development. The tenant mix in these galleries serves to complement the product mix in the main store and typically include travel agent, bank, hairdresser, and a few small specialist stores. In France, the Auchan and Rallye companies and the operators of stores associated with the Paridoc chain had begun exploring this type of development by 1966 but most of these early schemes contained fewer than 25 shop and service units, as is shown in Figure 10.3.

Associated with the structural changes, the spatial diffusion process became established relatively quickly after the early experiments had proved themselves. It is possible to discern two spatial processes in operation that result from different corporate policies. First there is the spread of developments within the local region of an operating company. This may be termed the *neighborhood effect*. The ASDA company in Britain, for example, concentrated early development in north England, particularly the

FIGURE 10.3
Focused Shopping Centers Based on Hypermarkets in France

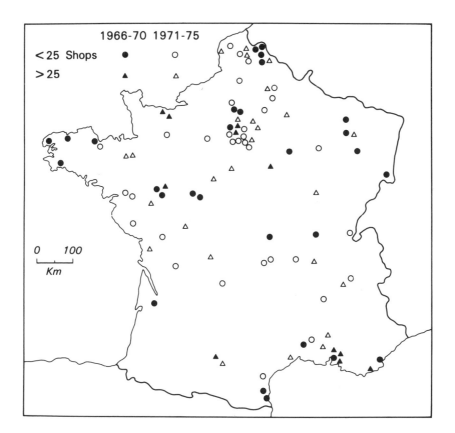

region around its headquarters at Leeds. Jones, in a review of ASDA operations on which Figure 10.4B is based points to the "early concentration of the ASDA stores in the north of England," reflecting "that the parent company's traditional area of operation had been here." Not all the stores shown on Figure 10.4A rate as hypermarkets, but the map serves to show this pattern.[18] Figure 10.4C shows the stores of the Rallye Group in France and a similar conclusion can be drawn as with ASDA.

Secondly, a spatial pattern emerged indicating the presence of only a single hypermarket in each major market center. In this establishment phase, such a pattern suggests the avoidance of competition and may be termed a *noncompetitive* effect. Figure 10.5 shows the locations of hypermarkets opened in France between 1968 and 1979, and in very few cities was more than one store opened. This pattern results from the presence of relatively few operating companies, who tended, in the establishment phase, to avoid direct competition with each other. Even in a large regional market such as greater Paris, there was a tendency to avoid direct interhypermarket competition until the rapid expansion phase of the early 1970s. Mettain shows in the Paris region, for example, how hypermarkets developed before 1971 were concentrated in a zone around Paris 15 to 25 km out from the city center.[19] The suggestion is that trade areas were sectoral, with stores located to command a particular sector stretching from inner city to outer suburb. This seeking of major unserviced markets during the establishment phase is seen elsewhere in Europe. In Belgium, the pattern is particularly marked because the small compact national market (9.5 million in the late 1960s and no major city more than 180 kms. from Brussels) results in Brussels-based companies' activities producing the neighborhood effect,but with the nation serving as the neighborhood. Furthermore, the dominant position of a single company in hypermarket development in Belgium leads to an enhancement of the *noncompetitive* effect.

The structural and spatial changes discussed in the above paragraphs relate to a phase of development that has been termed an *establishment* phase. The beginnings of hypermarket retailing occurred in an origin or *innovation phase*. When the trading technique had become established, a period of rapid growth in numbers of units and rapid spatial diffusion of the retail technique occurred, and this may be considered as a third phase and termed the *rapid-growth phase*.

Rapid-Growth Phase

Figure 10.1 provided an indication of the rapid rate of growth of hypermarket numbers in several countries during the 1970s. In France and Germany, new stores were opening at an average rate of one or more per week in the early 1970s. Jones has suggested that in Britain at this stage

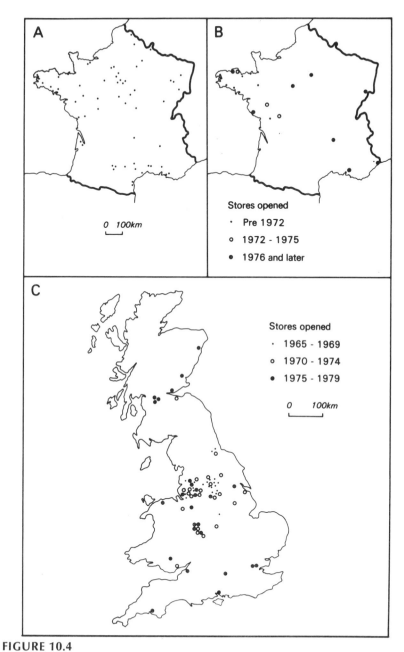

FIGURE 10.4

(A) Location of New Hypermarkets Opened between 1968 and 1970 in France; (B) The Spread of Rallye Hypermarkets 1968–1981 in France; (C) The Spread of ASDA Stores 1965–1979 in Britain (after Jones, 1981)

FIGURE 10.5
Dates of Hypermarkets Openings in the Paris Region

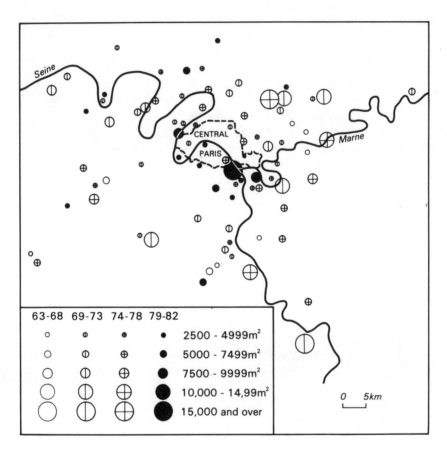

"companies were very keen to get on the bandwagon and were prepared to undertake risk ventures wherever an opportunity arose."[20] The expansion of this form of retailing led to its taking a significant share of retail sales volume and so created conflict over market share with other retail types. The period may be seen as one of increasing conflict between hypermarket operations and the existing network of stores and operators. As hypermarket operations expand, so other retail formats are impacted, and frequently their operators lobby government for controls over hypermarket development. Characteristic of the later part of the growth period, therefore, are attempts to introduce public policy controls on the spread of hypermarkets. The rapid-growth period ends either with approaching market saturation or the imposition of effective government controls. During the period of rapid growth, the share of food sales accounted for hypermarkets passes 10 percent and the share of nonfood sales passes 5 percent. In France, this level of market penetration was achieved in 1973. Hypermarkets become integrated into channels of distribution and, for some products, become major institutions taking the leader's role within the distribution channel.

A number of evolutionary features characterize the hypermarket during this phase of development. These features can be seen in many countries but at different dates because of the different stages of development. The characteristics of the rapid-growth phase are:

1) Growing domination of large enterprises in the development and operation of stores.

2) Increasing size of new units in the major markets, but also the development of small-store units located in the smaller markets.

3) More sophisticated shopping environments with hypermarkets developed as part of focused shopping centers.

4) Increased awareness of the impact of hypermarkets on other types of trading and on urban form.

5) A spatial pattern of provision showing approaching market saturation in some regions, with only areas of very low population density having no opportunities to visit hypermarkets.

6) A spread of hypermarket retailing to smaller towns or *middle markets*.

7) Growing interhypermarket competition.

8) At least 8m^2 of hypermarket sales-space per 1,000 population.

9) Some mergers and takeovers among operators, with hypermarkets being traded on the property market.

In the early 1970s, the success of the units of the major companies in France provided the capital necessary to finance the corporate growth programs. The British group, ASDA, depended heavily on its generated profits to provide capital for expansion. Furthermore, if it became necessary to borrow on established money markets to finance growth plans, then the larger companies, often with considerable existing capital assets in property, usually found the borrowing exercise easier than new, small companies with no track record. A further reason for the increasing dominance of large groups was their ability and expertise in managing a program of rapid expansion. When growth is through replication of similar stores, then organizational scale economies may be developed in the research and development sections of already large retail companies. Within hypermarket development generally, and even more so during the rapid-growth phase, there are few opportunities for small, independent companies. Countries currently entering the rapid-growth phase show particularly clearly the domination by large enterprises, since the high nominal interest rates over the last two years have discouraged even the few interested independent firms. In Spain, for example, not only are almost all the units operated by major companies, but more than three quarters of the stores are operated by foreign-owned companies and the proportion rises even higher if companies having a substantial, though minority, foreign interest are included. Of ten units opened in a two-year period beginning in early 1979, only one was not developed by a large corporate chain group. In this single case, development was undertaken by a cooperative.

The increasing size of new units during the rapid-growth phase is shown in Figure 10.2. The large corporate chains seek to exploit scale economies to their limit and so experiment with increasingly large units. But also in this phase there is evidence of a growing interest in smaller units in smaller markets, for example towns of 25,000 urban population but with a substantial rural trade area. These stores represent one of the few opportunities open to independent retailers who have been able to obtain sites in these middle markets while the larger groups have been concentrating on the major centers of population.

Typical of the rapid-growth phase therefore is a bimodal distribution of new store size. Table 10.6 shows the size distribution of new stores in Belgium and the bimodal pattern is evident. In France, a similar pattern may be seen, for example, in 1972 at the peak of the rapid-growth phase, when 62

TABLE 10.6
Size Distribution of New Hypermarkets in Belgium

Year of opening	Number of units*	Sales floorspace categories in m^2 2500–4500	4501–6500	6501–8500	over 8500
1961	3	1		2	
1963	2	2			
1965	1	1			
1966	2				2
1967	1				1
1968	5	3			2
1969	4			3	1
1970	10	3		5	2
1971	20	3	2	9	6
1972	17	4	2	6	5
1973	2				2
1974	5	1			4
1975	2		1		1
1976	1			1	
1979	1	1			

*Excludes extensions

TABLE 10.7
Associated Activities in French Hypermarkets

			Percentage of hypermarkets with			
Date	Number of stores	Cafeteria	More than 10 boutiques	Auto center	Garden center	Furnishing center
January 1, 1970	71	69	46	30	32	
January 1, 1973	209	77	59	45	27	20
January 1, 1976	305	79	62	61	23	26
January 1, 1979	392	71	61	57	19	21
January 1, 1982	406	63	55	47	18	21

hypermarkets were opened. Of the 62, 21 were under 4,500 m², 11 between 4,500 m² and 6,500 m², 15 between 6,500 m² and 8,500 m² and 15 over 8,500 m². The medium-sized units appealed neither to developers looking toward middle markets nor to large companies concentrating on major metropolitan centers.

While operators were experimenting with larger units, they also were exploring the commercial potential of adding additional facilities to new units. Table 10.7 shows the proportion of hypermarkets in France having various auxiliary facilities. It can be seen that, during the rapid-growth period between 1970 and 1976, the number of stores within associated cafeterias increased whereas the proportion of associated garden centers have declined. In 1974 a widely held view in France was that "future hypers will form the hub of small towns."[21] Not only were new units opened with commercial and social facilities associated with them; these facilities were also added to existing stores. In Britain, a similar pattern is apparent with the incorporation, particularly during the late 1970s, of hypermarkets within shopping centers. In the forefront of this trend have been ASDA, the pioneers of British hypermarketing. The first important scheme of this type developed by ASDA was at Dyce in suburban Aberdeen. The center, comprising a hypermarket and 21 other shops, was developed jointly by ASDA and the local government land-use planning agency, and opened in 1976. The period of rapid growth in Britain dates from 1976 and, although tempered by land-use legislation, is marked by a notable increase in stores designed to be part of a larger shopping center in which the hypermarket is the dominant tenant.

The increase in number, size, and complexity of hypermarket operations resulted in a growing awareness, among the more conservative retail groups as well as the public, that hypermarkets were having an appreciable and clearly apparent effect on other shop types and on urban form. Various impact studies were produced which showed that hypermarkets attracted shoppers who previously had used supermarkets.[22] The greatest impact of hypermarkets was originally thought to be on small independent traders, but most impact surveys showed that local small stores could coexist with widely spaced hypermarkets and it was medium-sized supermarkets that were most seriously affected by hypermarket development. In many cases these were the more progressive independent retailers who had expanded from small stores to small supermarkets, and this group of independent traders raised their collective voice in protest against the growth of the network of corporate chain hypermarkets.

The period of rapid growth results in some regions achieving market saturation of hypermarkets. During the late 1970s in Britain, for example, the northwest region of England, through the development activities of regionally based corporate chains and consumer cooperatives, came close to market saturation for hypermarkets. Similarly, in France in the early 1970s there was massive development around Paris, with 33 new units opened in as many months between 1972 and 1974. The outer suburbs in the northeast and west were particularly favored for new stores. Figure 10.5 shows the dates of hypermarket openings in the Paris region. It must be stressed that in this rapid-growth phase market saturation is regional, with some regions—in England, for example, the London region—having relatively few units while others—for example, northwest England—are crowded with them. The reasons behind this pattern are, first, the growth strategies of a few large firms. In France, for example, Carrefour and Euromarche focused their growth on Paris. Second, there is the availability of suitable sites. Third, a regional bandwagon effect occurs whereby developers, retailers, and landowners try to avoid being left out of a lucrative market and so development decisions are made with a view to keeping other companies as much as from positively entering the market. Once begun, this bandwagon effect only stops with regional market saturation, and results in a regional concentration of investment. Furthermore, it generates a much higher level of interhypermarket competition in certain regions than in others.

The rapid-growth phase usually ends with approaching market saturation in the major regional markets, coupled with the introduction of new public policy controls on hypermarkets or the more rigorous application of existing policies. Then begins a phase of *public policy control.*

Public Policy Control Phase

With the increasing market power of hypermarkets and their greater impact on traditional store types come demands for public policy intervention to "regulate competition." Often the plea to regulate competition is a request for protection of the less efficient from the competition of the more efficient.

Almost as soon as rapid growth is evident policy makers become or are made aware of the potential need for intervention. Both independent supermarket and small shop lobbies become vocal. The responsiveness of public policy makers is dependent on both the organizational efficiency of these lobby groups and on precedents within the historical framework of international hypermarket development. Thus in France, Belgium, and Sweden, where hypermarket development began early, there were no precedents for control and policies were introduced relatively late in the growth phase. In Italy and the United Kingdom, growth began later but policy controls were applied early in the growth stage because lobbyists and policy makers could look to developments elsewhere to serve as precedents. In Spain, where rapid growth is just beginning, we may see public policy controls become effective quite quickly if a protectionist lobby emerges rapidly.

Public policy intervention in this phase of hypermarket development generally takes one or two forms, and although aimed at competition control, usually takes the form of controls over store location. In essence, spatial policies are applied to a problem created by distribution structure. In the first case, control is effected through the existing land-use planning machinery, possibly through some specific decree or circular or simply by creating general land-use policies that limit the role of the hypermarket. Second, control may be effected through special, unilateral policies that create a bureaucracy and the control machinery to deal specifically with hyper-markets (and perhaps one or two other selected forms of distribution). The control policies in the United Kingdom, West Germany, and the Nether-lands are of the first type and those in France, Belgium, and Italy are of the second.

It is not proposed to consider, in this chapter, the various legislative measures in operation in different countries. Some general comparative points with respect to Europe have been made by the Commission of the European Communities[23] and more detailed reviews of specific countries are covered in Davies[24], Dawson,[25] and Guy.[26]

Generally, the control policies are delegated to local government agencies with ultimate authority retained by central government. Developers or retailers usually are required to obtain individual permission for a hypermarket at a specific site. The application for development permission is reviewed, within the framework either of general land-use policies or of the specific legislation, in respect to the location of the proposed development and its form and character. When considered under general land-use policies, the review usually will focus on the land-use and environmental impacts of the proposal, while in countries with specific legislation the reviews also frequently consider the effects on business structure and existing retailing as well as the interests of consumers. The decisions taken by local government are usually the responsibility of nominated or elected committees on which various social and political pressure groups are represented. Local small supermarket owners may well be members of the committee ultimately responsible for reviewing an application for a hypermarket. Because of the local or subregional nature of the control machinery, it is possible for the control policies to be applied in significantly different ways in different parts of the country.[27] Some areas may have committees that oppose all hypermarket development; other areas may take a more liberal view. No national coordinated plan of development exists in any of the countries with control legislation.

The effectiveness of the public policy controls varies enormously both within and among countries. In a review chapter such as this, it is not possible to consider the effects and effectiveness of controls in detail. Much does depend, however, on the timing of the introduction of controls in respect of national levels of market saturation for hypermarkets. In Belgium, for example, effective control legislation was not introduced until 1975, by which time market saturation was very close. In consequence, the effect has been minimal. In France, where effective legislation was introduced in 1973, the result was certainly a slowing of development, but it is doubtful whether there are many less hypermarkets in 1982 than there would have been without legislation. The real effect has been to slow the rate of development, encourage smaller units, generate a more even density of hypermarket provision, and encourage location at city center sites as well as suburban and peripheral locations, thus maximizing consumer access to hypermarkets. In Britain, these same four results are apparent from controls stemming from general land-use planning legislation. The public policy phase is characterized by a change in the form and location of hypermarkets and a reduction in the speed of development so that market saturation comes later than would have otherwise been the case.

Inevitably, the imposition of controls introduces additional complexities into the development process. Developers, usually retailers, have to bear some of the costs of these additional stages in the development process. The introduction of controls in a country certainly has been one factor (incipient market saturation is another just as potent factor in this connection) in the growth of multinational hypermarket operations during this fourth phase of hypermarket development. Retailers have looked to other countries, which lack effective controls, as a means of expanding their corporate network of hypermarkets. A notable characteristic of the public policy phase of hypermarket development in a country is the increase in international investment by hypermarket operators. The French-based Carrefour company, for example, has been associated, since the introduction of controls in

France, with 32 hypermarkets outside France in five different countries. Most notable, and largest, are the investments in Spain and Brazil, where public policy controls are minimal. As an alternative to looking overseas for investment opportunities, some hypermarket companies have diversified into other types of large-unit retailing, such as Do-It-Yourself stores and furnishing stores. This has occurred in both Belgium and Sweden. The search for alternative investments is as much a response to market saturation for hypermarkets as it is to the imposition of policy controls but nevertheless characterizes this last stage of hypermarket development.

A final noteworthy characteristic of the public policy phase is increased land-cost. Higher land costs result from several factors. First, a policy of permissions inevitably means that land with permission has an enhanced value. Second, as hypermarket numbers increase, sites with market potential decrease in number and increase in value. Third, with a small number of large companies looking for sites, the available sites become locations of intense development pressure, increasing land prices. Finally, as locations other than peripheral ones are considered, more expensive land in inner suburbs and city centers is purchased for hypermarket construction.

The public policy control phase of hypermarket development differs in detail from country to country, but several common characteristics may be cited. The effects of public policy are not always what was aimed for and policy makers in countries where hypermarkets are becoming established should beware of some of the mistakes made in Europe. The strength and vitality of the economic and commercial processes generating the rapid growth of hypermarkets are not easily halted or even redirected. Controls on "hypermarkets" result in them being called "superstores"; controls on stores over 5,000 m^2 results in a surge of units of 4,950 m^2 followed by plans for extensions; and so on. Hypermarket controls, like taxes, are there to be avoided. From the policy makers' viewpoint, public policy intervention is aimed at creating a more orderly distribution system—this, however, does not always occur.

Hypermarkets in the Late 1980s

This chapter has described the operational character of hypermarket retailing, has shown that this retail format has spread, with minor variations, to many countries, and has suggested a four-stage developmental model of the spatial and structural aspects of the hypermarket sector. From these discussions, some pointers emerge for hypermarket development through the 1980s. Many countries are in the relatively early stages of the developmental model and development over the next few years might be expected to broadly follow the stages of the model. But it must be remembered that public policy intervention appears to become progressively earlier in the overall model as case law and case lore emerge from other countries. Using Table 10.4, it is not difficult to attempt a forecast of where growth is likely to occur in the next few years, nor is it difficult to forecast the countries where hypermarkets will appear for the first time. Greece and Portugal, for example, are particularly noticeable by their absence from this list. Somewhat more difficult to forecast is what will happen in countries such as Belgium, West Germany, Sweden, and, to a lesser extent, France, where little opportunity appears to exist for more hypermarket floorspace. When the hypermarket sector matures, how does it then evolve? Does it stagnate and then decline? Does it evolve from within? Is it changed by borrowing new ideas from other retail formats? A number of possibilities exist, and experiments by operators are already underway. To create a framework for such forecasts, it is useful to consider changes in the operating environment, marketing technique, and business organization of the hypermarket sector. Changes likely in the operating environment are:

1) the development of smaller units of 3,000 to 3,500 m² to serve small towns.

2) the use of hypermarkets as nodes at which to locate a wide range of social services.

3) the use of hypermarkets as economic catalysts in depressed inner-city areas.

Changes likely in marketing techniques are:

4) the development of computer-based information systems linking hypermarkets to homes and social centers.

5) even more vigorous attempts to reduce operating costs with advanced technology. Competition seems likely to continue to be based on price rather than on service, as has often occurred with other matured retail types.

Changes likely in business organization are:

6) merger and takeover among hypermarket operators, creating even larger chains with multinational interests.

7) diversification of hypermarket operators to create vertically integrated and horizontally coordinated distribution system.

Many distribution types are now megacultural phenomena existing in quite different economic, social, and political circumstances. The hypermarket is one such type, and its study in a comparative marketing framework makes it possible to adapt concepts developed in one country to the distribution system of another. In the development of hypermarkets, the role of the individual as an innovator and risk-taker is apparent from the early experimental years of the early 1960s. The idea of hypermarket retailing was spread through formal and informal intercompany communication. As the concept matured, so international growth has taken place increasingly within an intracompany structure. During the expansion of the hypermarket sector, competition problems have been created and government has been called on to intervene in market mechanisms. Within 20 years, through a complex interrelationship of structural and spatial processes generating change in consumers, business, and government, the hypermarket has become an established and potent retail force in postindustrial society.

Notes

1. J. A. Dawson, *Commercial Distribution in Europe* (London: Croom Helm 1982).

2. International Chamber of Commerce, *International Uniform Definitions for the Distributive Trade*, Paris, 1979.

3. P. M. Jones, "Trading Features of Hypermarkets and Superstores," *Unit for Retail Planning Information*, Report, U7, 1978.

4. Libre Service Actualité Quo, les hypermarchés offrent bien les prix les plus bas, *Libre Service Actualité*, 697, 1979, pp: 16–17.

5. Libre Service Actualité Investir à quel priz? 1: Les cas des supermarchés, *Libre Service Actualité*, 638, 1877, pp: 107–10; and Libre Service Actualité Investir à quel priz? 3, Le cas des hypermarchés, *Libre Service Actualité*, 652, 1978, pp: 81–84.

6. R. Muir, "Mainstop: A Young Superstore Group Finds Its Feet," *Retail and Distribution Management*, 10:1, 1982, p. 9.

7. E. Thil, Speech in London to a Presentation: Retail Revolution: Britain's Dilemma, 1970.

8. R. Tanner, "40 Departments Enrich New Combo Store," *Progressive Grocer*, 61:1, 1982, pp. 82 and 86.

9. A. D. Bates, "The Superstores: Emerging Innovations in Food Retailing," in J. L. Grimm, ed., *Marketing Strategies in Food Distribution*, American Marketing Association, Chicago, 1976, pp: 65–92.

10. A. D. Bates, "Warehouse Retailing," *California Management Review*, 20:2, 1977, pp: 74–80.

11. Chain Store Age Hypermarkets: Une Force Majeure, *Chain Store Age*, 57:5, 1981, pp: 89–94.

12. Progressive Grocer, "Anatomy of the U.S. Superstore." 52:5, 1973 pp: 44–51; A. Roberts, "Superstore and Hypermarket Impact Analysis." *The Planner*, 68:1, 1982, pp: 8–11; and S. Seale, *Impact of Retail Outlets on Patterns of Retailing: A Synthesis of Research Results in Great Britain*. Scottish Development Department, Edinburgh, 1977.

13. E. Thil, *Les inventeurs du commerce moderne*. Arthaud, Paris, 1966.

14. M. Cauwe, "Genese du libre-service et des hypermarchés en Belgique," *Distribution d'Aujourd'hui*, 21:10, 1982, p. 13.

15. Business Week "Will It Go in Britain?: GEM Supercenters," *Business Week*, January 9, 1965, pp: 86–89.

16. S. Burt, J. A. Dawson, and L. Sparks, "Bibliography on Hypermarkets and Superstores," University of Wales, Saint David's University College, Department of Geography, Seminar Discussion Paper 9, 1982.

17. P. M. Jones, "Hypermarkets and Superstores: Future Growth or Saturation?" *Estates Gazette*, 262, 1982, pp: 813–47.

18. P. M. Jones, "Retail Innovation and Diffusion: The Spread of ASDA Stores," 1981, *Area*, 13:3, p. 199.

19. A. Metton, *Le commerce et la ville en banlieue Parisienne*, Courbevoie, 1980.

20. P. M. Jones, "Hypermarkets and Superstores," p. 845.

21. Institut für Selbstbedienung und Warenwirtschaft, *SB-Warehaus Report*, Köln, 1982; and International Association of Department Stores, *Development of Large Selling Units in Europe 1953–1980*, Paris, 1982.

22. M. J. Breheny, J. Green, and A. J. Roberts, "A Practical Approach to the Assessment of Hypermarket Impact." *Regional Studies*, 15:6, 1981, pp: 459–74.

23. J. A. Dawson, A Note on the Law of June 29, 1975 in Control Large Scale Retail Development in Belgium, *Environment and Planning*, A14, 1982, pp: 291–96 and E. E. C. Commission Aspects of Establishment, Planning and Control of Urban Retail Outlets in Europe. Commerce and Distribution Series, 4, E. E. C. Commission, Luxembourg, 1977.

24. R. L. Davies, ed., *Retail Planning in the European Community*, Saxon House, Farnborough, 1979; and R. L. Davies and D. A. Kirby, "Retail Organization," in J. A. Dawson, ed., *Retail Geography* (London: Croom Helm 1980), pp: 156–92.

25. J. A. Dawson, "Control Over Large Units in France: The Loi Royer and Its Affects," *Retail and Distribution Management*, 4:6, 1976, pp: 14–18; and J. A. Dawson, "The Impact of Changing Marketing Practices on the Urban Environment," in G. Enyedi and J. Meszaros, eds., *Development of Settlement Systems*, (Budapest: Akademia Kiado 1980), pp: 99–122.

26. C. Guy, *Retail Location and Retail Planning in Britain*, (Farnborough: Gower 1980; and Institut Français du Libre Service, *Hypermarchès contre supermarchès: trois années de concurrence* (Paris, 1971).

27. J. Sumner and B. K. Davies, "Hypermarkets and Superstores: What Do Planning Authorities Really Think," *Retail and Distribution Management*, 6:4, 1978, pp: 8–16.

11

INTERNATIONAL DISTRIBUTION SYSTEMS: A COMPARATIVE APPROACH

John R. Stock and Douglas M. Lambert

In recent years a large number of companies have expanded the scope of their operations beyond their own country and have become multinational. A survey of the thousand largest industrial firms in the United States, reported in the *Chicago Tribune* on February 4, 1981, revealed that management in 70 percent of these companies expected international growth to exceed their firms' domestic growth over the next five years.[1] The expansion into international markets has not been limited to any specific industry or nation; rather, it has included almost every country in the world, and firms from the consumer, industrial, and service industries.

A significant aspect of international marketing activities is the physical distribution of goods and services. As part of the firm's marketing mix, distribution can be used to effectively and efficiently penetrate international target markets. A good physical distribution system can result in improved customer service, lower inventories for buyers and sellers, and a lower delivered cost for the manufacturer's products. The benefits to the firm marketing its products and services internationally include increased sales, market share, and profits. "Physical distribution provides the means by which the customer receives the goods and the credibility of the whole company image may depend upon the way in which the physical distribution process is planned and executed.[2] A firm may have a well-conceived and well-manufactured product, priced right, and with good promotion, but if the physical distribution system fails to deliver the product in good condition when and where customers expect it, the entire marketing mix may be rendered ineffective. This occurs when customers do not reorder the manufacturer's products or do not purchase them because of the firm's reputation for physical distribution failures.

It is vital that firms seeking to become international in scope understand the distribution environment that exists in world markets. Therefore, the objectives of this chapter are to:

1. Examine methods of international physical distribution.

2. Identify components or elements of the international marketplace that are uncontrollable by the marketing and/or physical distribution manager.

3. Examine those components of international distribution that can be directly controlled by the marketing and/or physical distribution manager.

International Channels of Distribution

Companies involved in international distribution can enter foreign markets in one of two basic ways: production in their home markets or production in the foreign market. If a firm chooses to maintain its production facilities in its home country, it can employ a direct or indirect exporting strategy. With direct exporting, the company performs the exporting task without intermediaries. Examples of direct exporting include use of foreign distributors, agents, and/or foreign marketing subsidiaries. Examples of indirect exporting include trading companies and/or export management companies.

If foreign product sources are utilized, methods of international distribution can take the form of licensing, contract manufacturing, coproduction, joint ventures, and direct ownership (assembly and/or manufacturing). The type of foreign operation chosen by a company depends on many factors, including the flows of goods and materials, financial capital, physical capital, and human capital. Table 11.1 illustrates the flows associated with various forms of entry into international markets.

International Physical Distribution Environment

All forms of entry into international markets require an awareness of the environmental variables that can affect the firm's distribution system. Some of these factors can be controlled by the physical distribution executive. Others, unhappily, are not subject to control but must be addressed and dealt with in any international marketing undertaking. The major uncontrollable elements include social and cultural factors, political and legal aspects, economic conditions, competition, technology, and geography. Controllable

TABLE 11.1
International Flows by Level of Involvement

Type of Foreign Operation	Flow of Goods and Materials					Flow of Financial Capital							Flow of Physical Capital		Flow of Human Capital		
	Finished Products	Semifinished Products	Parts	Spare Parts	Raw Materials	Payments	Fees	Royalties	Interests	Equity Capital	Loan Capital	Profits, Dividends (Repatriations)	Machinery	Equipment, Tools	Know-how	Industrial Rights	Personnel
Indirect export	x[a]			x[a]		x[a]											
Direct export	x			x		x											
Own export (Marketing subsidiary)	x		x[c]	x		x				x	x	x			x		
Licensing								x	x	x	x		x[d]	x[d]	x	x	x
Contract manufacturing						x	x	x					x[d]	x[d]	x[d]		x[d]
Co-production							x		x	x			x	x	x[d]	x	x
Own assembling	x[b]	x	x		x	x	x	x[b]	x	x	x	x	x	x	x	x[b]	x
Own manufacturing	x[b]	x	x		x	x	x		x	x	x	x	x	x	x		x

[a] If the middleman in the home country is a buying middleman, the different flows in the first stage of operation take place in the home country.
[b] May be included as a suboperation or as a supplementary operation.
[c] Easily assembled parts may be assembled in a sales outlet.
[d] May be included in the contract.

SOURCE: Vern Terpstra, *International Marketing*, 3rd ed. (Hinsdale, IL: Dryden Press, 1983), p. 358. This table was originally presented in Reijo Luostarinen, "Foreign Operations of the Firm," mimeographed (Helsinki, Finland: Helsinki School of Economics, 1970), p. 10.

FIGURE 11.1

The International Physical Distribution Environment

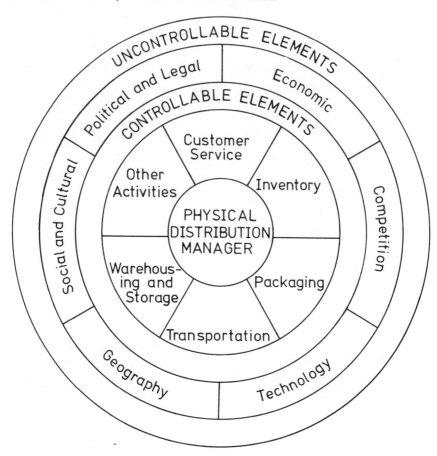

SOURCE: Douglas M. Lambert and James R. Stock, *Strategic Physical Distribution Management* (Homewood, IL: Richard D. Irwin, Inc., 1982), p. 448.

elements include customer service, inventory, packaging, transportation, warehousing and storage, and other activities (see Figure 11.1).

Uncontrollable Elements

Major differences in distribution systems exist among international markets because of uncontrollable elements. In the following sections, each uncontrollable element will be discussed briefly, including an explanation of how each one affects distribution activities.

Social and Cultural. A country's social and cultural environment includes such components as language, education, religion, aesthetics, attitudes, and social organization.

The importance of communication in international distribution makes it imperative that the role of language be understood. Throughout the world there are literally thousands of different languages and dialects that must be considered when determining the labeling requirements for products being distributed across international borders. All facets of the order cycle, including order transmittal, processing customer orders, answering customer inquiries, completing international bills-of-lading, and negotiating with distribution intermediaries such as transportation companies, warehouses, and suppliers are made much more complex because of language differences.

The availability of a trained workforce will depend upon the education system in each country. Generally, the more educated the workforce, the easier it is to increase labor productivity and implement more advanced or automated distribution systems. The channel of distribution in a foreign culture also will be affected by the educational level of its population. Channel relationships, the level of cooperation, and channel performance are partially dependent upon the education and skill levels of the channel intermediaries.

Overall, management must recognize that distribution activities and channel structures should be planned giving full consideration to the social and cultural environment of the host country.

Political and Legal. The impact of import quotas, duties, government ownership of transportation modes, and laws can significantly affect distribution activities. For example, in the United States, governmental agencies such as the Interstate Commerce Commission, Department of Transportation, Federal Maritime Commission, and Civil Aeronautics Board regulate economic and safety aspects of modes and carriers. The existence of regulatory bodies and their concomitant regulations will affect transportation rates, competition, equipment safety, customer service levels, and intermodal coordination. The political and legal environment also can determine channel structure.

A major reason for the lack of growth in efficient large-scale retailing in Belgium, France, and Italy is the legislation in these countries. Though France was one of the creators of the hypermarket . . . in 1973 France passed the "Loi Royer" regulating the establishment or expansion of

retail stores. The effect of this law, and similar laws in Belgium and Italy,
is to give existing retailers a veto over the establishment of any new large-
scale retailers. . . . Japan has a similar law, "Daiten Ho."[3]

The results of laws restricting normal development of the channel of
distribution can be inefficiency and excessive costs or low levels of
service.

Government ownership of transport may give preferential treatment to
national companies in terms of lower rates and/or preferential service, which
can place "outsiders" at a serious competitive disadvantage. Even when the
political and legal system of a foreign country does not favor domestic firms,
the differences that exist in laws, regulations, and regulatory enforcement
among countries may result in a complex legal structure difficult to
understand, control, and manage. "Outboard Marine in Norway tried to
implement a selective distribution system but the Norwegian courts ruled
against the company, saying that this practice would reduce competition in
outboard engines to the detriment of the consumer."[4]

In addition, political issues can cause unexpected changes in the
physical distribution system. In many countries, the possibility of international terrorism, strikes, nationalization of foreign investment, and other
internal strife makes decision making and forecasting difficult.

Economic. The economic aspects of international distribution include the
financial characteristics of the foreign market and the costs of doing business
in that country. Financial characteristics include GNP, per capita income,
rate of inflation, capital costs, and currency fluctuations. The costs of doing
business refer to the actual expenses incurred by a firm in carrying out
marketing/distribution activities.

Economic conditions vary considerably throughout the world. For
example, factors such as inflation, capital costs, and currency fluctuations
make distribution planning difficult and uncertain. Inventory carrying costs
may fluctuate significantly due to interest rate variations. The possibility of
currency revaluations will have an impact on both the amount of inventory
held and the preferred storage location. High rates of inflation will affect the
desirability of holding inventory as well as result in frequent increases in
transportation rates, storage charges, and the costs of land, labor, and
capital.

International economic conditions will cause the costs of doing business
to fluctuate, making individual markets more or less profitable, and a firm
may be required to make significant changes in its international transportation, warehousing, and/or order processing systems in response to
changing conditions. Financing for working capital, inventory, credit, capital
investment, and merchandise adjustments will increase costs for the

international firm. The time lags caused by distance and crossing international borders make cash-flow planning very important. Even for a simple transaction, money may be tied up for extended periods of time while products are being shipped from one part of the world to another; customs clearance may add days, weeks, or months to the cycle; payment may be held up while the international payment documents are being transferred from one nation to another; and breakage, commercial dispute, or governmental restrictions may add still further delay. The international business may appear to be profitable in terms of the profit and loss statement, but the high costs of holding inventories and the slower cash flow may result in an inadequate return on assets. One way of overcoming this difficulty is to include opportunity costs such as inventory carrying costs and a charge for accounts receivable and other assets employed in segment profitability reports.[5]

It is vital that firms entering foreign markets fully understand the economic environment of each country.

Competition. During the 1980s, multinational firms can expect to encounter an increase in the degree and type of competition encountered in foreign and domestic markets. Canadian, German, Japanese, and U.S. firms will find that competition from third world and other countries will increase. As governments turn to protectionism as the means to protect domestic producers, the competition will intensify in unprotected markets.

In response to the threat of protectionism, Japanese, French, and German auto producers have built manufacturing facilities in the U.S. Many foreign-based multinationals have purchased U.S. firms in order to gain to the lucrative U.S. market.

> Nestlé acquired Libby and Stouffer Foods; a French firm acquired a major position in A&P, the food retailer, and other U.S. firms such as Baskin-Robbins, Saks-Fifth Avenue, Kentucky Fried Chicken, and Capital Records are either owned outright or substantially owned by foreign companies. Among the largest exporters of grain, minerals, chemicals, and machinery from the United States are subsidiaries of Mitsui and Mitsubishi of Japan. If Fortune's 50 Top Exporters list included nonindustrial companies, Mitsui U.S.A. would have ranked fourth on the Fortune list just behind Boeing Company, General Motors, and General Electric.[6]

As a result of these actions by foreign producers, U.S. multinationals are also experiencing more competition in domestic markets. The types and sources of competition must be understood by management if domestic and foreign operations are to remain profitable.

Technology. Technology refers to the level of industrial development of a country. In highly developed nations such as the United States, Japan, Germany, France, and the United Kingdom, there are likely to be sophisticated distribution and marketing support systems. Lesser developed countries (LDC's) typically lack sophisticated distribution networks.

Generally, in LDC's it is more difficult to achieve high levels of customer service, make effective cost/service tradeoffs within the channel of distribution, and realize other marketing/distribution synergies. Firms entering foreign markets must adapt their distribution strategies to the marketing channels that exist in each market area. An example of such an adaptation has occurred in Europe and Japan as a result of "cold chain" developments.

> Cold Chain refers to the availability of refrigeration in warehouses, trucks, and retail outlets. Unilever found the major deterrent to growth to be the retail link of the cold chain. Many retailers could not afford the freezer unit. Unilever helped retailers finance a frozen-food unit in the expectation that the growth in the company's frozen food sales would be enough to cover financing costs and leave a satisfactory profit.[7]

Although the fundamental marketing concepts and principles are always the same, when a company enters foreign markets with differing levels of technology/industrialization, the emphasis placed on the various components of the marketing mix must change as must the tactics used to implement the marketing programs.

Geography. Physical and climatic conditions vary significantly between regions of the world and also within countries such as the Soviet Union, China, India, United States, and Canada. Such differences can directly influence distribution patterns and systems.

> In Canada . . . vast distances and extreme winter weather have a major influence on distribution. Reorder points and safety stock levels must be higher than normally expected for given inventories since large cities such as Montreal can be isolated suddenly and completely because of heavy snowfalls. At such times, delivery delays of three to four days are common. Additionally, shipment delays can result from a shortage of insulated rail cars and trucks, and the high cost of heating rail cars on long hauls in such extreme weather can add 10 percent or more to a company's freight bill.[8]

Many illustrations exist that identify the need for multinational firms to take into account the geographical differences in foreign markets.[9] Geography is an important uncontrollable element to which distribution and other marketing mix components must be adapted.

Other aspects of geography include population densities, topography, and availability of navigable rivers and ports/harbors. The concentration of population will affect channels of distribution, physical distribution networks, and communication systems. Topography influences the distribution network as well as the costs of providing distribution service. For example, level terrain usually means relatively easy land movements by truck or rail. Uneven terrain, perhaps including mountains, will increase transportation costs. In some parts of the world such as Europe, the availability of numerous navigable waterways and ports/harbors allows water transportation to compete effectively with other transport modes, both from a service and cost perspective.

Within an international environment containing many uncontrollable elements, the marketing manager must manipulate the various components of the distribution mix so that the firm's long-term profitability can be maximized. The controllable distribution elements will be discussed in the following sections.

Controllable Elements

In the same way that a marketing manager controls the marketing mix within an uncontrollable environment, the distribution manager controls the physical distribution mix. The controllable physical distribution mix includes customer service, inventories, packaging, transportation, warehousing and storage, and the order processing and communications systems. The objective is to manipulate these elements so that customers receive the necessary level of service at the lowest possible cost. However, a firm's cost/service mix will vary in international markets. In the United States and Japan, distribution costs as a percentage of sales are much higher than in Australia or the United Kingdom. Table 11.2 shows the cost differential that may exist between industrialized nations.[10] Firms operating in, or exporting to, those countries, may have to follow different distribution strategies because of varying cost structures. In firms involved in international distribution, especially those that own foreign subsidiaries, management must be cognizant of the differences that exist between the administration of domestic and foreign distribution activities.

Customer Service. Typically, the customer service levels provided in domestic markets are higher than those in foreign markets. This is because international product movements tend to be longer and can involve many transportation carriers, multiple transfers and handlings, and the crossing of a number of international boundaries. Consequently, time-in-transit can vary significantly from one shipment to the next.

If a firm is physically located in a foreign market, customer service levels may be higher. In Japan, for example, order cycle time is generally

TABLE 11.2
Distribution Costs as a Percentage of Sales

Country	U.S.	U.K.	Japan	Australia
Transportation	6.4%	5.5%	13.5%	2.5%
Receiving and dispatch	1.7	} 2.5		1.4
Warehousing	3.7			1.8
Packaging and storage	2.6	2		1.7
Inventory	3.8	3	} 13	3.6
Order processing	1.2	1		2.1
Administration	2.4	2		1
TOTAL	21.8	16	26.5	14.1

SOURCE: Peter Gilmour and Peter J. Rimmer, "Business Logistics in the Pacific Basin," *Columbia Journal of World Business*, Vol. II, No. 1 (Spring, 1976), p. 65.

shorter than in the United States. Due to the geographical differences between the two countries, more than 80 percent of all consumer goods orders are delivered in 24 hours or less in Japan. Only rarely does it take longer than 48 hours to deliver a product to the customer if it is available at the wholesale level in the channel of distribution.[11] For that reason, many international firms operate owned facilities in foreign markets in order to compete effectively on a customer service basis.

If a firm is attempting to provide a uniform level of customer service in several foreign markets, usually management will discover that physical distribution costs exhibit sizable variations. Therefore, each target market must be evaluated individually to determine its optimal cost-service mix.

Inventory. Effective management of inventories is especially important to the international firm. Inventory carrying costs can vary significantly by industry, company, and country. In the United States and Canada, the major components of inventory carrying cost are the opportunity cost of money and the value of the inventory. The value of the inventory for carrying cost purposes is the cash flow associated with producing or purchasing a replacement unit and moving it to the storage location. Only variable out-of-pocket costs are relevant. The cost of money used in the carrying cost should reflect how the cash made available from an inventory reduction would be invested or, conversely, the opportunity foregone by increasing the amount of cash invested in inventories.[12]

The cost of money and the variable cost of production will vary depending upon the country in which the product is manufactured. The opportunity cost of money will be influenced by the economic environment, national monetary policies, and interest rates. Variable production costs as a percentage of total manufacturing costs will depend upon the age of the manufacturing facilities and the level of industrialization. For example, in highly automated chemical processes variable manufacturing costs can represent less than 50 percent of the total manufactured cost. However, a relatively old plant in an underdeveloped country may experience variable costs in excess of 95 percent of the full manufactured cost. Other costs associated with holding inventory that will vary by country include taxes, insurance, storage costs, and the costs associated with obsolescence, pilferage, and damage. While these costs usually are less than 5 percent of the inventory value for most products inventoried in the United States and Canada, they can be much larger in less developed countries.

When companies are involved in exporting, management must be concerned with the amount of "pipeline" inventories. The long transit times and delays associated with international shipments may require firms to supply distributors or other foreign intermediaries with higher inventories than are necessary in domestic markets and for many products the inventory carrying costs can be substantial.

In addition, inventories may have a sizable impact on the international company due to the rapid inflation that exists in some countries of the world. In inflationary economies, it is very important to use the proper inventory accounting procedure because of the affect on company profits. For example, products in inventory will be carried at a substantially lower value than current replacement costs when inflation exists. A FIFO (first in-first out) accounting method will give the firm a larger profit figure than LIFO (last in-first out) because old costs are matched with current (inflated) revenues. Similar results occur when depreciations in currency take place.[13] Therefore, marketing management must be aware of the financial/accounting dimensions involved in international distribution.

In markets where channels of distribution are different, shopping patterns of the population are very important when determining inventory strategies.

> There are more wholesalers and retailers in Japan than in all of the U.S. . . . Purchases of wholesalers or retailers are characterized by very small amounts per order. Most of the shops are small and display space is also very small—about 20 to 40 square meters. Wholesalers do not have enough space for stocks because of high land prices. Therefore, they order small lots nearly every day, though the order items differ from day to day.[14]

Different distribution channels necessitate different inventory policies and control procedures.

Management in the United States usually can exercise greater control over inventories because they can influence the amount of product ordered by their customers through discounts that vary by the size of the order. This may not be a viable strategy in some international markets. For example, in Japan "manufacturers change the unit price considering the average amount of the customer's monthly purchases; or they pay rebates once or twice a year taking the annual amount of orders into consideration."[15] A similar situation exists in Canada, where discounts must be paid on the basis of annual volume, not order size. As a result of differences among foreign markets, management must develop inventory policies and control procedures that are appropriate for each market area.

Packaging. "Among the major factors involved in designing the package are transportation and handling, climate, pilferage, freight rates, customer duties, and most importantly, the customer's requirements. It is well-known that the greater the number of handlings to which goods are subjected, the greater the possibility of damage. International trade may require several such handlings."[16]

International shippers must be much more concerned with the protective and handling aspects of packaging due to higher rates of loss and/or damage in nondomestic product movements. For example, redesigning the package resulted in annual freight savings in excess of $1 million for a large Japanese importer.[17] While the package protected the contents and could be efficiently stacked on flatbed trucks in Japan, it allowed only 50 percent capacity utilization of the intermodal containers used aboard ship and of the trailer vans used for transportation in the U.S. Redesigning the protective package increased utilization of transportation equipment capacity to 90 percent. An additional benefit was that the efficiently loaded intermodal container could be used for transportation across the U.S. to the east coast, reducing overall transit time by more than two weeks.[18]

In order to facilitate product handling and to protect the product during movement and storage, many firms have turned to the use of containers. Containers are widely used in international distribution, especially when air and/or water movements are part of the transport network.

Related to the packaging component of international distribution is labelling. From a cost standpoint, labelling is a relatively minor aspect of international distribution. However, labels must contain customer information and comply with government regulations. Consequently, accurate labelling is essential to the timely and efficient movement of products across international borders. Even if labels are standardized in format and message, language differences may make it necessary to use labels in different languages for most foreign markets. This is particularly important if the label contains information for consumers. Although the costs of printing separate packages or labels may not be significant, the increased costs of production and the need to carry separate inventories of product in each language may substantially increase costs. One way of minimizing the costs associated with multiple labels is by using multilingual labels. For example, products destined for the European market might carry labels in four languages— English, French, German, and Italian. Bilingual labels in English and French have been used in Canada for many years.

Transportation. Successful international marketing requires an awareness of the different transport services, costs, and modal availabilities in each country. The differences that exist between nations can be due to taxes, subsidies, regulations, government ownership of carriers, and other factors. Rail service in Europe is usually much better than in the United States because equipment, track, and facilities are in better condition due to government ownership and/or subsidies of the rail system.

Japan and Europe utilize water carriage to a much larger degree than the United States or Canada. Due to the length and favorable characteristics of coastlines and inland waterways, water transport is a viable alternative for many shippers. For many companies shipping between or within the borders of foreign countries, it is necessary to thoroughly reevaluate the transport alternatives, costs, and services. As an example, air and surface transportation directly compete for trans-oceanic shipments. Many factors must be considered when a firm compares the two alternatives. It should be noted that each international shipment must be evaluated separately in order to ascertain the cost differential between air and surface transport.

In the European Economic Community (EEC), member nations are attempting to develop a long-term multinational transportation infrastructure. Similar to other countries of the world, EEC nations have developed transportation networks that were designed and constructed with "national objectives and trading structures rather than in accordance with the EEC's goal of removing barriers to trade between member countries, including physical distribution barriers."[19] A specific illustration can be seen in the area of transport labor.

> Under EEC international rules, drivers may only work for eight hours a day, although nine hours is permitted twice a week for those in charge of non-rigid vehicles over 20 tons. No driver may drive for more than four hours consecutively without a break of half-an-hour. Such regulations have vitally important implications for transport scheduling and depot locations.[20]

Other service factors that may affect a firm's mode choice include variability in transit time, loss and/or damage rates, and on-time pickup and delivery.

Warehousing and Storage. Product storage is a challenging and often complex aspect of multinational distribution. It is further complicated by the fact that in countries such as the United States warehouses that provide storage to customers on a rental basis may also provide nonstorage services such as billing, packaging, labelling, inventory record keeping, and transportation.

> One Dutch firm . . . in addition to warehousing, offers customers brokerage, freight forwarding, packaging, insurance, and transportation service to all of Europe and the Middle East. In a product introduction for an American appliance manufacturer it also co-ordinated promotional material to assure that promotional packets and displays were available for the firm's marketing teams in the target cities.[21]

In a study of 40 multinational corporations (seven European and 33 American) during 1978–79, Picard developed a descriptive classification of international warehousing strategies. Four basic models were described as follows:

> (a) The classical system: Among other functions, the subsidiary serves as a warehousing system. Merchandise is shipped to subsidiary warehouses and released as orders come in. This model is generally characterized by a relatively large storage system (which might include several warehouses located in different parts of the country), reducing the need for frequent and speedy transportation. Large quantities of merchandise are shipped by the cheapest possible means of transport from the country of manufacture to the subsidiary.

> (b) The transit system: In this sytem, the subsidiary warehouse(s) serves only as a transit center. Consequently, merchandise will be sent there only a short time before being sent on to the next level of the distribution channel.

> (c) The direct system: In this system, merchandise is sent directly from production site to the final user or to the next intermediary in the subsidiary's distribution channel. Although the subsidiary will have organized the transaction, it will never have possessed the merchandise from a strictly physical point of view.

> (d) Multi-country warehouse: When a company has subsidiaries in a few countries in an area, it might have a central warehouse serving all those countries. Goods will be shipped from the manufacturing plant to the central warehouse. From there, shipments will be made either to various subsidiaries' warehouses or directly to the next level of their channel of distribution. The multi-country warehouse concept incorporates a few variations. It can be used as "a transit warehouse" or as a "stocking warehouse" (as in the classical system). In Europe, the central warehouse

will generally be established in one of the countries where a subsidiary is located and under its control. Some companies, however, have a bonded central warehouse (sometimes located in a free-trade zone) with a management independent of any of the subsidiaries it supplies. In some cases, though, the central warehouse will be located outside the geographical area it serves. That is the case, for example, of an American company whose central warehouse for South America is located in Miami, Florida (geographically close to the market, with high frequency of airflights to all important South American cities, etc.).[22]

If a company is involved in exporting to foreign markets, products may be stored in the country-of-origin and shipped only after orders are received. As a result, no foreign storage is required. When foreign distributors or other types of channel intermediaries are utilized, inventories will have to be stored or warehoused at other locations within the channel of distribution.

The ability of the manufacturer or supplier to "push" the inventory "down" the channel of distribution will vary by country depending upon the size of demand for the product by final customers, storage costs, and customer service levels required to serve each market. In Japan and many EEC countries, the retail network is made up of many small shops, each having little or no room for storing safety or buffer inventories. As a result, they must place orders frequently with wholesalers and manufacturers for product replenishment. The inventory burden is shifted from the retailer to another member of the channel of distribution. In the United States, conditions are quite different, and, in general, retail outlets are of greater size. Therefore, the storage function can be performed by many of these retailers. Although physical facility limitations will generally not exist in the U.S., retailers will be reluctant to maintain large inventories for financial and other reasons.

When warehousing facilities are needed in a foreign market, a company may find an abundance of high-technology, modern warehouses in some industrialized countries. In Japan and the EEC, there is an increasing usage of high-cube warehousing coupled with automatic storage and retrieval (AS/AR) systems.

In many lesser developed countries, storage facilities may be nonexistent or extremely limited. The product package or shipping container may have to serve the warehousing purpose when proper warehousing is unavailable. Like all distribution activities, warehousing and storage must be managed differently in each foreign market. It is important to recognize how the storage activity differs and adjust the firm's distribution strategy as necessary.

Order Processing and Information Systems. One of the best opportunities that exist for improving customer service levels and reducing the costs of providing that service is to automate and integrate the order processing and information systems of the firms participating in the channel of distribution.[23] Transmitting orders by telephone using computer-to-computer or voice methods of communication, and automating internal information flows can lead to improved customer service by reducing order-cycle variability, improving in-stock availability, and improving communications with customers. More timely information flows will enable the manufacturer to reduce inventories and achieve transportation and production efficiencies.

While these opportunities still exist in international markets, lack of standardization of documents, computer protocol, and communication systems make truly integrated systems much more difficult to achieve. Another problem is the availability of "canned" computer systems. "Although order entry systems have been developed and used in larger firms for both domestic and export orders and domestic order entry packages are available from software houses and computer bureaux, there are few commercially available export packages."[24]

Summary

In most industrialized countries, the strong economic growth of the sixties and most of the seventies will not be present in the 1980s. Firms in mature markets will have a particularly difficult time achieving the desired growth in profitability in domestic markets. Further, protectionism threatens to reduce the attractiveness and even availability of some of the most desired foreign markets. The result will be more firms entering international markets and increased competition for those markets from existing multinationals. Significant advantage can be achieved if physical distribution is integrated into the planning process of international marketers. Although each of the activities of physical distribution must be performed in the international marketplace, the execution of the various distribution functions will be different in foreign markets.

The concepts of "integrated physical distribution management" and "cost trade-off analysis" are very important in international physical distribution, but the relative importance and the cost of each distribution component will vary from market to market. If the firm's international business is to be profitable, marketers must understand the cost/service differences that occur in foreign markets and incorporate them into their planning processes.

Notes

1. Kenneth L. Block, "International Business Strategies for the Eighties," *From the Podium . . .* , (Beta Gamma Sigma, 1982), p. 3.

2. Alan Slater, "International Marketing: The Role of Physical Distribution Management," *International Journal of Physical Distribution and Materials Management*, Vol. 10, No. 4 (1980), p. 160.

3. Vern Terpstra, *International Marketing, 3rd ed.* (Chicago: Dryden Press, 1983), pp. 377–78.

4. Terpstra, *International Marketing*, p. 388.

5. The interested reader is referred to Douglas M. Lambert and Howard M. Armitage, "An Information System for Effective Channel Management," *MSU Business Topics*, Vol 27, No. 4 (Autumn, 1979), pp. 13–22.

6. P. R. Cateora, *International Marketing*, 5th ed. (Homewood, IL: Richard D. Irwin, Inc., 1979), p. 39.

7. Terpstra, *International Marketing*, p. 393.

8. Cateora, *International Marketing*, pp. 217–18.

9. See David Ricks, *Big Business Blunders: Mistakes in Multinational Marketing* (Homewood, IL: Richard D. Irwin, Inc., 1983).

10. These numbers should be treated as rough estimates since evidence in the U.S. and Canada supports the conclusion that corporate accounting systems do not accurately collect the true costs of physical distribution. Since most estimates of distribution costs are based on industry surveys their results may be inaccurate.

11. Mikio Ideda, "The Progress of PD in Japan," *Transportation and Distribution Management*, Vol 14, No. 1 (January/February, 1974), p. 41.

12. See Chapter 7, "Financial Impact of Inventory" in Douglas M. Lambert and James R. Stock, *Strategic Physical Distribution Management* (Homewood, IL.: Richard D. Irwin, Inc., 1982), pp. 232–73.

13. See E. J. Kolde, *International Business Enterprise*, 2nd ed. (Englewood Cliffs, N.J.: Prentice-Hall, Inc., 1973), p. 387.

14. Ikeda, "The Progress of PD in Japan," p. 42.

15. *Ibid.*

16. R. Kahler and R. L. Kramer, *International Marketing*, 4th. ed. (Cincinnati, OH: South-Western Publishing Co., 1977), p. 204.

17. *Ibid.*

18. L. E. Gill, "Beware of Booby Traps in Multinational Distribution," *Handling and Shipping*, Vol. 17, No. 3 (March, 1976), p. 45.

19. Gordon Wills and Angela Rushton, "UK Progress in PDM," *International Journal of Physical Distribution and Materials Management*, Vol. 12, No. 6 (1982), p. 41.

20. *Ibid.*

21. Kahler and Kramer, *International Marketing*, p. 216.

22. Jacques Picard, "Typology of Physical Distribution Systems in Multi-national Corporations," *International Journal of Physical Distribution and Materials Management*, Vol. 12, No. 6 (1982), pp. 28–29.

23. See Douglas M. Lambert and James R. Stock, "Using Advanced Order Processing Systems to Improve Profitability," *Business*, (April-June, 1982), pp. 23–29.

24. G. J. Davies "Computer Based Export Systems," *International Journal of Physical Distribution and Materials Management*, Vol. 11, No. 5/6 (1981), p. 49.

12

COMPARATIVE TRANSPORTATION SYSTEMS

John L. Hazard

The goal of comparative studies of transportation, as in comparative marketing, is the systematic identification, classification, measurement, and interpretation of similarities and differences among national systems.[1] The objectives will differ from group to group. Transportation authorities will be more interested in whether the circumstances are sufficiently comparable that the results of substantive findings and policies are transferable between the nations.[2] Marketing professionals, on the other hand, are apt to be more concerned with what comparative transportation studies contribute to defining and measuring markets,[3] determining where they are located and whether they are accessible,[4] and how they are structured and behave in different national environments.[5] In this analysis, we shall be concerned primarily with policy-level comparisons that make a significant difference in marketing, and not with obvious differences in transport technology, procedures, documents, and regulations that are the daily and detailed concern of individual practitioners. From this perspective, it is well to define our terms of reference carefully and place some qualifications on the usefulness of comparative transportation studies.

Scope

If transportation encompasses the carriage or movement of persons and goods, then the scope raises the literal question of from where to where.

Should comparative transportation analysis be limited to movement within different nations, or include movements between nations (international) and even movements between different areas within the same nations (interregional)? Generally, transportation analysts have adopted a systems approach (Manheim-Morlock) which, as one of its principles, requires examining movements from original origin to final destination.[6] Transportation operates within several types of distinct markets, i.e., urban, regional, national, and international.

National boundaries seldom define markets. Frequently, movements cut across all types of markets en route to destinations, and this tends to obliterate national political boundaries. Where common markets are formed and work, as in Western Europe, movements between nations that are still regarded as international have become interregional movements between members of a larger European community. As Ohlin indicated some time ago, international trade is really only a special case of interregional trade.[7] In larger nations, there are usually several regional markets. Grether made this principle explicit in his studies of interregional marketing in the U.S.[8] Observing the trend toward an increased blending of interregional and international commerce, this study will examine some of the similarities and differences in international transportation systems as well as those between national systems. It will also observe that many of the so-called national systems are really not national markets because of the limitations of geography, transport development, and accessibility.

With increasing urbanization in the United States and elsewhere, another transport market emerges for comparative analysis, and that is the urban transport market. In some countries, these urban markets have spread out into high-density population corridors or conurbanizations, as in the Tokyo-Osaka Corridor in Japan, the Northeast Corridor in the U.S., and the North-South and East-West Corridors in Western Europe. These corridors have given rise to a whole new mode of high-speed rail transport, the results of which have been extremely monitored and the subject of many exchanges between nations.

Qualifications and Limitations

This chapter will focus primarily on policy-level facets of transportation experience. In many instances, the policy experience abroad is as valuable as technological innovations, and frequently the lessons (failures and successes) are as easily transferable.

It is important to understand the circumstances that gave rise to the differences in national approaches to transportation, as well as the conditions that must be fulfilled to foster an exchange. In some instances, the transportation experience abroad is not comparable and the lessons are unique to the foreign circumstances. In others, the conditions are sufficiently similar that the foreign experience is relevant to the United States and may in some circumstances be transferable. Each prospective candidate for transfer must be missible not only with the demographic conditions, but also with cultural traditions and political circumstances of the prospective host.

Merchant Marine Policies

Comparative foreign policy studies have provided some insight into the U.S. merchant marine dilemma. Maritime studies have focused primarily on comparative promotional, regulatory, and competitive policies. A comprehensive analysis of the promotional policies of six of the major maritime powers by the U.S. government provided a detailed analysis and quantification of the numerous types of subsidies employed by countries to assist their merchant fleets.[9] The interpretation of the data left a good deal to be desired. The U.S. Maritime Administration seemed to be utilizing the foreign assistance programs as justification for the U.S. subsidies that they administer.

A second look at the same data concluded that U.S. direct (differential) subsidies have been ineffective and had provided an incentive for the excessive utilization of high-cost U.S. resources and labor. A shift toward indirect subsidies, such as utilized abroad, would provide incentives for improved performance by the U.S. merchant marine and reduce the public costs of the subsidies.[10] Evidence has accumulated over the years that the U.S. shipbuilding industry is so inefficient that, even with construction subsidies of up to 50 percent of the total costs, the operating lines are handicapped by being required to purchase U.S.-built ships. Congress acknowledged that handicap by allowing the U.S. lines to purchase ships abroad for the first time in 1981.

There is also evidence that the operating subsidy is counterproductive. At least some of the nonsubsidized lines (Sea Land and U.S. lines) have been more successful than those lines receiving subsidies. At this point subsidies have become so widespread that no maritime power can unilaterally withdraw them. Ultimately, a multilateral approach, such as was utilized in tariff reductions, will be required to reduce competitive maritime subsidies. Yet multilateralism is the weakest link in U.S. maritime policy.

Caught between the conflicting maritime traditions, the U.S. Congress and the Reagan administration have been attempting to make the first major revision in U.S. maritime policies in the past 50 years.[11] The initiative consists of a three-pronged effort to reform regulations, reduce subsidies, and establish a posture for international negotiations. Congress has assumed the lead in maritime regulatory reforms but separate bills initiating it in the House and Senate failed to be reconciled and cleared in time for approval by the 97th Congress. The administration assumed primary responsibility for reducing maritime subsidies but is experiencing increasing opposition from maritime industry and labor. It has been successful in separating the interests of the U.S. lines from the shipbuilders by permitting the lines to acquire lower-cost foreign ships in lieu of the construction subsidy. No one appears to be working on establishing an effective international negotiating posture. With the UNCTAD anti-competitive Code of Linear Practices and the Law of the Sea Agreement about to become international law, it would appear to be time that the United States established an effective and on-going international negotiating policy.

International Air Policies

U.S. international air policies have pursued a different course from that of the merchant marine, with very different results. The first regular commercial passenger service was international. Aeromarine West Indies airways operated flying boats between Key West, Florida, and Havana, Cuba in 1920—five years before the first domestic U.S. service. From 1926 to World War II, Pan American Airlines became the "chosen instrument" of U.S. international air policy and negotiated many of its own agreements. As the war drew to a close, the allied community turned its attention to establishing a basic framework for the exchange of international aviation rights. A multilateral agreement was discussed at the Chicago Conference in 1944, but it was rejected primarily because of the opposing views of Great Britain, which was fearful of the dominant position of U.S. carriers. The divergent views of the U.S. and Great Britain were reconciled in Bermuda in 1946 in the Bermuda I Agreement, which formed the basis for U.S. international air policy for the next 30 years. Under that framework, the U.S. negotiated bilateral agreements with major nations extending reciprocal landing and service rights to U.S. and foreign flag carriers.[12] It was a comfortable arrangement often referred to as regulated competition. The CAB certified carriers, the State Department negotiated bilateral agreements with foreign countries, and the CAB generally approved of rates set by the International Air Traffic Association (IATA), a conference of carriers that sets rates and coordinates services from the Hague.

This comfortable arrangement started to come apart in 1975, when the Ford administration shifted to a policy of deregulation of air transportation. An attempt was made to implement the competitive U.S. policy in the negotiation of Bermuda II during the Carter administration. Most U.S. carriers and economists felt that the United States gave up too much for the benefits of liberalized competition received in Bermuda II.[13] Each of the subsequent bilaterals negotiated by the U.S. (with Japan, West Germany, and Israel) has attempted to incorporate more competitive provisions in the agreement (more carriers, points of service, and freedoms).

For a while the CAB refused to approve U.S. carrier participation in IATA rate agreements—creating an open and competitive international market. This brought U.S. competitive policies into direct confrontation with the cartel policies of IATA and the national control practices of most of its members. These differences were papered over by the Reagan administration, and the CAB again accorded rates and fare agreements filed by U.S. members of IATA antitrust exemption. However, the confrontation between U.S. competitive and international cartel practices is not over by any means. Instead, the differences in policy will continue to produce issues until some type of international accommodation is reached.

National Comparisons and Contrasts

A number of basic factors influence the national choice of transportation policies and decisions on infrastructure development, including geography, stage of development, differences in national objectives, and regional alignments. Geography, in all its aspects—configuration, location, and endowment—is probably the most important influence. The United States, for example, is one of the few continental-sized nations that has developed a truly integrated transportation system serving nationwide markets. The Soviet Union, in contrast, is an oblong nation almost entirely north of the United States, with mountains in the center and low rainfall and short growing seasons. It pursues a policy of decentralized transportation development within almost autonomous federal regions. This facilitates economic development without enormous investments in national transportation infrastructure and creates a multiple-centered economy less vulnerable to external attack. In similar geographic circumstances, the United States might also have foregone an integrated pattern of national market development. All of the other factors, however, must also be taken into account. Stages of development, national objectives, regional alignments, etc., impact directly on transportation policies and choices as well as geographic influences.

Analogous Conditions—Western Europe

When all factors are considered, the U.S. transportation system can be compared with best results to the systems of Western Europe. That, fortunately, is where most of the work has been done. The European Economic Community forms a fairly useful analog for the United States. It occupies only about one-sixth of the land area of the United States. The EEC, however, has a somewhat larger population, which produces about the same volume of economic activity as the U.S. and a good deal more foreign trade. Actually, in terms of population density and economic activity the EEC is more like the older northeastern region of the United States and has progressively less in common with regions to the south and west. It is also similar in terms of location, climate, ocean and energy reliance, and proximity to trade routes. Western Europe is somewhat ahead of the United States in the aging of its cities, in energy shortfall, and in having to deal with congestion. At these leading edges the U.S. has much to learn from Western Europe.

The United States, on the other hand, is ahead of Western Europe in establishing a common market among its separate states. This has resulted primarily from the federal use of the "commerce clause" to conform state and local trade and transport practices. In this respect, Western Europe has much to learn from the United States. There are still many national constraints to the transport integration of the European Common Market.

Institutionally, Western Europe is not as different from the United States as commonly assumed. Financial participation by western European governments in the total economy (government expenditures are 33.7 to 55.1 percent of the GNP) is not much higher than in the U.S. (31.5 percent).[14] While most Western European countries participate more prominently in transportation than the United States, their share of the total transportation capital expenditures is only slightly higher.[15] When state and local expenditures for transportation are included, the U.S. has about the same share of government capital in transportation as Western European countries.[16] One important difference is that European countries have a parliamentary system with the same party controlling the legislative and executive functions. That probably assures easier legislative acceptance of executive policy initiatives than is the case in the United States—where separate parties often control legislative and executive functions.

Goals and Objectives

Despite institutional and historic differences, the general goals of transportation policy in Western European countries are remarkably similar to the United States. Most European countries and the United States look on transportation as a means to serve other national goals such as:

- Economic growth and development
- General welfare and interest
- National defense and security
- Resource conservation and the environment.[17]

To serve these goals well, the first objective of the transport systems in Western Europe is economic efficiency. Most legislative mandates describe the ideal system in basically the same terms as does the United States, i.e., transportation must be safe, fast, low-cost, energy conserving, and as environmentally pure as investment resources permit.[18] The major differences here between the U.S. and Western European nations are in the administration of policy.

European nations pursue three-to-five year economic development plans in which transportation is an important element. The United States makes short-range economic forecasts but no long-range plans. Even long-range forecasts of U.S. transportation needs were discontinued in 1977.[19] Without a plan or a forecast, it is increasingly difficult for state and local governments, private individuals, and corporations to gear their long-range transportation commitments and investments to any established guidelines at the federal level.

Organization

One of the recurring questions for comparative consideration among Western nations has been how to organize and administer their transportation activities. Some consensus is beginning to emerge around the concept of a functionally organized, comprehensive transportation department or ministry with a broad portfolio. Experience of the United Kingdom with attempting to subsume the Ministry of Transportation in a super Department of the Environment did not work well. As a consequence, the Ministry of Transportation is being stripped out and operated independently. That experience had some dampening effect on plans of splitting up the U.S. Department of Transportation, and placing parts of it in new departments of Economic Development and Community Development in the mid 70s. Fragmenting transportation functions and placing them in separate ministries has not worked particularly well in Belgium and France. This impression is reinforced by the experience in West Germany, where all transportation modes function efficiently under a small single Ministry of Transport using the most advanced methods of analysis, budgeting, and control.[20]

Three organizational innovations utilized abroad are potentially useful to the United States. The first is the use of economic regulation as simply one of a number of instruments of transportation policy. This may be especially valuable to the U.S. in an age of economic deregulation. It suggests that the residual regulatory functions of the independent commissions (CAB, ICC, and FMC) might well be taken over by the Department of Transportation with no loss in effectiveness and some gains in uniformity of policy.

Another feature is the movement of the more progressive ministries abroad toward functional forms of organization (planning, finance, operations, control, etc.) in place of modal organization (highway, air, railroad, etc.). If the United States ultimately moves toward a more functional type of organization, it might overcome the biases implicit in its strong modal administrations (aviation, highway, railroad, Coast Guard, etc.) in DOT. It could also result in some gains in intermodal coordination and service effectiveness and in reducing destructive modal rivalries.

The unique ways in which Western European countries have utilized public incorporations in transportation operations is also of interest to the United States. These government-owned-and-operated entities, known as boards and corporations in the U.K., *sociétiès* in France, *régies* in Belgium, and *Bundesbahn* in Germany, are used extensively throughout Western Europe and Canada but have only recently taken hold in the United States (Amtrak, Conrail, and U.S.R.A.). By tradition, the government-owned enterprises in Europe and Canada have been given considerably more budget autonomy then their counterparts in the United States. They have been extremely useful in areas where private capital was reluctant or market failures have occurred. On the other hand, they have also been remarkably defensive about retreating gracefully in the face of growing competition or obsolescence of their services.

Differences in Western European and United States transportation policies are most significantly reflected in approaches to the three fairly distinct transportation markets—intercity, urban, and regional.

Intercity Markets

Despite the relative modest distances between major urban centers in Western Europe and Japan, both areas are much more committed to rail transportation as the "backbone" of their systems than is the highway-oriented U.S. Western European railroads haul a good deal larger share of the intercity passengers (9 to 10 percent) than do the U.S. railroads (less than 1 percent),[21] even though they carry a smaller share of the freight traffic (17.5 to 31.4 percent) than the bulk-hauling U.S. railroads (33.5 percent).[22] Basically, European railroads are passenger-oriented while U.S. railroads are freight-oriented. Not understanding these contrasting approaches, many U.S. citizens return from European tours critical of the U.S. railroads and wondering why they are not as "successful" as their European counterparts.

Several factors help to explain the European proclivity for railroads. The first is that highway modes did not snap back as quickly in Western Europe as they did in the United States after World War II. There were only 5.7 million automobiles in Western Europe, in 1950, in comparison with 37.3 million in the United States.[23] Both were verging on 100 million in 1977. Another rationale for European railroad preference is that most Europeans have assumed that rail transport was less energy-intensive and environmentally damaging than other modes, although this assumption does not hold up for intercity buses, waterways, or pipelines. The capital costs of new highway infrastructure was also a consideration. The Economic Commission for Europe had identified the improved utilization of existing systems (railroads) as an early policy alternative preferable to large public expenditures for new modes (highways).[24] The United States by contrast had proposed the massive Interstate Highway System as early as 1944 as a public works and employment product to facilitate the transition to a civilian economy.

The relatively inefficient European railroad freight services (1/5th to 1/10th the ton/kilometers per employee hour of the U.S. railroads)[25] are the beneficiaries of policies designed to reinforce European intercity rail passenger service.[26] This is the opposite of the U.S. case, in which freight services subsidized passenger services for many years. In some countries, such as West Germany and Australia, railroads have become a means of government sponsored employment. As a consequence, they have evolved into powerful bureaucracies that are difficult to compete with on commercial terms and hard to cut back after their services are no longer required.

Intercity Passenger

Whatever the rationale, most Western European countries do favor railroads, even at the expense of competing modes of transport. In most continental European countries, buses are not allowed to enter intercity markets already served by rail. In the United Kingdom, buses serve primarily low-density population areas unable to support rail service.[27] In Spain, buses pay an extra tax if they parallel or compete with railroads.[28]

Airline services in Western Europe are not a truly integrated system of transport. Fewer than 10 percent of the major airports are even interconnected.[29] Where they are, fares are frequently higher than transatlantic discount fares covering several times the distance.[30] Within Western Europe, air fares have been held up above rail fares even for the long-haul services where air may be cost-advantageous. This protection of rail fares may be coming to an end with the easing of economic regulation.

Highway competition with the railroads has been similarly restricted by the assessing of fuel and other taxes on the automobile to generate a net surplus over and above the costs of providing highways. This differs appreciably from the U.S. case, where assessments against vehicles have not covered full highway costs and the Highway Trust Fund has been depleted. Fuel taxes alone in Western Europe are placed at several times the U.S. level (federal and state combined). In France, the fuel tax is over $2.00 per gallon, and tolls are charged on many intercity expressways. In Australia, national revenues from user fees exceeded costs imposed on the highways, resulting in a net government surplus. The highway user-fee surpluses in West Germany are used to subsidize the railroads. Only the large trucks of Western Europe may be paying fees less than their fair share of the costs. As in the United States, trucks are frequently subsidized by overpayments on passenger automobiles.

Western European countries did not artificially control the price of energy as long as the U.S. Free markets resulted in fuel prices several times the U.S. level in the mid- and late 1970s. The result was a hastening of the down-sizing of automobiles and a restraint on fuel consumption and automobile use. Despite these contraints, automobiles have taken over 80 percent of the intercity passenger traffic in Western Europe, leaving only a residual share to the railroads and airlines. In this respect, the automobile by 1976 had become almost as important in intercity service in Western Europe (80 percent) as it had in the United States (87.1 percent).[31] The only major differences in commercial market shares is that railroads are the dominant carrier of the residual commercial share in Western Europe, while the U.S. airlines (with 12.9 percent) dominated rail (0.7 percent) and bus (1.3 percent) in 1980.[32]

Intercity Freight

Intercity freight services in Western Europe appear to be something of an afterthought, while they are at the forefront of carrier activity in the United States. While most European authorities still regard the railroads as the backbone of the European system, that is clearly not the case in freight services. By the mid-1970s, trucks had become the dominant carriers within every major country in Western Europe, with the major share of ton/kilometers of freight hauled as well as value of traffic and revenue (Table 12.1).

The United States has a more balanced freight transport system, in so far as modal participation is concerned, than does Western Europe. The U.S.

TABLE 12.1

National Shares of Freight Traffic—1970s (in percent of intercity ton/kilometers)

	United Kingdom	France	W. Germany	United States
Truck	65.1	48.5	32.5	20.1
Rail	17.5	35.6	31.4	33.5
Water	14.9	4.9	27.3	25.8
Pipeline	2.5	10.9	8.6	20.4
Totals[a]	100.0%	100.0%	100.0%	100.0%

[a]Rounded to 100% with air freight excluded.

SOURCE: Data collected from transport ministry officials in a 1977 visit.

system is also much more effectively integrated across state lines, with fewer border obstacles than exist at the European national boundaries.

Truck transportation had to overcome a number of obstacles, constraints, and discriminatory regulations to become the dominant freight mode in Western Europe. There were a number of competitive obstacles. Entry and rate deregulation were accomplished for the railroads first in France and the U.K., and that gave the railroads the upper hand over other modes in pricing and developing innovative services. Policies discriminatory to nonrail carriers also played a prominent role. The U.K. and France, for example, placed quantitative controls on the truck fleets used at home, and the U.K. has placed proportional limits on growth of the trucking industry. Similar capacity controls were employed by Japan to protect its government-owned railroads from coastal shipping competition.

Western European governments also contribute social payments to the railroads to cover mandated reductions in fares or free service to select groups—the old, the young, unemployed veterans, widows and children of military deceased, etc. They make payments to railroads for what is called "normalization of accounts" to equalize the burden between railroads and other modes and to achieve uniformity of subsidies as between nations. This normalizing subsidy includes payments to offset any advantages that heavy trucks may have because of insufficient user charges.

In West Germany, high prices are paid for truck vehicle-operating certificates. Trucks are restricted from operating on weekends, holidays, and tourist seasons and in urban areas in Switzerland, France, and West Germany. In a number of countries, including Canada, regional development is promoted by subsidized rail service and less than cost-based rates for transport by railroad but not by other modes. In most countries, trucks are limited in access to certain urban areas. Britain controls the access of trucks to certain intercity roads—even though a large share of British trucks are nationalized.[33] Though the heavier trucks in some European countries appear not to be paying the costs they impose on the system, user charges are moving up rapidly.[34]

How did the trucks succeed in achieving a dominant position in the face of such obstacles? Primarily because of geographical and service considerations. The European cities are within a relatively short haul of each other (150 to 500 miles), and that is the area within which the flexible, fast, and complete services of trucks have their greatest advantages.

Despite the difference in treatment that the Europeans and Americans accord their railroads, neither side has been able to escape the necessity for substantial rationalization of their systems in the face of growing obsolescence and increased competition from other modes. Though European countries differ in the extent of their disenchantment with the use of railroads as instruments of national policy, all are attempting to rationalize their existing systems to some degree. The British Railway System, which was nationalized in 1948, has made the most drastic cutbacks. It has eliminated 387,000 jobs (60 percent of its work force) and 9,000 miles of track (about 45 percent of the total).[35] The privately-owned U.S. railroads have reduced employees nearly commensurately (from 1.3 million in 1948 to 560,000 in 1977) but have found reductions in trackage and services harder to come by except where major bankruptcies and reorganizations have occurred. The Japanese National Railways are also considering a substantial cutback in thinly utilized lines, but are at the same time extending the high-speed Shinkasen line north to Hokkaido and south to Kyushu in order to spread population and industrialization away from the high-density Tokyo-Osaka corridor. West Germany has probably been the least successful in rationalizing its rail employment and plant—having 4/5th's of the employees of the U.S. railroads to render only a small fraction of the U.S. service.

U.S. railroads have been able to generate a modest return on capital investment over the past decade and in that capacity they stand almost alone.[36] Despite strong promotion and support, most nationalized railroads incur huge deficits and, in fact, no nationalized railroad has reported a profit since 1964.[37] Admittedly, some of the nationalized railroads have different social responsibilities to perform. But most of the nationalized systems are now receiving earmarked government payments for the performance of specific social services. Only in Japan are the railroads required to absorb social costs. There is still much room for better studies of broader benefits and costs of railroads. As losses have skyrocketed, however, countries have taken a more sober look at the social performance of their railroads and most are examining the prospects for drastic cutbacks.[38]

In many respects, the management of U.S. and European railroads is becoming more alike. The European railroads, in the face of overwhelming losses, are becoming more cost-conscious if not profit-oriented. Unprofitable segments of U.S. railroad passenger and freight services have been taken over by public corporations (Amtrak and Conrail) for purposes of rationalization and revitalization. Railroads on both sides of the Atlantic have been substantially deregulated and have assumed more responsibility for pricing their own services. Neither the government-supported railroads of Western Europe nor the private-owned systems of the U.S. have been successful in stemming the rise of highway modes of transportation. As the systems grow more alike and struggle with similar problems they have more to learn from their respective experiences—both the successes and failures.

Notes

1. Jean J. Boddewyn, "Comparative Marketing: The First Twenty-Five Years," *Journal of International Business Studies*, 12:1, Spring/Summer Issues, 1981, p. 61.

2. "Comparative Transportation Policies in Other Countries," Chapter 4, *National*

Transportation Policies Through the Year 2000, Final Report of the National Transportation Policy Study Commission, Washington, DC, US Government, Printing Office, July 1979, pp: 69–82.

3. Reavis Cox underlined the importance of studying the physical flow of goods in "The Search for Universals in Comparative Studies of Domestic Marketing Systems," in *Marketing and Economic Development: Proceedings of the 1965 Fall Conference*, American Marketing Association, P. D. Bennett, ed., Chicago, Illinois, 1965, pp: 143–62.

4. As set forward most effectively in Part V, "Marketing Within and Between Regions," *Marketing in the American Economy*, Valie, Grether and Cox, New York, The Reynold Press, 1952, pp: 487–555.

5. Boddewyn, "Comparative Marketing," pp: 61–79.

6. As most extensively developed by Professor Marvin Manheim of MIT and Professor Edward Morlock of the Transportation Centre-Northwestern University during the 1960s and 1970s.

7. Bartel Ohlin, *Interregional and International Trade*, Cambridge: Harvard University Press, 1935.

8. As carefully documented in "The Theory of Interregional Marketing," Ronald Savitt; and Chapter 16 of *Regulation of Marketing and the Public Interest*, Balderson, Carman, and Nicosia, eds., (New York: Pergamon Press, 1981).

9. U.S. Maritime Administration, Office of Policy and Plans, *The Maritime Aids of the Six Major Maritime Nations*, Washington, D.C.: Government Printing Office, 1977), pp: 1–223.

10. "Relevant Maritime Policies of Other Countries," John L. Hazard, *Papers on Selected Transport Policies of Developed Countries*, U.S. National Transportation Policy Study Commission, Washington, DC, NTIS, No. PB 80-219231, November 1979.

11. The U.S. differential subsidy policies were established in the Merchant Marine Act of 1936 as amended, but the regulatory policies and exemptions reach back to The Shipping Act of 1916.

12. The Civil Aeronautics Board (CAB) extended certification to other U.S. carriers and that ended the dominant position of Pan American.

13. Nawal K. Taneja, *U.S. International Aviation Policy*, Lexington, Mass., Lexington Books, 1980, p. 22.

14. *The OECD Member Countries—1981*, Washington, D.C. Organization for Economic Cooperation and Development, 1982, p. 4.

15. "The National Role in World Port Development: United States and Western Europe," in John L. Hazard, ed., *Maritime Policy and Management*, 1978, No. 5, p. 271.

16. State and local government expenditures for transportation in the U.S. are about twice the federal expenditures.

17. John L. Hazard, "National Transportation Policy Administration—Lessons from Home and Abroad," *Transportation Journal*, Summer 1977, p. 6.

18. The author was able to compare legislative objectives as the U.S. representative to the *Council of European Ministers of Transportation* during the 1972 and 1973 meetings of that organization in Brussels and the Hague.

19. The biennial *National Transportation Reports* containing forecasts to the year 2000 were discontinued by order of the Secretary of Transportation in 1977.

20. Interviews with Ministry officials in the United Kingdom, France, Belgium, the Netherlands, and West Germany in the summer of 1977.

21. Market shares are measured in terms of passenger kilometers and ton kilometers in the mid- to late-1970s.

22. Hazard, "National Transportation Policy." p. 8.

23. "Urban Transportation in Europe" and "European Intercity Passenger Trans-

portation," C. Kenneth Orski, *Papers on Selected Transport Policies of Selected Countries*, Special Report No. 5, Washington, D.C. NTPSC-NTIS, November 1979, pp: 159 and 168.

24. "Comparative Transportation Policies for Other Countries," Chapter 4, *Transportation Policies to the Year 2000*, National Transportation Policy Study Commission, Washington, DC, U.S. Government Printing Office, June 25, 1979, p. 78.

25. *Transportation Policy—A Consultation Document*, 1, London, Her Majesty's Stationary Office, 1976, and the Association of American Railroads, *Yearbook of Railroad Facts*, Washington, DC, 1975.

26. C. Kenneth Orski, "European Intercity Passenger Transportation," *Selected Transport Policies*, NTSPC, Washington, DC, NTIC, 1979.

27. United Kingdom, Department of Transport, Scottish Development Department, Welsh Office, *Transport Policy, White Paper* presented to Parliament, June 1977, London, Her Majesty's Stationary Office, 1977, pp: 174–76.

28. World Bank, *The Economic Development of Spain: Report of a Mission*, Baltimore, MD: Johns Hopkins Press, 1973, p. 224.

29. Organization for Economic Cooperation and Development, *The Future of European Passenger Transport*, Final Report, A, Paris, OCED, 1977, pp: 174–76.

30. *National Transportation Policies Through the Year 2000*, National Transportation Policy Study Commission, Washington, DC., U.S. Government Printing Office, June 1979, p. 73.

31. Hazard, "National Transportation Policy," p. 8.

32. *Transportation Facts and Figures*, Transportation Association of America, Seventeenth Edition, December 1981, Washington, DC. TTA, 1982.

33. *U.K. Transport Policy*, pp: 42–43.

34. J. R. Nelson, Surface Transportation in Europe," in *Selected Transport Policies*, Washington, DC, NTPSC, November 1979.

35. "Comparative Transportation Policies in Other Countries," Chapter 4, NTPSC *Final Report*, p. 70.

36. Averaging about 1.7 percent between 1970 and 1980, and slightly higher in the 1980s.

37. Jim Loveland, *Southern Pacific Bulletin*, 62, May 1978, pp: 6–7.

38. In each major European country railroad losses exceeded $1 billion in 1975 and were up from 22 percent in West Germany to 400 percent in the United Kingdom. Source: national budget accounts for each country, 1975.

VI

COMPARATIVE MARKETING STRATEGY: SPECIAL MARKETS

In this part on special markets, the first chapter examines the nature of the marketing evolution which is an on-going process in Eastern Europe. Five key issues related to East European marketing are explored in this chapter. First, the development of the evolutionary process of marketing in East European countries is examined. Second, the significant influences of this evolutionary process on the marketing systems of the member countries is looked at. Third, the kinds and extent of marketing information systems that are required in the process of this evolutionary movement are formulated. Fourth, the critical changes needed in overall marketing functions/processes, as the evolutionary marketing system progresses, are examined. Finally, the role that is attributed to marketing/functions, based on the relative emphasis that is put on the ultimate consumer satisfaction at a profit in East European countries, is explored.

In dealing with Japanese environments, a few comparisons are made between Japanese and American perceptions of trade, the Westernization of Japan, Japan as an economic power, and the role of competition and cooperation. Lazer, in the section on Japanese consumers, briefly examines various aspects of Japanese consumer behavior. The management and labor discussion focuses on the outlook and responsibilities of Japanese managers, the role of workers and labor unions, and the direct transferability of Japanese approaches to the U.S.A. The chapter concludes with a discussion of common problems and errors of the U.S. companies marketing in Japan. In the final chapter of this part, Kin-chok examines the structure and development of marketing as a managerial function in the Peoples Republic of China. The problem faced by China's plan-based command system and the growing role of marketing in her reformed plan-based and market-directed systems are also viewed. In particular, the discussion focuses on the state-owned enterprises in the manufacturing sector of the Chinese economy.

13

COMPARATIVE MARKETING SYSTEMS IN EASTERN EUROPE: AN ILLUSTRATION OF MARKETING EVOLUTION

A. Coskun Samli

Despite the general use of terms like Iron Curtain, communist-bloc, or socialist countries, thus far East European countries has evolved significantly different socioeconomic technological and marketing structures. Furthermore, in these countries the relative role and importance attributed to marketing varies in important ways. Finally, the relative speed of socioeconomic, technological and marketing progress in these countries has been different. Thus, along with marketing structures and the role attributed to marketing, significant variations can be observed in the countries' marketing functions.

At the present time, the marketing systems of Eastern European countries can be viewed in terms of a spectrum having totally centralized systems at one end and substantially decentralized systems on the other. The countries in this region have been slowly decentralizing. However, all of them have not been following exactly the same socioeconomic development route, nor have they been changing at the same speed.[1] This is why the spectrum exists. It is important to understand the characteristics of the key points on this spectrum, which in turn would enable one to understand the nature of the marketing evolution which is an on-going process in Eastern Europe. Five key issues are explored in this chapter. First, the characteristics of the evolutionary process are examined. Second, the significant influences of this evolutionary process on the marketing system is examined.

Third, the kinds of marketing information that are required in the process of this evolutionary movement are evaluated. Fourth, the critical changes in overall marketing functions, as the evolutionary process progresses, are explored. And finally, the role that is attributed to marketing, based on the relative emphasis that is put on the ultimate consumer satisfaction in East European countries, is examined.

The Characteristics of the Evolutionary Process

In order to understand the changes that have taken place in East European marketing, it is necessary first to examine the macroeconomic systems and the changes that have taken place in these systems. The macroeconomic system in a society determines the nature and characteristics of total economic activity. The latter, in turn, specifies the characteristics of total societal production and the nature as well as the specifics of distribution. In other words, it is the macro economic activity that has the final say on what and how much should be produced as well as what and how much should be distributed to whom and how. The decision process underlying total economic activity in East European countries is composed of two types of key linkages—macro and micro types. These linkages facilitate the information and the authority flow necessary for commencement and continuation of economic activity. The two types of linkages reflect two basic types of economy, *command* and *demand*. The command economy has primarily *vertical* linkages. Orders and directions come from the top and economic institutions are linked vertically. The demand economy, on the other hand, has horizontal linkages which transfer information and provide guidance from the market place on up. Thus, the emphasis here is on the market and on competition rather than central authority. The horizontal linkages are owned and controlled by the private sector and influenced by the government only nominally. The vertical linkages are planning linkages owned and controlled by the central authority.

Thus, the macro system that emphasizes planning linkages is heavily centralized and has many planning and administrative layers between the planning of production and actual distribution.

The micro system, on the other hand, that emphasizes market linkages is quite decentralized. In such a system there exists only a few market-oriented independent layers between production and distribution. Horizontal linkages provide the information and direction for market-oriented planning of production and actual distribution. Since both of these activities are performed at the same layers, or at layers very close to each other, more coordination and communication is expected to take place between production and distribution.

FIGURE 13.1
Spectrum of Macroeconomic System*

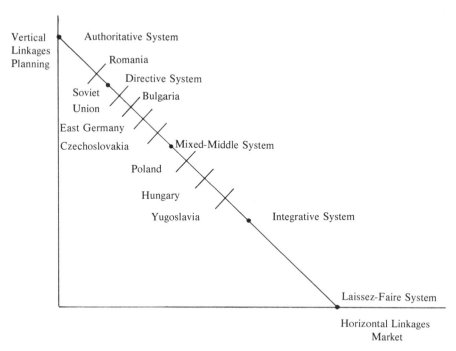

SOURCE: A Coskun Samli and Wladyslaw Jermankowicz, "The Stages of Marketing Evolution in East European Countries," *European Journal of Marketing*, 17:2, 1983, p. 28.

*Since it is almost impossible to quantify the exact degree and scope of the decentralization in developing this exhibit, the author employed a Delphi process. The opinion of some fifteen experts on East European affairs was solicited as to where each country stands on the authoritative/laissez-faire spectrum.

A purely planned macro system with a sole emphasis on planning (or vertical) linkages, such as the one that existed in the U.S.S.R. during the 1920s, also had a totally planned distribution system. At the other extreme, a purely competitive system functions only through market (or horizontal) linkages. Such a system existed in the United Kingdom in the seventeenth through the eighteenth centuries. As the system relies more on vertical linkages, its reliance on horizontal linkage is limited. The reverse is also true, as the system emphasizes horizontal linkages more readily, it de-emphasizes vertical linkages.[2] Between the two ends of the spectrum exist a virtually unlimited number of mixed systems. In fact, all prevailing macroeconomic systems are located between the extremes of this spectrum. (See Figure 13.1). The spectrum has five major divisions: authoritative, directive, mixed middle, integrative, and laissez faire.[3] Of these, only the first four are feasible for East European countries, since socialism, by definition, excludes laissez faire.

The four possible systems feasible in East European countries can be described as follows: 1) authoritative systems where total dependence is on vertical planning stages and total centralization; 2) directive systems still heavily dependent on vertical planning linkages, but relying on at least some information from a few remotely located market linkages; 3) mixed middle systems combining planning linkages with market linkages. Although still planned economy, the plans are based primarily on the needs and desires of market linkages; and 4) integrative systems putting more emphasis on market linkages, freeing them to make all of their major decisions as long as they fall within the constraints of a national development plan. In essence, these are market systems guided by a long-term planning process.[4]

This spectrum indicates the parameters of the economic evolutionary process in Eastern Europe. The key parts of the spectrum are briefly summarized in Table 13.1. Regardless of where they may be positioned on the spectrum, all of the East European countries are moving in the direction of point #4 on the spectrum, i.e., integrative macroeconomic system.

TABLE 13.1
The Four Key Points on the Macroeconomic Systems Spectrum

	Characteristics
1. Authoritative	All aspects of production and distribution are administered and controlled by central authorities. All the planning and authority for economic decisions are concentrated at the top, e.g., Russia before 1920.
2. Directive	Market operates within a direct planning system where the self-regulation of the market function is limited and the distribution system is based on strict central authority. Some research information filters through the market upwards to decision-making authority, e.g., Romania.
3. Mixed-Middle	A planned economy operating with central indirect layers where market functions within certain rules, e.g., Hungary.
4. Integrative	Based on self-management, in which business enterprises and cooperatives are in a free market within a certain set of conditions, e.g., Yugoslavia.

SOURCE: A. Coskun Samli, *Marketing and Distribution Systems in Eastern Europe*, Praeger, 1978, Laszlo Szabo, "The Methods of Market Research in Socialist Countries," Ill.: Millimetro, Palermo 1972.

However, no two of the East European countries are presently at the same position on the spectrum. In fact, each is clearly positioned at a different point. Furthermore, even if all of them were to start again from the same position they would not all end up in the same position. This is due to the various supporting conditions of the evolutionary process as well as to the differences in the individual countries' ability to successfully decentralize.

The evolutionary process discussed in this chapter is related to the attempts on the part of the East European countries to move away from their original position on the spectrum in the direction of the integrative system. Perhaps the most important aspect of the evolutionary process is that all of the countries of this region have gotten away from the authoritative system. This movement away from that extreme of the spectrum was preceded by some economic and political evolution, which is represented by a slowly emerging decentralization in, if not the planning, at least the execution of the development plans.[5] Following economic and political evolutionary activity has been the marketing evolution, which in essence brought control over distribution and product choice closer to the consumer.

Evolutionary Process as It Affects the Marketing System

Even though most East European countries are quite far from it, they all have been proceeding in the direction of the integrative system. Table 13.2 depicts all four stages of the four-stage evolution from a marketing point of view. An increased degree of concentration on marketing and an increasing degree of marketing sophistication are the two necessary key ingredients of this evolution.[6]

A few key trends emerge as an East European country moves from an authoritative to an integrative system. Among these, the following stand out:

- While the market enterprise virtually has no identity in an authoritative system, since the whole economy is treated as one big national enterprise, it comes very close to its Western counterpart in the integrative system.
- Consumers face extreme shortages in authoritative systems. As the country moves in the direction of the integrative system, there is more consumer credit, consumer input in product design, and some market segmentation and product differentiation take place.
- The distribution system becomes more decentralized, with the burden of performance switching from central authority to the enterprise entity.
- The responsibility for the decision-making process regarding marketing decisions at enterprise level shifts from, again, the central authority to the enterprise entity.

TABLE 13.2

The Four Stages of Marketing Evolution in East European Countries

Stage 1   *Totally Planned and Controlled Distribution Systems (Authoritative Economic System)*
- National economy is treated as a big nationwide enterprise.
- All decisions about structure of production and directions of investment are made at the central governmental level in the planning council.
- Directive form of management.
- Ration-card type distribution system.
- Nationalized retailing structure with virtual monopoly of sales in urban areas.
- Nationwide seller's markets.

Stage 2   *Directly Planned and Controlled Distribution Systems (Directive Economic System)*
- An enterprise is regarded a ministry association.
- Some competition among ministries.
- Some pressure on the producers to attract customers.
- Introducing of input-output analysis at the governmental level.
- Large-scale advertising of an ideological character is utilized.
- Better method of estimating, thanks to input-output analysis, where, when, and what the consumers will buy.
- Increased choice for the ultimate consumer.

Stage 3   *Partially Planned and More Indirectly Controlled Distribution Systems (Mixed-Middle System)*
- An enterprise is regarded an industrial association.
- Some competition among the industrial associations.
- Moderate degree of decentralization.
- Planning of market consumption goods and services is decentralized.
- Some product differentiation—particularly, free-market mechanisms for individual consumption products.
- Increased availability of consumer credit.

Stage 4   *Indirectly Planned and Controlled Distribution Systems (Integrative Economic System)*
- The focal point in the economy is the market enterprise.
- Competition among the enterprises.
- Government influences the behavior of enterprises indirectly only by the use of economic parameters.
- Free-market mechanisms for all goods and services.
- High autonomy for enterprises to improve their marketing efforts.
- Ability to fluctuate prices.
- Increased discretionary income and luxury items.

SOURCE: A. Coskun Samli and Wladyslaw Jermankowicz, "The Stages of Marketing Evolution in East European Countries," *European Journal of Marketing,* 17:2, 1983, p. 29.

As movement takes place from an authoritative system towards an integrative system, it involves not only economic decentralization but organizational decentralization as well. In an authoritative system, the entire national economy can be regarded as one big market, while in an integrative system enterprises become autonomous entities. Hence, at stage four, the market enterprise carries out its own plans with substantial degree of autonomy. At this stage, its executives function with a relatively high degree of independence.[7] However, national economic development plans to establish the parameters of this autonomy. The marketing environment shows a drastic difference as authoritative and integrative systems are contrasted.[8] First, the distribution system, while a national monopoly in the authoritative system, becomes a regulated private industry. Individual enterprises gain more autonomy in making strategic marketing and management decisions. Consumers gain more power in terms of being able to make an impact as to what may be produced and distributed by the existing economic system. This power stems from the fact that almost invariably consumers have greater discretionary income in integrative systems than in authoritative or directive systems.* As the country moves from an authoritative system towards an integrative system, the need for and the use of marketing research changes substantially.

The Need for and the Use of Marketing Research

In Eastern Europe, marketing research, like marketing itself, is a relatively new phenomenon. In order to systematically analyze marketing research activity in this region, it is necessary to consider at least three key factors: approximate degree of economic development, where the country is on the authoritative integrative spectrum, and existing degree of marketing sophistication.

Degree of Economic Development

Although marketing has an undeniable impact on economic development, historical evidence indicates an increasing market sophistication as countries develop economically.[9] As marketing sophistication increases, the need for information becomes more noticeable. Hence, marketing research

---

*It is not implied here that the consumer in the integrative system has more discretionary income because this system works better and generates more income. It is the author's contention that, at the beginning of economic growth in many less-developed countries, a system similar to directive is quite workable. As progress has been made, that system gives way to other systems in the direction of integrative system. The causal relationship, i.e., whether income and wealth determine the system or the system determines the level of income and wealth are not scientifically established and hence one can only hypothesize.

lies behind marketing development, which in turn lies behind economic development.[10] From the point of view of economic development, Bulgaria and Romania can be considered developing; Yugoslavia, Hungary and Czechoslovakia are almost developed; and Poland and East Germany are developed countries.

There is a relationship between marketing research utilization and economic development (Table 13.3). A relatively more developed country has a greater appreciation and/or need for marketing research information, for there is a higher level of consumer needs and wants and the marketing process is more complicated. For instance, Yugoslavia may be considered the heaviest user of marketing research in East Europe. It is also the most decentralized of the whole group. Its five-year plans are based on consumer research.[11] Bulgaria and Romania, on the other hand, are relatively light users of marketing research.

Relatively less-developed East European countries use macro marketing research to provide government with proper direction in the distribution of goods and services. In Romania, for instance, it has been established that certain past expansion figures of trade space and sales per square meter can be used as benchmarks for planning business expansion. Such benchmarks are used only as a suggested guideline in Yugoslavia.

Enterprises in relatively less-developed countries require less research information. The status of marketing described by Fedor Rocco in the early 1960s is quite similar to the present-day marketing system in Bulgaria and Romania:

> ... Volume of demand has exceeded the volume of supply ... The problem of inventories did not exist ... buyers were searching for connections to enable them to find the goods they needed.[12]

Under such circumstances, the individual enterprise, because of its monopoly power and the progress it automatically makes, does not need much marketing sophistication, much less marketing research. Today, however, the relatively more developed East European countries are able to obtain and use marketing research.[13]

The Position on the Authoritative-Integrative Spectrum

There is no measure to determine exactly where an individual country is on the authoritative-integrative spectrum, which somewhat overlaps with a "centralized-decentralized" spectrum.[14] To a substantial extent, however, the nature of the marketing information needed and its specific uses are determined by a country's relative position on the spectrum.

TABLE 13.3
Use of Marketing Research by East European Countries

Country	Approximate Degree of Economic Development	Macro Economic System	Approximate Degree of Marketing Sophistication	Utilization of Marketing Research
Bulgaria	Developing	Directive System	Unsophisticated	Relatively light
Romania	Developing	Directive System	Unsophisticated	Relatively light
Hungary	Almost Developed	Almost Integrative	Relatively Sophisticated	Medium
Yugoslavia	Almost Developed	Integrative System	Sophisticated	Medium-Heavy
Czechoslovakia	Almost Developed	Almost Mixed Middle	Sophisticated	Medium
Poland	Developed	Mixed Middle	Relatively Sophisticated	Medium
East Germany	Developed	Directive but close to Mixed Middle		

SOURCE: Compiled by the author.

225

In authoritative and directive economies, the central government, in order to create a balance between the purchasing power of the population and the supply of goods and services, has to make plans and provide direction for the enterprises.[15] On the other hand, as the country is closer to the integrative system, enterprises are forced to make their own decisions, and hence they need decision-oriented marketing research information.

In order to regulate the present consumption patterns so that a balance between supply and demand is created, in East Germany the Market Research Institute, under the direction of the Ministry of Home Trade, performs at least four types of market studies:[16]

- Gathering basic data on trends in consumption and consumers' buying and living habits;
- Development of consumption models based on changes in the sales of various food stuffs, textiles, and other manufactured consumer goods;
- Investigations of the sale of key consumer goods, availability of which primarily determines the sales of other goods;
- Investigations of consumption trends and patterns of different segments of the population.

Less than half of the studies undertaken by the institute are done strictly for the ministry. The rest of the studies are conducted for various enterprises. Further down on the spectrum, in the direction of the integrative system, enterprises in Czechoslovakia, Poland, and Hungary have a greater tendency to be involved in marketing research themselves rather than relying central agencies or ministry of home trade for information. In Poland, for instance, a major company, PREDOM/POLAR, which manufactures refrigerators and washing machines for household use, is engaged in widespread marketing research activity in an effort to support its domestic and international marketing efforts. Typically, the company's marketing research group is engaged in some eight kinds of research projects: 1) level of appliance ownership; 2) ultimate demand; 3) motivation analysis; 4) product/price ratio analysis; 5) consumer preference research; 6) test marketing; 7) retail sales and inventory analysis; and 8) long-range forecasting.[17]

Degree of Sophistication

The need for and the use of marketing research is also conditioned by the degree of marketing research sophistication. There are three indicators of marketing research sophistication: 1) marketing research education; 2) availability and the use of computers; and 3) development of marketing research activity in the universities. On the basis of these three criteria, Yugoslavia and Czechoslovakia are judged to be relatively more sophisticated than other countries in the group. Finally, marketing research utilization as a whole (including both governmental and individual enterprise utilization) varies substantially among the East European countries.

Critical Changes in Overall Marketing Functions

Each of the four macroeconomic systems discussed earlier in this chapter has a series of marketing functions attached to it. Given the macroeconomic and political systems, these marketing functions are basically appropriate to perform the total societal marketing function. As a country moves in the direction of the integrative system, its marketing functions change substantially to facilitate the economic and political changes. Table 13.4 illustrates the major differences in key functional areas of marketing as the authoritative system is contrasted with the integrative system.[18]

TABLE 13.4
The Contrast in the Marketing Functions

The Functional Area	Authoritative System	Integrative System
The Market	Strictly a Seller's Market	Sum Zero Market or a Buyer's Market
	No Competition	High Degree of Competition
	No Market Linkages Between Enterprises	Market Linkages Are Dominant
Marketing Research Information	Macro Marketing Information Needed for Detailed Planning	Micro Marketing Information for Enterprises to Make Decisions
Product	Standardized	Some Differentiation and Segmentation Depending Upon the Characteristics of Submarkets
Distribution	National Monopolies	Competition Among Enterprises
Advertising	Product Advertising with Ideological Overtones	Enterprise Advertising
Price	Centrally Administered Pricing	Enterprise-Administered Pricing

SOURCE: Adapted from A. Coskun Samli and Wladyslaw Jermankowicz, "The Stages of Marketing Evolution in East European Countries," *European Journal of Marketing*, 17:2, 1983, p. 30.

The market in the authoritative system may be considered strictly a seller's market, since on the basis of national economic development plans supply in this system is always kept short of demand. Almost by definition, this situation is reversed in the integrative system. Nonetheless, national economic development plans do not allow supply to exceed demand. Hence, under typical circumstances, a buyer's market is not allowed to exist. The authoritative system does not allow competition to take place. There is some degree of competition among ministries (directive), industry associations (mixed middle), as well as some competition among enterprises (integrative). The integrative system, as shown in the Yugoslavian experience, is very close to a market system. As long as they do not exceed the boundaries established by the economic development plans, enterprises in that country can and do compete.[19]

In general, products under an authoritative macro organization have been, and are, simple and standardized. They reflect frugality and a lack of consumer orientation on the part of the decision makers. Since supply is kept rather short of demand, choice for consumers is virtually nonexistent. Usually, the same products are available at the same prices throughout the country. These products are highly standardized.[20]

A substantial degree of product differentiation and some segmentation exists in the integrative system. Here, consumers have a reasonable choice within the general constraints of frugality, national resource management, and priorities reflected in economic development plans. There are substantially more new products in the integrative system. Most new product ideas come from research at the enterprise level. New product ideas are more scarce in authoritative or directive systems. They are (if any) generated, to a larger extent, at the administrative level or borrowed internationally.[21]

The structure of distribution in the authoritative system is strictly one of national monopoly. Central authority owns, manages, and decides on the logistics of the total distribution system. Different enterprises and different trade associations may have their own outlets in the same area.[22] The outlets may be in direct competition, or sometimes they are in partial competition because of the partial overlay of the product lines carried. The control exerted upon the distribution system in the integrative system is illustrated in central disapproval if the outlet or some of its activities do not fit the national economic plan.

Advertising in the East European systems is not well-developed. This can be attributed to two key factors. First, there is a doctrinarian anti-advertising sentiment stemming from a Marxist stance that advertising is totally wasteful. Second, since many of the economies of the region still enjoy a sellers' market, there is no immediate pressure felt towards advertising in order to stimulate sales. Advertising, however, exists in this region. It has a far different mission, however, than in the Western free market systems. In the authoritative system, advertising is used for ideological purposes. When the central economic plan dictates the production of certain commodities, e.g., shoes, or when the general consumption of a key national product, e.g., milk in Bulgaria, is deficient, advertising is used as a last resort to manipulate the populace and stimulate the consumption of these products. The integrative system, on the other hand, allows advertising for enterprises so that they can promote themselves as well as their products. In addition, through advertising they provide information for the consumers as to where the products are available and how they should be cared for or used.[23]

Pricing in socialist systems, in general, is highly complex and multi-faceted. This complexity stems from the fact that governments typically try to prevent inflation, match supply and demand, stimulate foreign trade, encourage savings and frugality, and still provide a certain desirable quality of life to the populace. These opposing goals and objectives make administered or controlled prices very difficult to manage.

In authoritative systems, all prices are government-administered, so that the discrepancies between supply and demand are partially eliminated. Administered prices are also utilized to assure that the country's role in international trade will not be jeopardized by excessively high prices, which might be the case if the price controls were to be lifted. Except for sections of agriculture and arts and crafts, fixed prices are uniformly set for the whole country by various agencies of the central government.

Integrative systems, on the other hand, call for only a few centrally levied price controls. Prices are established by enterprises as long as the constraints established by the central authority are not violated or undermined.[24] In certain cases, to cope with inflation, the state may establish maximum price levels for certain key industries. The state also indirectly manipulates prices by encouraging competition through opening up import channels.

The Role of Marketing

The perceived role of marketing in the economy is not exactly related to the structure of the economy or the degree of economic development in different East European countries.

In the most decentralized East European country, Yugoslavia, for instance, while enterprises primarily make their own marketing decisions, only a limited degree of emphasis is put on marketing. The role of marketing in this country is conceived to be the coordination of supply and demand. Thus, although it is seen to be necessary to carry on the decentralized functions, marketing, at best, is a neutral force from a macroeconomic point of view.

In Romania, on the other hand, despite the fact that this country is on the opposite end of the authoritative-integrative spectrum, marketing is considered to be an accelerator of economic development. In this respect, marketing plays an active role as a key contributor to the country's economic growth. This is considered to be possible if marketing can stimulate consumers' wishes for better standards of living and speed the realization of these higher standards.

In most of the other East European countries, marketing is attributed a lesser role than in Yugoslavia or Romania. In Hungary, for instance, although it has been agreed that a marketlike mechanism is needed for the economy to fulfill the specific objectives, it is believed that Western marketing methods cannot be adopted as they are. Because of the prevailing political and economic differences, the marketing methods developed and utilized in the West would have to be scrutinized and adopted to the particular needs of the socialist countries.[25]

Future Directions

Almost all East European countries have gone through an economic reform, most of which has represented some evolution in the direction of an emerging quasi-market economy or integrative system. As East European economies faced difficulties with totally centralized and planned decision systems, they started decentralizing; that is, introducing market linkages in the economic system.[26] This decentralization process has not been uniform and, hence, different East European countries have reached different stages of the spectrum. While Yugoslavia is considered to be the most decentralized country, and can be placed on the above spectrum between integrative and laissez-faire systems, Romania is on the opposite end of the spectrum between the authoritative and directive stages.

If one examines the reforms and outcomes that took place in Eastern Europe in general, and in Hungary, Poland, and Yugoslavia in particular during the 60s, it becomes clear that all countries of the region are moving toward the integrative stage. It is also reasonable to observe that nonsocialist countries such as France, Japan, and the United Kingdom are moving further and further away from the laissez-faire state toward the integrative stage. Thus, Eastern and Western macroeconomic systems would seem to be converging. This does not mean, however, that the political systems are moving in the same direction and becoming similar. The East European countries still remain socialist and the Western countries capitalist. This necessarily influences the power structure and the criteria for distributing the national income. The macroeconomic system, therefore, can also be regarded as a means to achieving macrosocietal goals that are different in the two separate political systems. To what extent the convergence process is likely to continue, and how effective it *will become*, remain to be seen. These questions pose serious challenges to researchers dealing with East-West relationships.

Conclusions

This chapter, by attempting to explore the dynamic and changing nature of marketing in Eastern Europe, focused on five key areas: 1) characteristics of marketing evolution; 2) significant influences on the marketing systems; 3) marketing research needs and uses; 4) critical changes in overall marketing functions; and 5) the role attributed to marketing. The emphasis was placed on the fact that, because of the variations in their starting points and the differences in their development patterns, the East European countries present a spectrum of authoritative-integrative macro systems. The characteristics of their respective macro systems determine the conditions for varying market and distribution systems. The general direction for all of these countries has been one of decentralization. All East European countries, at different speeds and with varying degrees of success, have been moving from an authoritative stage toward an integrative stage. Consequently, the marketing systems in these countries have been going through a process of evolution. Through this evolutionary process, the roles that are attributed to marketing systems are changing as well as the system itself. Along with these changes, the need for and the use of marketing research has grown.

Critical changes in marketing functions can be analyzed in terms of the market itself, marketing research, product distribution, advertising, and price decisions. An attempt was made in this chapter to contrast the nature of these functions in an authoritative system with that of those in an integrative system. In this manner, the nature of the overall economic change in East Europe and the specific direction of this change in terms of marketing functions are identified.

The general conclusion of this chapter is that, while significant differences may currently exist in their marketing systems, East European countries are all becoming integrative systems at their own pace and in their own styles. It is further concluded that the Western countries are slowly but surely getting further and further away from the laissez-faire system. Hence, in the future there may be a convergence of the economic and marketing ideologies in these two groups of countries.

Notes

1. Morris Bernstein, "Economic Reform in Eastern Europe," in *East European Economies Post-Helsinki*, Joint Economic Committee, Washington, D.C.: U.S. Government Printing Office, 1977.

2. J. Kormai, *Anti-Equilibrium on Economic Systems Theory and the Tasks of Research*, Amsterdam: North Holland Publishing Company, 1971.

3. W. Jermakowicz, "An Attempt to Classify Management Styles in the Socialist Economic Systems," in Prace INES PW/Warsaw Technical University Publications, 1975;

A. Coskun Samli and Wladislaw Jermakowicz, "The State of Marketing Evolution in East European Countries," *European Journal of Marketing*, 17:2, 1983, pp: 26–33; and Wladislaw Jermakowicz and William A. Ward, "Organizational Structures in the R & D Sphere of Activity," *Clemson Review of Industrial Management and Textile Science*, 1978.

4. Laura O'Andrea Tyson, "The Yugoslav Economy in the 1970s: A Survey of Recent Developments and Future Prospects," in *East European Economies Post-Helsinki*, Joint Economic Committee, Washington, D.C.: U.S. Government Printing Office, 1977.

5. Morris Bernstein, "Economic Reform" and Peter Y. Lauter, "The Changing Role of Marketing in the Eastern European Socialist Economies," *Journal of Marketing*, 35, October 1971, pp: 16–20.

6. Fedor V. Rocco, "Marketing in the Socialist Economy of Yugoslavia," *MSU Business Topics*, Summer 1968, pp. 14–19; A. Coskun Samli and Irene Lange, "Eastern European Markets and Marketing Systems," *Proceedings of Southern Marketing Association*, 1973 Conference, Robert L. King, ed., 1974.

7. Bernstein, "Economic Reform."

8. Wladislaw Jermakowicz and William A. Ward, "Organizational Structures in the R & D Sphere of Activity," in *Clemson Review of Industrial Management and Textile Science*, 1980.

9. Reed Moyer and Stanley Hollander, eds., *Markets and Marketing in Developing Economies* (Richard D. Irwin, Chicago: Illinois), 1968.

10. A. Coskun Samli, *Marketing and Distribution Systems in Eastern Europe* (New York: Praeger Publishers, 1978).

11. A. Coskun Samli, "A Comparative Analysis of Marketing in Romania and Yugoslavia," *The Southern Journal of Business*, 5, July 1970, pp: 110–14. and Laszlo Szabo, "The Methods of Market Research in Socialist Countries, (Palermo: Ill. Millimetro, 1972).

12. Rocco, "Marketing in the Socialist."

13. Robert L. King, "Insight into the Structure and Practice of Marketing Research in a Socialist State: The Polish Experience," in *The Proceedings of Association of Advertising Agencies*, 1982; and Robert L. King, "Enterprise-Level Marketing Research Activity in Poland: The Pardom/Polar Experience," *Journal of Academy of Marketing Science*, 1982b.

14. Samli, *Marketing and Distribution*.

15. Andrzy Hodoly, "Organizations and Methods in Marketing Research in Poland," *Handel Wewnetrzyn*, July/August 1967.

16. Samli, *Marketing and Distribution*.

17. Robert L. King, "Enterprise-Level Marketing."

18. Samli, "A Comparative Analysis," pp: 113–14; and "Marketing and Distribution."

19. Laura O'Andrea Tyson, "The Yugoslav Economy"; and Samli, "Marketing and Distribution."

20. Samli and Jermakowicz, "The State of Marketing," pp: 26–33.

21. Samli, *Marketing and Distribution*.

22. *Ibid.*

23. Leslie Szeplaki, "Advertising in the Soviet Block," *Journal of Advertising Research*, 24, June 1974, pp: 13–17.

24. Rocco, "Marketing in the Socialist," pp: 14–16 and A. Coskun Samli, "Marketing and Distribution."

25. Lauter, "The Changing Role," pp: 16–20.

26. *Ibid.*, pp: 16–20; Morris Bernstein, "Economic Reform"; and Jozsef Bognar, *Balance of Achievements of Twenty-Five Years of Hungary's Economic Development* (Budapest: Hungarian Scientific Council, 1982).

14

COMPARATIVE INSIGHTS INTO JAPANESE MARKETING: MYTHS AND REALITIES

William Lazer

Introduction

The purpose of this chapter is to deal with four main topics, namely: perceptions of Japanese marketing environments, Japanese consumers, management and labor perspectives, and common errors in marketing to Japan. In dealing with Japanese environments, comparisons are made between Japanese and American perceptions about trade, the Westernization of Japan, Japan as an economic power, and the role of competition and cooperation. The section on Japanese consumers notes but a few aspects of consumer behavior. The management and labor discussion focuses on the outlook and responsibilities of Japanese managers; the role of workers and labor unions; Japan, Inc.; Ringi-sho; and the direct transferability of Japanese approaches to the U.S.A. The chapter concludes with a discussion of common errors made by U.S. companies marketing in Japan.

Differences in Perceptions

Free Trade or Protection

If there is one topic now on the minds of both Japanese and U.S. marketers, it is trade. Americans have raised issues about Japanese trading practices, aggressive export policies, and protectionistic market measures. A common view is that if Japan would merely open their markets wider to the U.S. imports and reduce the pressures on their exports, most of our trade difficulties would be resolved. But would that really happen? I think not. At best, it would only serve as a partial short-term stop-gap measure. For rather than protecting markets and easing competition, one should seek to reduce trade barriers in both countries.

What are the reasons for Japanese trade surpluses? Their success in international markets is not, as has been suggested, mainly attributable to cheap Japanese labor, tariff or nontariff barriers, lifetime employment, weak unions, the use of quality circles, or the U.S. free-trade posture. My analysis suggests that a whole host of other factors must be considered, including productivity increases, rational wage policies, consumer savings rates, monetary exchange rates, differences in financial arrangements, government and business relationships, management and labor harmony, labor motivation, modern plant and equipment, and well-designed, quality products.

The main trade problem of the United States is simply that we are not competitive in world markets and, as a result, are losing market share. The situation is exacerbated by barriers erected by Japan and other countries. But the remedy is not additional trade barriers; rather, U.S. companies must find ways to compete efficiently. Japanese competition is now forcing a discipline on U.S. management and labor that is inducing them to take the actions that they should have taken long ago on their own initiative. In turn, U.S. reactions stemming from our own economic distress will stimulate Japan to do what it should have done earlier, namely, open up Japanese markets.

The Westernization of Japan?

A myth exists that Japan has been modernized along the lines of Western ideas and culture. While it is true that Japan has successfully introduced some of our customs, concepts, technology, and products, that does not mark the Westernization of Japan. Rather, Japan has borrowed what applies, absorbing the borrowings into its own fundamentally unchanged society. What has occurred is a massaging of things Western to adapt them to the Japanese culture, resulting in the Japanization of Western culture rather than Westernization of the Japanese culture.

For example, when Western companies tried to introduce cereal into the Japanese breakfast market, the idea of eating cereal with sugar and milk first thing in the morning was not palatable to Japanese tastes. Nevertheless, Westernization did occur because the Japanese began serving Western-style packaged soups to their families for breakfast.[1]

To be successful in Japan, U.S. marketers should recognize the fundamental, distinctive, unique characteristics of the Japanese culture and should reflect them in their marketing approaches. Several Japanese executives have informed the author that this is a major reason for the success of the marketing approaches of companies like Meiji/Borden, 7-Eleven stores, and Coca-Cola.

To highlight what U.S. businesses must do to cultivate Japanese markets, an analogy is often drawn between the Japanese market opportunities and the walnut. The "walnut's rich and nutritious contents are covered by a hard shell. Once one cracks the shell, one may enjoy the tasty contents. But to extricate the meat in its entirety one must carefully maneuver around a complicated and fragile internal structure. Without an understanding of the inner complexity, one may be able to obtain only small crushed pieces of the meat."[2]

Japan, Inc.

It is difficult for Americans to grasp the relationship between government and business in Japan that has been termed Japan, Inc. It usually conjures an undesirable image of government directing and controlling businesses, giving Japanese firms unfair advantage so they achieve great success in international markets. While governmental agencies, such as MITI and the Bank of Japan, exert directional influence and stimulate or deter industries, the Japanese government does not rule by decree, but adopts an "administrative guidance procedure" built on consensus about what would be best for all concerned. The guidance procedure has no legal basis or sanctions, and if companies do not heed, there can only be indirect penalties. Highly coordinated and integrated government/business planning does not exist. Rather, the initiative is taken by a very dedicated bureaucratic group that works closely with businesses without a lot of undue interference by politicians.

The underlying objectives of administrative guidance are to protect and promote Japanese industry such as the government's tobacco monopoly. While businessmen can act against the advice of the bureaucracy, usually they do not and they are particularly good at maintaining harmonious relationships and working out compromises. Businesses deem connections and friendships with government officials to be very important and work hard to maintain and reinforce them. Business and government personnel who graduated from the same class in the same university maintain close liaison and comprise "a club," a very cohesive group. Bureaucrats who retire from the government may be brought into companies that they have dealt with to maintain contacts with the personnel in their old government units.

It has been pointed out to the author that, if Japan, Inc. is seen as a partnership with the bureaucrats, one should be able to identify the bureaucrats and their common objectives. But the objectives of MITI may differ from those of the Bank of Japan, the Ministry of Finance, or the Fair Trade Commission; moreover, the objectives of specific bureaucrats in each would vary. Responsibilities for administrative guidance is not assigned to a specific agency, as integrated government control would suggest.

Americans should remember that many of today's large Japanese business institutions were initially organized by the government and, when they became successful, were sold to private entrepreneurs for relatively low prices. A close working relationship has been maintained whereby business informs the government about key decisions, projects, and strategies when government interests are involved. Moreover, the good relationships maintained with government become essential aspects of such activities as promoting products, gaining market entry, establishing market position, and financing ventures. Japanese executives, unlike U.S. leaders, see government contacts as an important factor in business success and their actions have always been very closely intertwined with the national policy in creating modern Japan.

Japan as a Superpower?

Americans generally conceive of Japan as a highly industrialized, efficient, wealthy nation; a true economic world superpower. After all, Japan produces about 53 percent of the world's ships, 26 percent of the autos, over 25 percent of the TVs and about 15 percent of the steel. Its GNP between 1955 and 1980 increased about ten times, compared to the two-fold U.S. increase, and 14 of the world's top 50 banks are Japanese while only seven are American. Japan's productivity has eclipsed that of the U.S.A., and the quality of their products have set world standards.

But Japanese executives seem to see a different Japan: a small, island country that is poor and lacking in resources, where hard work and group cooperation, rather than rugged individualism, is the best route. They feel they will have to work very hard just to keep up and that they must do their best to cultivate foreign markets and export aggressively to make up for their deficiencies.

Both the Japanese and U.S. perspectives should be brought into a more realistic focus. Americans should look at the total Japanese economy and not at just a few of the powerful, more advanced economic sectors. It is true that there are a small number of highly significant Japanese industries and companies that are very efficient, and it behooves Japanese leaders to recognize this and their changing role as an economic power. However, there also exist a large number of inefficient sectors, including many service industries, wholesaling and retailing institutions, agriculture, housing, as well as such public-sector services as sewer systems, health and medical coverage, and recreation facilities.[3]

The Japanese Way

Americans observing Japanese marketing success have made the error of believing that there can be direct transference of Japanese methods to U.S. situations. But it is not possible to take Japanese approaches rooted in a different culture and put them directly into place in our environment. Moreover, there is no universal model of Japanese organizations. The policies and practices of large firms are, of course, different from small ones. Smaller, new firms do not offer the benefits of security, lifetime employment, and promotions based on length of service, which are often heralded as being typical. And there are even substantial differences among large organizations.

Americans seem to believe that such business qualities as lifetime employment, acquiescent labor unions, large-scale integrated businesses, and cooperation are historical methods of Japanese business operations that have been handed down to contemporary business executives. All of them, however, are really part of postwar Japanese developments, and it must be remembered that, after the way, the Japanese did not have too many alternatives but to cooperate, which may explain how many of the policies of large integrated companies got started.

Inter-Japanese Competition or Cooperation?

Americans do not see Japanese companies competing vigorously among themselves, but see them cooperating and developing monopolies. For Japan is a group society, and the author has been told that cooperation is a Japanese value while competition is not. The Japanese society emphasizes loyalty, harmony, cooperation, and group behavior.

But the Japanese culture is full of paradoxes, and an important factor in Japan's economic development is keen competition within industries. The existence of many independent Japanese companies in industry sectors is sometimes contrasted with our active merger movements and the resulting concentration of power.

Japan, with a population of about 115 million people, has eight different automobile manufacturers compared to our four. Also, about 20 or 25 years ago, U.S. economists explained that if Japan had fewer automobile manufacturers, their industry would be more stable, but that this, however, was opposed by small automobile manufacturers such as Honda and Mazda, who felt that competition would be beneficial.

The Japanese concept of competition does not correspond totally to ours. They want "fair and hard competition," two words used to connote a resistance to mergers and takeovers, which, in view of lifetime employment, would not be acceptable to either labor or management. This also implies limitations by small retailers on larger ones, curbing the excessive competition that results in exceedingly low prices, driving companies out of business, and the acceptance of some forms of business cooperation that are probably illegal in the U.S.A.

Japanese Consumers

Japan is now the second largest consumer market in the free world: roughly 40 percent larger than West Germany and 2.8 times that of Great Britain. It has about 32 million households versus 81 million in the United States, and single-person households account for about 10 percent of the market, while the U.S.A. proportion is over twice as large. Japanese household consumption patterns are generally affected by summer and winter bonuses, which together may account for 20 percent to 40 percent of salaried workers' annual income. Whereas the U.S. has over one-half the wives gainfully employed, in Japan the figure is about one-fourth, but the number is growing. And, like the U.S.A., Japan's population exhibits the same tendencies of aging so that retirement, social security, and medical services are becoming problems.

Americans often reach conclusions about Japanese consumers by observing the so-called visible culture and noting similarities among Japanese and American consumer reactions to products, entertainment, life-styles and family life. But to understand Japanese consumers, attention must be paid to the invisible culture, which is rooted in Japanese values, mores, attitudes, opinion, motivations, and perceptions. For example, Americans often note that Japanese consumers have a high savings rate—a rate three to four times that of U.S. consumers. Can one conclude, therefore, that Japanese consumers are thrifty by nature; that they have a natural propensity to save? Part of their savings behavior relates to the desire to own a home in the light of very high housing costs. It has been estimated that $200,000 spent in suburban New York, as compared with suburban Tokyo, would buy about four times as much space with 20 times as much land area. Part of it also results from high education costs, and the need to provide for retirement, which often occurs between the ages of 55 and 58, in the light of totally inadequate retirement plans, pension funds, and medical insurance.

U.S. manufacturers seem to believe incorrectly that their products meet the needs of Japanese consumers when, in reality, products often have to be redesigned before they can be marketed successfully in Japan. Consider the differences in body dimensions, the size and shape of homes, the size of retail stores and supermarkets, and the host of cultural and environmental factors that are markedly different.

While Japanese housewives spend less time cleaning their houses, they spend more time washing clothes. For instance, they do not want dirty clothes spread around small enclosures. They spend more of their time shopping and less in the kitchen. They are not as likely to develop shopping lists before going to the stores, but do set budgetary limits, along with a plan of how the money will be spent, to guide them. This permits them to indulge in creativity in shopping while limiting expenses.[4]

Japanese consumers have been characterized as being more concerned about quality and not as willing to put up with the shoddy workmanship and poor services that U.S. consumers do. That is one of the reasons stated for the lack of success of U.S. products in Japan. As far as exports are concerned, Japanese producers send their best products abroad and specifically redesign them to meet the needs of U.S. markets.

Japanese consumers are very interested in status. Students compete for positions in prestigious universities, not for the money they will eventually earn, but for the status associated with becoming a member of a powerful Japanese corporation or governmental unit. Employees try to enhance their company's market share and well-being so that they can further their own status expectations. Japanese corporations pay great attention to status and image considerations and take special pride in announcements about prestigious awards, such as the Deming Award or company achievements that have been recognized.

Marketing Management Considerations

Human Factors and Company Loyalty

Many misunderstandings exist in the U.S.A. about lifetime employment, often referred to as one of the underpinnings of the Japanese system. This system is not rooted in antiquity, but began after the war. Not everyone who works for a Japanese company has lifetime employment and not all companies offer it. Small businesses do not generally offer lifetime jobs. Estimates suggest that about one-half the working population, particularly women, are not included. Women tend to be hired as part-time workers and can be laid off, especially if their wages rise too rapidly. Those who work on an hourly or a daily basis, as they are needed, are considered temporary workers, even if they have worked over 40 hours a week for a long time.

While U.S. marketers tend to identify with their professions and occupations, Japanese marketers identify with their companies. To a Japanese, the place of employment is exceedingly important because it is the source of both security and satisfaction. Hiring marketing personnel is not merely a matter of buying marketing skills, but of establishing a very important relationship between the management and employees, since the persons hired are expected to spend the rest of their lives with the company and become an integral part of it.

The company pervades every aspect of one's personal life and there is a real sense of joining. One's attitude towards the company and work is as important as one's skills and competencies. The value of getting along in the group, acting harmoniously, cooperating, and being a contributing member to something that is larger than any person is stressed. Hard work is accepted as a way of life and employees develop the right attitude to enjoy their work.

U.S. executives hiring marketing personnel pay particular attention to industry experience, technical competence, educational backgrounds, and the marketing duties and responsibilities involved. By contrast, Japanese executives see the main duties of marketing personnel as being involved with developing people. And it is this very perspective that marks a key difference between Japanese and U.S. marketing executives. Whereas Japanese executives consider business and marketing to be units of human activity, Americans consider them to be units of business activity.

Japanese marketing managers are responsible for getting marketing personnel to agree, cooperate, work harmoniously for the good of the company, and contribute as much as they can. They know their fellow managers, the clients and subordinates, and strive to get along with them. They spend a great deal of time on personal counselling of subordinates, looking after them and trying to help them out of any difficulties. Contrast this approach with the managerial activities normally considered responsibilities of U.S. marketing managers.

Loyalty is a fundamental Japanese value: loyalty to the nation, to the family, and, indeed, to the company. In exchange for this loyalty, the company may offer lifetime employment. Groups of people enter the company together, go through very similar training and advance at the same time, which results in an escalator effect of a total group. The longer people remain with a company, the greater the benefits they receive for their loyalty.

Even with the group escalator effect, however, not all candidates will make the grade. But just singling out one outstanding individual for promotion and ignoring the rest of the group is considered to be inhumane and is not done. The whole group moves together and, somewhere along the way, a few leaders will emerge. But, unlike in the U.S.A., most company leaders maintain a low profile. No matter how dynamic they are, they concentrate on becoming gentle and skilled in directing and manipulating people.[5]

Japanese companies do not hire university graduates and bring them in at the middle or top management levels, for they are not perceived to be professional experts. Rather, they begin at the bottom, receive beginners' salaries, gain experience, and are educated and trained in the ways of the corporation. Moreover, while Americans believe in the trickle-down theory, that upper management levels have the greatest knowledge and know what is best, in Japan the reverse is often true; the ideas and suggestions of experienced workers are valued and good ideas typically rise from the bottom.

Labor-Management Relationships

Japanese labor, as compared with U.S. labor, seems to be more moderate, practical, and realistic, for unions see themselves as an integral part of the business. Violence, sabotage, destroying equipment, or shutting down factories are not part of their pattern. Unions do not believe that uneconomic demands, or activities that hurt their company, help them; nevertheless, they are well aware of workers' needs and of their own power, and do make themselves felt. But strikes are very brief and the workers may merely wear red armbands or headbands, post their demands, or scream at management.

It is wrong to conclude, as Americans often do, that the lack of labor unrest stems from docile unions. It really results from management's good personal relationships with labor, for management works hard at determining what might be troubling their employees and identifying what can be done to maintain harmonious relations. Management does not permit labor situations to deteriorate to the extent that they do in the U.S.A. Conflicts do indeed exist, but they are resolved in the context of the company, rather than by a union considered to be outside the company.

Japanese workers have often been described as "economic animals" who work after hours and on their days off, do not take all of their vacation, and place their jobs above all else. But Japanese workers, unlike their U.S. counterparts, do not seek work as a matter of exploitation, or of doing something that one hates to do, but as a basic part of their normal life.[6]

Japanese workers assume that when companies are doing exceedingly well everyone has contributed, and that it will be reflected in their bonuses and wage negotiations. It is not merely top management that receives the tangible rewards.

The bases of payment in Japan differ from those in the U.S.A., where contribution made is said to be the fundamental criterion. Rather, people are paid on the basis of their seniority, position, and educational qualifications. In addition to their wages, employees expect a substantial bonus (perhaps two to three months salary, twice a year), leaves of various sorts, as well as a whole host of special allowances for heavy work, night work, or family situations. The seniority system, of course, creates problems of getting rid of incompetent people and placating frustrated, competent young workers who can not be promoted.

Financial Structure

Japanese businesses are less dependent on capital markets, with the result that financial performance does not depend on short-term indicators. Japanese companies are willing to accept lower margins, and ignore short-term profits and current return on investments to obtain larger market shares and better future returns.[7] Thus, U.S. firms with their short-term market share and profit maximization objectives are pitted against Japanese companies working towards long-term objectives.

A number of interesting correlates stem from these differences. For example, since there is no great need to answer to shareholders, Japanese companies pay more attention to growth in market share than they do to corporate profits. They adopt longer-range goals, perspectives, and performance measures. A large portion of their profits can be reinvested. They are more concerned with social responsibilities and Japanese companies are viewed as having major responsibilities to the whole of society and not just to the shareholders. But it should also be noted that such Japanese companies as Sony, Honda and Matsushita, and Ito Yokado are now financed with equity capital.

Ringi-Sho

U.S. observers have contrasted the Japanese ringi-sho decision-making process, a "bottoms up" process, with our own top-down approach. One can be led to believe that all decisions flow from the bottom to the top; unless those at the bottom agree and a consensus is reached, decisions are not made. But some decisions are made at the top and merely communicated downward via the ringi-sho system. Others merely permit various levels of management to express their opinions rather than exercise real decision authority. Moreover, getting a consensus should not be mistaken for total agreement, passive acquiescence, or unanimous approval. Reaching a consensus does not mean that everyone speaks with the same voice, but merely indicates that certain issues are being considered, consultation has occurred through committees, and that some agreement or accord is reached.

Ringi-sho results in duplication of authority, communications bottlenecks, and confusion because decision authority and responsibility are not clearly defined. The U.S. decision-making process takes less time, but decision implementation and execution takes more time. In the Japanese system, where consultation has occurred, those who have been directly involved and informed are motivated to implement decisions.

Understanding Marketing and Distribution Systems

Some writers have a tendency to stress similarities between Japanese and U.S. marketing systems, and to minimize or disregard important differences. A number of paradoxes occur in Japanese marketing that make it easy to be misled by apparent similarities in a few areas. It is prudent, when considering similarities, to remember there may well be other dimensions, less apparent or hidden, that reflect important differences.

U.S. observers of Japanese distribution systems must remember that, in Japan, substance need not follow form. In Japanese companies, marketing functions and responsibilities are defined quite loosely, overlap, and do not neatly fall into departmental units. Organization position is not equated with authority, and the way a marketing system actually functions cannot be deduced from an organization chart. Japanese marketers do not see their duties as being tied to a functional area, such as sales, advertising, or distribution, but to the total company.

Japanese distribution systems have been termed confusing and unintelligible; they have been criticized for their economic inefficiencies and praised for their effectiveness in excluding foreign products from their markets. Economically, they are less efficient than U.S. distribution systems and can present invisible barriers to market entry.[8]

Although distribution appears to present a formidable maze, Americans entering Japanese markets would do well to note the following: traditional Japanese distribution systems have a logic, even though it is foreign to Americans and takes a long time to understand. Innovation is possible, as is the development of new distribution systems, but it is costly and time consuming. The often heard American complaint about the antiquated distribution arrangements may not be as much a complaint about the lack of existing channels, their length, or the disadvantageous position of foreign companies as it is an admission of the lack of understanding of Japanese distribution approaches and rationale.

U.S. companies that have achieved success in the Japanese market have generally accepted the uniqueness of Japanese distribution systems with the attendant variety and layers of middlemen, the oversupply of distribution personnel, and the strong service emphasis. Although Americans are best advised not to meddle with the distribution system, it must nevertheless be recognized that companies can set up a different system and succeed, as both Coca-Cola and Sony did.

U.S. Marketing Approaches: Problems and Errors

When entering Japanese markets, U.S. companies are generally guided by their other international experiences, which tends to compound errors, for what will work in Japan need not work elsewhere and vice versa. The best guideline is to underplay what was done in other markets, emphasize the unique Japanese factors, and develop special marketing programs to account for them.

In the past, U.S. business viewed Japanese markets as offering a little add-on business yielding short-term returns for relatively little investment. Gaining a niche in Japanese markets, however, requires care and long-term commitment, similar to R & D expenditures. And, as Japanese environments change, so must products and marketing approaches, often a task difficult to achieve when U.S. companies are far removed from the scene and work through trading companies and licensees. Interestingly enough, Japanese companies marketing abroad have been careful to make the appropriate adjustments, which has meant replacing their own locally produced labor-intensive products with those imported from lesser developed countries. U.S. companies should adopt a similar posture and supply some Japanese markets from third-country bases. Examples exist of U.S. manufacturers that have successfully introduced new products into Japan over time, gained market position, and still not given these markets the attention and resources they deserved. The result was an invitation to Japanese companies to step in and take over, which they did.

Mistakes occur when the U.S. marketing model is assumed to exist in Japan. For example, in selling to Japanese retailers, U.S. manufacturers sometimes act as though they are dealing with American retailers and expect them to adhere to U.S. inventory standards. But Japanese retailers have severe space limitations, face exceedingly high space costs, and require suppliers with inventories located nearby and dependable, and frequent delivery schedules, perhaps daily, to meet their needs. Surely, this is inefficient by U.S. standards, but it is a requisite of successful marketing in Japan.

What can U.S. companies do to gain larger, more profitable shares of Japanese markets? That is a question this author has been investigating for almost 25 years by questioning prominent Japanese executives, professors, consultants, and graduate students, and by studying relevant research results. To date, although not listed in order of importance, the following eight conclusions have been reached.

1. U.S. companies do not work hard enough at understanding the Japanese culture, consumers' tastes, life-styles, and environments. The result is that important market factors are often neglected.

2. An unwillingness exists among U.S. companies to modify their products to better fit Japanese wants and needs. Rather, products that meet U.S. specifications are offered to Japanese markets.

3. There is a lack of understanding of the unique characteristics of Japanese marketing practices, particularly of Japanese distribution systems. The complexities of the distribution systems, including the role of trading companies and the variety of wholesalers and small retailers must be understood.

4. In dealing with Japanese employees, U.S. companies often disregard major differences between their own personnel management practices and those of Japanese companies. Included are such practices as basing compensation and promotion on seniority, lifetime employment, and the paternalistic treatment of employees, all part of the work culture.

5. U.S. firms have not attempted to understand the Japanese mind, or the reasons for various Japanese business approaches. They have sometimes refused to take seriously the advice and observations given by Japanese, glossing over marketing differences. Some have the serious mistake of viewing Japan as just an extension of the U.S. market, and attempted to do things in the "good old American way."

6. Americans often disregard important Japanese business practices. For example, it is not common practice to replace wholesalers or distributors in a short period of time just because they have not performed well economically. It is important to stress the human aspects and not just short-term returns. Companies do not engage in hostile mergers in Japan, and the standards of hard and fair competition have different meanings.

7. Informed Japanese executives keep on asking the same question, reflecting an isue that has been raised by others, namely, "What has happened to U.S. entrepeneurship? What has happened to the American willingness to work?" Perhaps, answers to that question will go a long way in helping U.S. business to succeed in Japanese markets.

8. U.S. businesses do not understand and appreciate the differences between U.S. and Japanese pricing arrangements, particularly the extension of credit, financing wholesalers, retailers and discount structures. Japanese arrangements can be quite different.

Conclusions

U.S. and Japanese economic well-being is inextricably intertwined: one cannot advance greatly without the other, and what one does affects the other. Japan and the U.S.A. will have to view each others' economic situation with insight, patience, understanding, and an appreciation of the differences in values and perceptions involved.

The solution to current trade problems is rooted in the long-term reduction of trade barriers and the advancement of free trade by both sides. At the same time, great sensitivities to the short-term economic and social problems of each nation must be maintained. And Japan must recognize the great changes that have occurred in its economic status, for it is a world economic power and some additional responsibilities have been thrust upon her.

U.S. companies will have to adopt a longer-range perspective in their marketing practices in Japan and become more sensitive to important cultural differences, Japanese business methods, and the Japanese mind. They should recognize that they can learn much from Japanese businesses but cannot transfer Japanese approaches and techniques directly to U.S. settings; rather, they will have to massage and modify them. Is it not interesting that Japanese businesses took a uniquely American technology—marketing—modified it, utilized it most effectively, and became marketers to the world. The new challenge to U.S. marketing is to make the appropriate adjustments so that its technology can meet the tests of the new international realities.

Notes

1. George Fields, "The Japanese Housewife: A Marketing Appraisal," in Paul Norbury and Geoffrey Bounas, eds., *Business in Japan*, Boulder, Colorado: Westview Press, 1980, p. 77.

2. Mitsuaki Shimaguchi and William Lazer, "Japanese Distribution Channels: Invisible Barriers to Market Entry," *MSU Business Topics*, Winter 1979, p. 49.

3. Jon Woronoff, *Japan: The Company Economic Crisis*, Lotus Press, Tokyo 1979, p. 168.

4. George Fields, "The Japanese Housewife", p. 79.

5. Jon Woronoff, *Japan: The Company*, pp: 65–75.

6. Shi-Ichi Takezawa and Arthur M. Whitehall, *Work Ways, Japan, and America*, (Tokyo: Japan Institute of Labor, 1981), pp: 49–73.

7. Paul Norbury and Geoffrey Bownas, *Business in Japan*, (Boulder, Colorado: Westview Press, 1980).

8. Mitsuaki Shimaguchi and William Lazer, "Japanese Distribution," pp: 49–62.

15

MARKETING IN THE PRC

Mun Kin-chok

Compared with the Soviet Union and other socialist countries of East Europe, China started her economic reforms at a much later stage. Before 1979 China basically followed the 1950s Russian model of adopting a highly centralized command system, under which the role and the scope of marketing had essentially been restricted only to fulfill the tasks inherent in the state economic development plans. The importance of marketing in China, however, has been growing ever since her economic and management reforms began in 1979.[1]

This chapter explores the problem faced by China's plan-based command system and the growing role of marketing in her reformed plan-based and market-directed system. To this end, the discussion will focus on the state-owned enterprises in the manufacturing sector of the Chinese economy.

Lack of Adaptability and Flexibility in the Plan-Based Command System

Enterprises Are Lifeless

Under China's command system, the whole national economy was treated as a single unit and the state-owned enterprises in the country as its branches. The state, including the central, provincial, and municipal authorities, was the superior, while the business enterprises became subordinates of the state. The state set the production targets for the enterprises, distributed their products, assigned their personnel, allocated their supplies and equipment, took over their profits, and covered all their losses. Since the enterprises were organizations for the implementation of state plans, they received neither decision-making authority nor economic responsibility from the state, thus making it unnecessary to adapt economic calculations and national marketing planning to changing social needs. The command system discouraged the state-owned enterprises from taking any initiative for their own growth and made them become lifeless entities.[2]

Irrational Product Planning

As production levels were generally used as the indicator of economic performance, the state-owned enterprises devoted exclusive attention to quantity and neglected quality. In order to achieve their quantitative targets in terms of production value or volume, many enterprises produced large quantities of unmarketable products. Thus, an acute shortage of many products coincided with large stockpiles of goods rotting and rusting in warehouses.

To achieve a high production value, the enterprises preferred the production of high-priced goods to low-priced goods, irrespective of the users' demand, resulting in irrational product planning. While the high-priced goods were overproduced, low-priced goods were limited in supply. In 1978, 24 percent of consumer goods manufactured by the industries in Shanghai faced the problem of overproduction while only 4 percent of the goods manufactured had an excess demand.

Price Rigidity

Since the prices of the products were fixed by the state, the enterprises had no authority to adjust them according to the changing conditions of production or demand. Price rigidity had left the enterprises no adaptability or flexibility.

Due to development expenditure, the costs of new products would generally be high. But, for the purposes of price stability, a higher price for a new product was rarely approved. One factory had developed an antiwind match, with higher production costs. To cover the costs, the new match, based on the calculations, should be sold for 30 cents Renminbi, which would be 10 cents higher than an ordinary match. But, for reasons of "price stability," the price control department of the state did not approve this new higher price. The Bureau of Commerce, which is the state organization responsible for purchasing consumer goods from the enterprises, had to stop further purchasing and so the factory dropped their new product.[3]

In response to social needs, the final prices of some new products had been set below their costs. The resulting losses to the Bureau of Commerce had been covered by the Ministry of Finance. To produce these new money-losing products, the enterprises were required to submit their proposals to the state for approval. But the bureaucratic procedures had discouraged initiatives on the part of the enterprises to develop new products.

Another unfavorable impact of the fixed-price policy on new product development has been the absence of cost reductions. The development of the watch industry in China started in the 1950s. The prices of the watches had purposely been set at a high level in order to stimulate enterprises to manufacture them, because the generally preferred high-priced goods were, as mentioned above, preferred over low-priced ones. With the increased production, costs of the watches had begun to decrease because of the increasing scale economies. Because the prices of watches were not reduced, demand was not stimulated. Consequently, the inventories of watches increased.[4]

Because of the fixed-price policy, a number of new products had to be eliminated from manufacturing plans. Also, the production of many old products was suspended due to the price inflexibility upwards. It has been estimated that the total number of consumer goods sold in the department stores of Beijing in 1978 was 6,000 less than the peak level in the past.[5]

Very often, prices for different sizes of the same product were fixed and hence led to a misallocation of the resources in the product planning of the enterprises. For example, in an electric light bulb factory, the price of a low-watt bulb (15w–45w) was so low that selling one bulb incurred a loss of two cents Renminbi, while a much higher price had been set for a high-watt bulb making a profit margin of 50 to 60 percent. Because of this price relation between low-watt and high-watt bulbs, the factory had been induced to concentrate its productive resources in manufacturing the high-watt bulbs, though the market demand for the former had been higher than that of the latter. As a result, the low-watt bulbs were short of supply while the inventory of high-watt bulbs increased.[6]

Price rigidity had also resulted in a different profit rate between manufacturing and distribution sectors. Generally speaking, the profit rates in the distribution sectors were higher than that of the manufacturing sectors. For example, in Guangxi province, the profit rate of shoes and leather cases for the manufacturing and distribution sector were 3 percent and 24 percent, respectively.[7] In 1979, the profits of one ton of sugar in the distribution sector were 200 Renminbi compared to 100 Renminbi in the manufacturing sector. One of the reasons for this was price inflexibility in the manufacturing sector when the input price of raw materials had been increased.

An Ineffective Distribution System

Theoretically speaking, there is great potential in China for organizing the socialist distribution system effectively, as all distribution channels are owned by the state. However, the Chinese distribution system is ineffective, as measured by out-of-stock products and overstocked inventories. The main reason for the ineffective distribution system in China is ideological. It's basis is Karl Marx's contention that "all expenses of circulation, which arise only from changes of form, do not add any value to the commodities."[8] In other words, any capital investment in the distribution or service sector is considered unproductive. For this reason, the compilation of national income in China, as in other socialist countries, has excluded the production value contributed by the service sector.

Investment in the distributive sector was 1.5 percent of total investment during the period of China's first Five-year Plan (1952–1957), after which it began to decrease. In 1978 the percentage of distribution investment of total investment was cut down to only 0.46. As a result, the total number of retail outlets of consumer goods in China has been reduced from 2.8 million in 1957 to 1.3 million in 1978, a decrease of 53 percent.[9] The number of retail outlets as per 1,000 persons in 1957 was 10, but it has been reduced to 1.5 in 1980.[10] In proportion to population growth over the past 30 years (from 600 million in the 1950s to 900 million in 1979), retail outlets have obviously been underdeveloped. Also, the percentage of persons employed in the distribution sector of the economy has decreased from 1.4 percent in 1957 to 1 percent in 1978.

In the industrial goods sector, the distribution method used in the past three decades has also been ineffective. Industrial goods, including raw materials, components, equipment, and tools have been distributed exclusively through a central allocation system. After a national allocation plan was set, the enterprises then formulated their production and supply plans according to the demand from the various central ministries and local authorities. The enterprises would receive a distribution list showing the buyers of their output and needed amounts. At an "order meeting," which generally was organized on an annual or semi-annual basis, the buyers (central and local authorities) placed their orders for the industrial goods needed. The enterprises were responsibile for delivery. Central government and local authorities had set up their own resource and supply departments responsible for the purchasing and allocation of these industrial goods.

This allocation system of industrial goods resulted in a communication gap between the producers and the users. The goods manufactured often did not meet the requirements of the users in terms of product quality, standard, and selection. The enterprises had to go their own way to get what they needed. Purchasers from the enterprises rushed for goods everywhere, a sign of the sharp contradiction between supply and demand.

To make certain that production would not be interrupted by inadequate supply, the enterprises intentionally overestimated their requirements for the necessary raw materials, components, and equipment.[11] Fighting for more supplies therefore became an important task of enterprise managers in China. The overrequest for supplies made by enterprises was not only to assure their own production; it also served to put the enterprises in a good position to exchange these surplus supplies with other manufacturers for goods that would be needed but not allocated by the state. As a consequence, many enterprises often stocked far more supplies than they really needed.

The Growing Importance of Marketing in the Plan-based and Market-directed System

Having recognized the low adaptability and flexibility in her plan-based command system, China decided in 1979 to introduce the market mechanism and incorporate it into her planned economy.[12] The market mechanism has been considered a supplementary device to a state plan-based system, aiming at an improvement in its adaptability to increasingly diversified social needs. To make the marketing system more adaptable and flexible, six major breakthroughs have been made by the economic and management reforms in China:

- Delegating the decision-making authority to the designated enterprises (about 6,000) in respect to profit-sharing, depreciation, purchasing, and marketing.
- Recognizing profit as the main criterion for evaluating enterprise performance.
- Recognizing competition as a means of increasing management efficiency.
- Recognizing the effectiveness of the price mechanism: permission of the use of negotiated or floating price as the regulator of supply and demand.
- Recognizing industrial goods as a commodity; distribution through open markets as a supplementary channel to the central allocation system.
- Recognizing the communication effectiveness of advertising.

Increasing Demand-oriented Product Planning

The pilot enterprises have been delegated the authority, after fulfilling the state plan, to develop prospective new products according to their capacity and market demand. To enable the pilot enterprises to develop new products, the state has cut down the production targets of the existing products originally set for these manufacturing units, thus releasing their productive capacity.[13]

Users' needs have become the focal point of the new product planning. To make a more reliable estimate of demand, market research has been conducted by these pilot enterprises—for example, the users' survey. In the planning for consumer products, the purchasing power of consumers has been studied as an information basis for setting prices. Some pilot enterprises have successfully developed good connections with foreign buyers. Products have been manufactured according to the specifications given to them. Sales representatives have been sent by some enterprises to overseas markets for the purposes of negotiation and collection of market information.

Because of competition, brand names of the products have been emphasized in order to distinguish higher- and lower-quality products. The use of brand names has had a favorable effect on increasing the enterprise initiative. It has been found that the profits of better brands were higher than those of ordinary brands. Generally speaking, brand names of the manufacturing enterprises in Shanghai have gained a much more favorable image as compared with that of other regions, primarily because of better technology and more skillful labor. As product development in the pilot enterprises has shifted from a production-orientation to a marketing-orientation, a tendency to increase the number of new products has emerged.

Introduction of the Floating Price

For the launching of new products, prices have generally been allowed to adjust downwards. Chungking Steel Mill produced 500,000 tons of steel in 1979, of which 100,000 tons were sold at a price lower than the fixed price set by the state. Also, a plastic materials factory in Chengtu solved its inventory problem and increased its exports by reducing the price by 13 percent. Under the floating price policy, competition has developed. When a machine tool factory in Jiangsu province reduced its price of a quality product, the manufacturer of similar products in other places had to follow in order to attract buyers.

In some cases, the enterprises have also raised their prices—though not by more than 5 percent above the state-approved price—just because the market would bear the new, higher price.

Distribution of Industrial Goods through the Open Market

The first open market for industrial goods set up in Shanghai in 1979 was named "the Shanghai Means-of-Production Exchange," playing the role of a Hongniang*—the matchmaker.[14] The form and organization of this "means-of-production exchange" is similar to that of an exhibition. Manu-

---

*Hongniang is a maid-servant in the Chinese classical drama *Western Chamber* who helps her mistress break the yoke of the feudal ethical code and marry her lover. Hence, in China this name is given to those who act as go-betweens, helping two parties to achieve a common objective. Here the common objective is to find potential trading partners.

facturers from different places or provinces set up a sales office here, dealing with the work related to selling, buying, negotiation, and consulting with prospective customers.

Previously, the collective enterprises, like other state enterprises, could only obtain their capital goods through a central allocation system. But now they are able to get them through this open market. The Shanghai Means-of-Production Exchange has also sent sales personnel to various parts of the country for sales promotion. Following the successful experience in Shanghai, about 60 similar open markets for industrial goods have been organized in different provinces of the country.

The Growth of Direct Sales

With the increased autonomy, direct selling in the manufacturing units of both industrial and consumer goods sectors has been growing.

In most enterprises manufacturing machinery, tools, and equipment, the production quotas assigned by the state have not been sufficient to fully utilize their capacity. The reason for this has been primarily due to a change in the economic structural policy in favor of developing consumer goods industries. The excess capacity has ranged from 60 percent to 90 percent. Consequently, the enterprises have been induced to start selling direct in order to offset the decreased income resulting from the reduced production orders of the state plan.[15] Factory managers and engineers have visited the users and potential buyers in different provinces of the country. Other selling methods to narrow down the gap between the enterprises and the users have also been used, such as setting up sales outlets, selling through cable, telephone, mail order, consignment, and exhibitions.

In the consumer goods sector, the distribution channels also tend to be shortened by reducing two or three levels. For example, some clothing factories sell their products not through the traditional channel of the state wholesale organizations but directly to the retailers. The average time period of the distribution of clothing from manufacturers to retailers previously had been two to three months, but this has been cut down to one month and in some cases to only three to five days.[16]

Developing Market Communications

Since the economic reforms, newspapers with large circulations at central or provincial levels are permitted to accept commercial advertisements, but the numbers placed have been rather small. Due to their emphasis on political contents, their poor printing, and limited number of pages, newspapers are unattractive to advertisers. *Renmin Ribao* (*People's Daily*), published in Beijing, is the leading newspaper in China, with a nationwide circulation of 7 million. Nearly all the advertisements in

Renmin Ribao are for industrial goods, an indication of the marketing problem in the industrial goods sector. Rate of advertisement per newspaper page ranges from US $10,000 to $20,000.

Market, a bi-weekly newspaper which began publication in October 1979, concentrates on the reporting of consumer goods. The response of consumers to this nontraditional newspaper has been very favorable; its circulation has increased to over 1 million in a short time. Compared with other newspapers, *Market* has obviously many more commercial advertisements, but the majority are in the area of industrial goods. The rate of a half-page in *Market* is US $3,000.

Television stations in China which accept TV commercials are the Central, Beijing, Tientsin, Shanghai, Nanking, Guangdong, and Guangzhou stations. Channel 2 of the Central TV station has an audience of 200 million, the largest among all TV stations. The rate for a 30-second spot charged by Central is about US $4,000. Other TV stations have a much lower audience rate, Beijing having 3 million and Guangdong 1 million. The total number of TV sets in China was estimated at 5 million in 1980, and the number since then has been increasing.

Radio appears to be the most effective mass medium for advertising in China, judging from its audience of 60 million. Almost every urban family owns a radio, and in rural areas the majority do.

Generally speaking, advertising in China is considered a means of providing information about and creating primary demand for a product class rather than a persuasive or competitive tool to stimulate selective demand for a company brand. However, when the number of companies increases, and with the advent of product proliferation, advertising will be used by more Chinese companies as a managerial-decision tool. A comparison of the marketing system of the Peoples Republic of China before and after economic reforms is given in Table 15.1.

Factors Affecting the Effectiveness of China's Marketing System

Although the role of marketing in the PRC has been growing since economic and management reforms, the effectiveness of China's marketing system will essentially be affected by the following factors:

1. Degree of enterprise autonomy
2. A rational price system
3. Market protectionism of regions
4. Underdeveloped transportation facilities.

Let's examine these factors in turn, thus highlighting the most important components of the Chinese marketing system.

TABLE 15.1
PRC Marketing System

	Under the plan-based command system	Under the plan-based and market-directed system
Environment		
Priority order of economic sector	heavy industry, agriculture, light industry	agriculture, light industry, heavy industry
Competition between enterprises	none	increasing
Cooperation between enterprises of different industrial ministries	none	increasing
Transportation facilities and system	backward	backward
Political movements	many	less
Standard of living	low	improving
State enterprises		
Relationship with the state	subordinate	subordinate
Nature of instructions given by the state	imperative	both imperative and indicative
Decision-making authority	little	increasing
Economic responsibility	little	increasing
Orientation of manufacturing	product-oriented	increasingly marketing-oriented
Plans to be implemented	state plan	state plan enterprise plans
Market Segmentation	undifferentiated	increasing differentiation
Sales organization	small and unimportant	expanding and increasing in importance
Marketing mix		
Market research and survey	none	increasing
Product design	local standard	increasing use of international standard
New product development	little	increasing

(continued next page)

TABLE 15.1 *(continued)*

	Under the plan-based command system	*Under the plan-based and market-directed system*
Marketing mix		
Test marketing	no	yes
Before-sales service	no	yes
After-sales service	no	yes
Price	rigid	fixed price, floating price, negotiated price
Quantitative discounts	no	yes
Personal selling	none	increasing
Sales promotion	none	increasing
Advertising	none	increasing
Channel of Distribution:		
Industrial goods:	allocation system	allocation system through market direct selling
Consumer goods:	single long channel	multiple shorter channels
Exports and Imports:	through the corporations of Foreign Trade Ministry	through the corporations of Foreign Trade Ministry
		corporations of the related Industrial Ministry

Degree of Enterprise Autonomy

Conflict has arisen between the uniformity of national policy and enterprise autonomy under the economic and management reforms, as with increased authority enterprises have been induced to seek their own interest. As a result, cases of the following sort have emerged:

a) Enterprises have tended to manufacture the goods showing higher profits, though they have not been included in the state plan originally assigned to the enterprises. Goods with lower profits but higher social benefits have been overlooked.

b) Some enterprises have tried to raise their selling prices for highly demanded goods without getting permission from the state.

c) To promote their sales, some enterprises have used rebates and bribes.

d) To promote their exports to Hong Kong, some enterprises have shipped their goods directly to the buyers, bypassing China's sole agent in Hong Kong. This illicit transshipment has brought difficulties for China's sole agent and dealers in Hong Kong.

e) Bonuses have been widely used in the enterprises to stimulate worker's production enthusiasm. In order to be able to dole out more bonuses and to increase their profits, some enterprises arbitrarily raised their product prices or even passed off their defective products as quality merchandise. Through giving bonuses, enterprises have been in the position to reduce the profits to be turned over to the state.

The increased autonomy may gradually weaken the degree of state control over the enterprises, and hence China's economic system may move to a Yugoslavian type, under which ownership of enterprises has been transferred from the "state" to "society." China appears, at least at present stage, to prefer not to move in this direction. Consequently, the state is once again emphasizing the importance of national uniformity and of an imperative order to the state enterprises. After a few years of experimentation with market mechanisms in the economy and increasing the enterprise autonomy, China is apparently considering whether a repositioning of her economic system closer to the Romanian one among the socialist countries is needed. The Romanian economic system is a more centralized type than that of Hungary and Yugoslavia. If China decides to move in that direction, the adaptability and flexibility of state enterprises in relation to social needs will be reduced, even though not necessarily to the old level. If China moves to an Hungarian-type economic system, the importance of marketing is expected to grow in the future.

A Rational Price System

Since economic and management reforms, price rigidity has been reduced slightly, a indicated earlier, by introducing floating and negotiated prices. This price flexibility, however, is rather small, particularly in respect to the upper limit for the upward price adjustments. Enterprises can generally achieve higher profits by reducing their manufacturing costs, but some of the input prices are fixed at a high level due to economic inefficiency of production or simply an improper price setting. This would discourage the enterprises from developing new products, as in the case before reform.

In contrast, input prices for coal, steel, and industrial raw materials have been fixed at a rather low level without any adjustments for many years. Consequently, enterprises producing these products have lost their initiative, while enterprises using these products as inputs have benefited from the low costs, particularly if the selling prices of their products are fixed at a rather high level.

Without a rational pricing system, the effectiveness of the marketing system in China will clearly be lessened. However, to set up a rational pricing system is not an easy task for China, as Martin Feldstein pointed out: "Achieving an appropriate realignment of prices is extremely difficult for China. Without a complete system of free markets, there is no automatic way to learn what input and output are really worth."[17]

Market Protectionism of Regions

Another factor affecting the efficiency of the marketing system in China is the market protectionism of provinces. For financial reasons, each province has tried to protect its regional market for its own manufactured goods, for example, by setting higher prices for the competing products from other provinces.

A similar situation has been found in the supply of raw materials. A province that has an adequate supply of raw materials and fuels might prefer to reserve them for its own production or for exports rather than to sell them to other provinces. This economic regionalism has reduced the flow of products and resources among the different regions, and resulted in a number of separated markets, lacking the economies of a nationwide market.

Underdeveloped Transportation Facilites

Lack of developing a nationwide market in China is not only affected by the market protectionism of different regions, but also hampered by her underdeveloped transportation facilities. A comparison of China's transportation facilities with those of Japan and the USA is shown in Table 15.2.

TABLE 15.2

A Comparison of China's Transportation with Those of Japan and U.S.A., 1977

	China	Japan	U.S.A.
Road length ('000 Km)	950	1,078	6,177
Commercial vehicles in use ('000)	685	11,610	27,610
Railway track ('000 Km)	65	52	600
Shipping ('000 gross tonnage)	3,589	39,812	16,188
Civil aviation (Kilometers flow million)	11	276	3,732

SOURCE: International Marketing Data and Statistics, 4th edition, Euromonitor Publications Ltd., 1979, pp: 300–03. Annual Economic Report of China (1981), Hong Kong, VI–18.

The backwardness of transportation in China has segregated a number of regional markets from the nationwide market, thus resulting in a less efficient marketing system.

Marketing in the Future

The successful experiences of the experimental enterprises have shown that the market mechanism is also workable and effective in the planning economy of China. The government has shown a great determination to change the present rigid system, which is production-oriented and allocation-based, into a more flexible system, in which the market mechanism is incorporated with the national economic planning. The scope of the national planning, as many economists suggested, should be restricted only to key industrial goods. On the other hand, production of most goods, particularly consumer goods, should be guided by the market mechanism. Academics and senior government officials have admitted that through the market mechanism productive resources can be better allocated and consumer needs better satisfied. The marketing concept has been introduced in enterprises only recently and is expected to be developed in the coming years.

As consumer satisfaction is becoming one of the major objectives of the new economic policy, as reflected by the higher priority order of light industry than agriculture and heavy industry, an increase in retail outlets, service, and entertainment businesses is expected. From the macroeconomic aspect, the expansion of the consumer goods industries will result in a higher derived demand for industrial goods and resolve a part of the marketing problem of the latter. Given expanding enterprise autonomy and increasing competition, distribution channels are expected to be shortened for the purpose of reducing costs. To make better decisions, marketing research will be used to a greater extent by both national and enterprise planners. During marketing development, the practice of employing advertising as a means of developing customer awareness in an initial stage will probably evolve into its use in brand competition at a later stage.

Notes

1. See Mun Kin-chok, "China's Management System and State Enterprise Behavior," *Journal of Contemporary Business*, 10:3, 1981.

2. Jiang Yinei, "The Theory of an Enterprise-based Economy," *Social Sciences in China*, 1, 1980, Social Science Publishing House of China, Beijing, p. 59.

3. Sung Young-yin, "The Relationship Between Planning and Price Mechanism," *The Relationship Between Planning and Market in a Socialist Economy*, Social Science Publishing House of China, Beijing, 1979, p. 208.

4. Kung Fai-hsin, "Encouraging the Development of Light Industry by Proper Use of the Price Mechanism," *The Relationship Between Planning and Market in a Socialist Economy*, op. cit, pp: 732–33.

5. Yong-yin, "The Theory of an Enterprise," p. 209.

6. Lo Yen-min, "The Important Problem of Handling the Relationship Between Planning and Market," *The Relationship Between Planning and Market in a Socialist Economy*, op. cit., p. 267.

7. Fai-hsin, "Encouraging the Development," p. 730.

8. Karl Marx, *Capital* (Chicago: Charles H. Kerr and Co., 1907), p. 169, as quoted by Reed Moyer in "Marketing in the Iron Curtain Countries," *Journal of Marketing*, 30, 1966, p. 3.

9. "More Attention Should Be Paid to the Distribution of Commodity," *Economic Research*, 5, 1980, Beijing, p. 33.

10. *Market*, 19, 1980, Beijing, p. 1.

11. Shih Hsiu-lin, "The Supply of Capital Goods Should Be Based on an Integration of Planning with Marketing," *The Relationship Between Planning and Market in a Socialist Economy*, op. cit., p. 297.

12. Xue Muqiao, "A Tentative Study of the Reform of the Economic System," *Economic Research*, 6, 1980, Beijing, p. 3.

13. Lin Zili, "The Initial Reforms of Chinese Economic System—Comments on the Experiments in Increasing the Enterprise Autonomy in Sichuan, Anhui and Zhejiang Provinces," *Social Sciences in China*, 3, 1980, Beijing, p. 4.

14. Economic Readjustment and Reform, *Beijing Review*, special feature series, 1982, p. 136. See also Zhang Yongnian, "A Survey of the Market for the Means-of-Production in Shanghai," *Social Sciences in China*, Shanghai Academy of Social Sciences, 2, 1980.

15. Zhang Pinqian and Ziao Liang, "After Capital Goods Enter the Market—A Report on the Distribution of Machinery and Electrical Appliances through the Market," *Social Sciences in China*, 5, 1980, pp: 162–65.

16. "Promoting Garment Industry by Integration of Production and Marketing," *Economic Management*, 6, 1980, Beijing, p. 39.

17. Martin Fieldstein, "China's Experiment with a Market Economy," *The Asian Wall Street Journal*, July 3, 1982.

VII

COMPARATIVE MARKETING SYSTEMS: AN EVALUATION

The purpose of the first chapter in this part by Kaynak is to explore the methodological framework of comparative marketing systems studies. To this end, a comprehensive search of the literature has been carried out to help describe and evaluate the comparative marketing studies undertaken to date. An attempt has also made to identify unresolved research issues in the area, and an alternative methodology is suggested to develop an improved conceptual basis for studies in comparative marketing systems.

In the last chapter, the editors argue that it is desirable at this point to have some suitable body of scholars map out the comparative marketing systems field by: a) establishing some research priorities, e.g., what countries, what periods, what sectors, what problems, how and with what resources?; b) suggesting suitable conceptual schemes of analysis; c) designing methodologies that can be used and applied in more than one country over a period of time and; d) presenting a critical evaluation and interpretation of existing research. There is also an urgent need for mutually supportive theoretical and empirical research in comparative marketing research. A greater effort is required to bridge the gap between normative and empirical studies in comparative marketing. In the future, emphasis should be placed on analytical and synthesizing research endeavors rather than mostly on descriptive studies. More micro-oriented comparative studies should be conducted. Additional insights into rural marketing systems as well as rural-urban linkages are needed.

16

COMPARATIVE MARKETING SYSTEMS: PAST, PRESENT, AND FUTURE

Erdener Kaynak

Introduction

Comparative studies have been used widely in many fields, including comparative studies in the behavioral sciences, including marketing, are and hypotheses.[1] The term "comparative marketing" has traditionally meant any type of marketing study conducted outside North America. Generally, comparative studies in the behavioral sciences, including marketing, are thought to focus on the universality of the phenomena studied in different systems, societies, and countries.[2] It is the process whereby two or more marketing systems and practices can be compared and/or contrasted.

The purpose of this chapter is to: (a) describe and evaluate the comparative marketing, where it is necessary to construct and test theories existing comparative analyses; (c) identify unresolved research questions, implications, and issues; and (d) suggest an alternative methodology which may be practical in reality as well as logical in general. Every effort will be made to encourage further research in this area and to highlight unresolved research questions for the benefit of prospective researchers.

What Is Comparative Marketing?

Comparative marketing generally tends to emphasize differences among markets and marketing practices resulting from variations in factors such as socioeconomic level, state of technology, cultural systems, and legal frameworks. This emphasis has resulted in a casual and uncritical political use of comparative marketing techniques and concepts, but one that has had acceptance because of the ease with which visual comparisons or contrasts can be made by researchers observing two or more business systems.[3] Examples of "comparative" evidence would include smaller distributive institutions in one country than another, buyers rather than sellers taking initiative in market search and negotiation, and management decisions made with either greater haste or greater deliberation. Strictly speaking, such evidence is descriptive rather than comparative.

A comparative marketing study is not simply a description of marketing in another country. It is an examination of the relationships existing between marketing and its environment in two or more countries. Studies stressing differences and providing descriptive material may be interesting but are not effective for either managerial decision making or rigorous comparative marketing analyses. While it may be interesting to compare how consumers buy or how products are distributed elsewhere, there is little value in such information for businessmen or academicians in different countries unless it can be operationalized and generalized. However, comparison without solid descriptive data would only deal with skeletons while descriptive data without some attempt at comparison will hold less promise of advancing the discipline of marketing. For this reason, the study requires recognition that differences in marketing practices are as important as similarities.

Differences that might be emphasized in simple comparisons may become similarities when related to an environmental frame of reference.[4] Environmental variables such as physical or geographical attributes, as well as socioeconomic and technological factors, cultural elements and political-legal factors, characterize a country's society, and influence its marketing systems.

Early Studies

Comparative marketing had its beginning in the early 1950s as a result of increased trade between North American and West European firms. The expansion of the United States business operations abroad has been explosive in the post-World War II period.[5] Increased trade with overseas countries spurred a concerted effort to develop basic concepts, ideas, and directions in comparative marketing studies, commencing with James A. Haggler in 1957. Two years later, comparative marketing as a subject for study was introduced at a national conference of the American Marketing Association.[6] Early work proposed guidelines and frameworks for undertaking comparative studies of domestic marketing systems.[7] An example is *Comparative Marketing: Wholesaling in Fifteen Countries*, published in

1963. Bartels, its editor, pioneered in the field by designing a framework upon which many succeeding works have been constructed.[8] Bartels argues that, in general, comparative marketing involves following three types of interpretations: (a) the relationship between social conditions in a country and the manner in which marketing is practiced; (b) the character and operation of the marketing mechanism itself; and (c) the patterns of personal behavior and interaction in the sociomarketing activity. On these bases, comparative marketing is considered to be the study of role relationships existing among different countries. Bartel's book, however, suffers from a lack of a common theoretical framework as well as a rather wide range in the quality of the contributions.

Carson,[9] on the other hand, focuses on comparative marketing as a whole, rather than on individual segments. Comparative marketing, as a discipline, has not matured to the stage where a definitive, integrated, coordinated exposition is possible. Vast areas remain almost entirely unexplored, especially those involving the collection, evaluation, and analysis of key quantitative data. However, in recent years, the use of the multivariate techniques in comparative marketing studies has begun to change this situation.

The first major survey article on comparative marketing was published by Shapiro in 1965.[10] In it he suggested that if more attention was paid to the problem of comparative marketing, fairly rapid progress would be made in developing an appropriate framework for the description and analysis of marketing systems. However, the "appropriate framework" mentioned by Shapiro has not yet materialized. There are two reasons for this: the slow development of comparative marketing as a subdiscipline and the scarcity of conclusive constructs in the field.

Researchers of domestic marketing systems abroad seem to disagree about which framework or construct is best suited for conducting such studies.[11] A number of comparative marketing models have been advocated by such scholars as Bartel,[12] Boddewyn,[13] Farmer and Richman,[14] Negandhi,[15] Estafen[16] and Koontz.[17] Some of these models have yet to be tested empirically. Nevertheless, one study by Chong made use of a modified version of Negandhi's comparative model by focusing on marketing practices.[18] Chong contends that the methodology for a comparative marketing study should combine the heterogeneous cultural environments in which marketing practice takes place with the concept of marketing held by the researcher. Hence, the studies of comparative marketing should take differences into consideration, but reduce those differences to a level of comparability through the conception of marketing as a social process with individuals interacting in role positions.[19]

In his study, Cox pointed to serious inadequacies in the knowledge base for North American marketing.[20] These inadequacies are compounded when other marketing systems are compared with that of the U.S. Efforts in comparative marketing have either assumed that universal rules exist, denied that universal rules exist, or enumerated superficial differences only. To counter this, Cox pleads for a concern with "universals" in marketing. The search for universals will teach us much about other markets and more about our own. It is proper that marketing scholars should search for universals, and comparative marketing has begun to do so.[21]

The socioeconomic, analytical approach places more emphasis upon interrelationships among a given set of socioeconomic conditions and marketing practices.[22] It also concentrates on environmental differences of particular interest to sociologists and cultural anthropologist.[23] Its main shortcoming is that results are frequently ambiguous and do not necessarily lead themselves to the support of predictions; the inherent macro-orientation prevents consideration of interpersonal and interfirm differences. It attempts to isolate the environmental variables that cause similarities and differences in marketing effectiveness.

The behavioral approach, on the other hand, looks at the effect of cultural differences in comparative marketing analysis. There is one lesson to be learned here. While some writers attribute everything to culture, it is more fruitful to determine empirically the nature and form of cultural influence on given types of human endeavor in comparative marketing studies. Otherwise one will deal only with the skeletons of the enquiry.

Contemporary Studies

A compilation and comparison of consumer attitudes in the United States and several European countries provides a substantial data in the critical area of sociocultural values and attitudes.[24] Individual country studies such as those by Yoshino,[25] Anderson,[26] Preston[27] and Glade and Udell also provide the field with valuable descriptive material.[28] A study by Green and Langeard developed a comparative profile of consumers in France and the United States along several dimensions of consumption behavior.[29] This study compares profiles of consumers identified as innovators. One conclusion of this study was that most of the differences could be attributed to social and environmental differences between the two countries. Sood, after comparing the marketing system of the United States with that of Finland, concluded that many elements of the marketing process are common to both countries.[30] However, he also found a number of critical differences, most of which occur in distribution and promotion. Although these differences were significant, it was thought they could be overcome through a marketing strategy consistent with Finnish culture, geography, and politics. Hawes, Gronmo, and Arndt examine consumers' use of time for shopping, and the impact of shopping time on other categories of time expenditure in Norway and the United States.[31] Using data from previous studies, they found great similarity in the time spent on shopping in Norway and the United States, but wide differences in the use of time for other activities. Other studies have dealt with crossnational comparisons of values, roles, activities, interests, and opinions.[32] These generally conclude that sellers need to adapt marketing strategies to the culture and institutions of the host nation.

Comparative marketing studies represent an attempt to develop concepts and generalizations at a level between what is true of all societies and what is true of one society at one point in time and space.[33] A particular contribution toward understanding comparative marketing in a specific business sector-distribution is the unique work of Boddewyn and Hollander: *Public Policy Toward Retailing*.[34] Their study grew out of two hypotheses that had gained wide support among marketers: (a) the richer nations were being transformed into a truly supernational market through ever rising standards of living, the reduction or elimination of tariff walls, the growing popularity of foreign travel, and an acceleration in the international transmission of ideas, tastes, and fashions; and (b) retailers from the richer nations were urgently needed by the less-developed countries in order to offer price and service competition to local middlemen, stimulate local production by helping rationalize local sources of supply, and make new merchandise available as an incentive to indigenous labor.

In recent years, despite the marked diffusion of multinational retailers across national boundaries, one can not overlook numerous instances of failures in such moves.[35] In spite of the increased number of multinational retailers operating in less-developed countries, consumers benefiting from these foreign distributive institutions are more likely from of the high-income group than the poor masses.[36] Retailing systems are found in various environments; that is, in countries at different stages of economic development, with different types of political regimes and social structures, and different value systems. The system can be analyzed in terms of actors connected in relationship structures, and interacting in activity processes (buying and selling, promoting, pricing, and storing) that result in various economic and noneconomic functions or contributions. However, it is hardly possible to detect universals when marketing phenomena are not comparable. What is needed, therefore, is a set of criteria that can be used to evaluate the appropriateness of comparing marketing phenomena in different countries.[37]

Quantitatively based methods for measuring external or environmental factors have also been proposed. In their study, Farmer and Richman have emphasized the use of the Delphi technique for obtaining a consensus of opinion of the educational, cultural, legal-political, and economic constraints affecting the economic development of a country.[38] They have also tried to present a general theory of comparative management in analyzing marketing situations and economic progress in any country.

A similar approach to organizing international data specifically for national marketing systems was used by experts of the Marketing Science Institute.[39] This study suggested the following methodological techniques for classifying countries as a basis for marketing decisions: (1) a developmental cluster analysis classifying countries according to five progressive levels of economic and technological development; (2) a regional typological approach focusing on five major geographical regions; and (3) a two-dimensional score measuring the degree of economic and demographic achievement. This was the first major attempt to cluster countries for planning and control purposes. The study suggested that there were two factors impeding greater use of clustering. First, there is the inherent difficulty of determining criteria for the grouping or clustering or markets. The second difficulty, arising perhaps from the first, is that many firms were just beginning to make the break from comparative to multinational marketing. Multinational marketing techniques are used by management to evaluate the effectiveness of its marketing in several countries. By noting the degree of similarity among countries, executives can determine the relative market potentials and establish more effective controls over the marketing effort.[40]

Unresolved Problems of Comparative Marketing

In its scientific form, the comparative marketing approach consists of the systematic detection, identification, classification, measurement, and interpretation of similarities and differences among phenomena.[41] There is a lack of consensus among scholars concerning this definition. This situation has developed because many scholars are interested in a variety of related topics for which the label "comparative marketing" is handy. Essentially, these other approaches tend to: (a) broaden the concept of marketing; (b) make the comparisons less explicit; and (c) focus on behavior in foreign environments.[42]

In contrast to Boddewyn, Douglas examined the relationship between environmental factors and the marketing system.[43] She studied the issue through a comparative study of marketing systems in countries at different levels of environmental development. Assuming that marketing is a universal social process existing in some form in all countries, differences in marketing system characteristics may be partially attributed to differences in environmental development. It was hypothesized by Douglas that environmental factors would affect channel relationships through their impact on the organizational characteristics of firms. However, she found little evidence to support the widely held theory that the development of marketing structure closely parallels that of the social, economic, and cultural environment. These results suggest that the influence of environmental factors on marketing structure may be considerably less important than is frequently postulated by marketing scholars.

To alleviate this shortcoming, the comparative approach should work toward: (a) building the discipline; (b) inducing learning; and (c) improving practice. These objectives can be met by the development of concepts, theories, and generalized ideas that can form the basis of a general theory of marketing. Such a body of knowledge would help to describe and explain the working of marketing systems, and lead to more accurate and less costly decision making on the part of practitioners.[44] The systematic comparison of different situations over space and time in a particular area of marketing should lead to generalizations that could not be discerned from a study of one country. Comparisons of the marketing systems of developed and developing countries could reveal what factors are specific to one level of development and which are common to all levels.[45]

Theoretical and Conceptual Constructs of Comparative Marketing

In this section various theoretical and conceptual constructs of comparative marketing systems will be classified and analyzed. Significant theoretical and methodological approaches to comparative marketing will be evaluated for their usefulness in ' conducting empirical research and in developing a comprehensive comparative marketing methodology.

Any theory of comparative marketing must embody the following functions as comprehensively and consistently as possible:[46]

1) A descriptive function by which the theory carefully examines the antecedent conditions explaining a marketing phenomenon in one country or region of the world.
2) A delimiting function through which the comparative marketing theory explicitly limits its scope by appropriately defining the marketing phenomenon to be explained, e.g. advertising or distribution practices, in a given country or region of the world.
3) An integrative function by which it systematically relates all relevant research and evidence. Findings of specific marketing practices (e.g., advertising and distribution) in more than one country are compared and contrasted to each other.
4) A generative function by which it provides deductive hypotheses for future testing, verification, and theory-building.

The existing theories of comparative marketing are for the most part descriptive rather than normative. They simply describe and explain, with a minimum number of theoretical constructs. For instance, they do not tell us much about how consumers living in different countries perceive, evaluate, and adopt products and services marketed by multinational corporations. However, the descriptive-analytical studies do provide a wealth of information for comparative marketing. These studies are of three types and are designed to find a better or ideal marketing structure. The first type is the study of one component of the marketing mix, in which comparisons are generally made on a broad multi-country basis.[47] Then, empirically eclectic studies are generally in-depth investigations of the marketing system of one country or area that make limited comparisons.[48] Still a third approach is the case-study method, in which a description and analysis of the marketing problems of firms in various countries and under different environmental conditions are made.[49]

In contrast, deterministic studies covering patterns of interrelations between marketing and external variables not only describe and explain but formulate generalizations, hypotheses, and laws. These studies also aim at analyzing the similarities and differences in marketing structure over a period of time.[50] Here comparative marketing theory admits of two types of variables: exogenous and endogenous. The exogenous variables constitute external constraints on the explanatory factors and are fixed in structure and over time. The endogenous variables are clearly pointed out, their network of relationships fully detailed. These variables are often quantified and any changes in them are explained and predicted by a set of determinants—micro- and macroeconomic factors. Figure 16.1 classifies the methodological framework for comparative marketing studies.

Alternative Methodology

Most of the research designs for comparative marketing studies are descriptive and exploratory rather than causal. Time and cost factors have been primarily responsible for this. Many of the researchers have made a concerted effort to emphasize the exploratory nature of their work. However, this heavy emphasis on the descriptive and exploratory aspects of comparative marketing could serve as a strong foundation for future planning endeavors. During the next decade, prediction and experimentation could become the watchwords of the new marketing discipline.[51]

Since a comparison is based on identifying and comparing relevant marketing dimensions of two or more systems, it must consist of two major components :

1) Determining what to compare. Here the comparison must focus on some features of the entities compared, i.e., identifying the relevant properties or dimensions of the marketing system in question.

FIGURE 16.1

A Methodological Framework for Comparative Marketing Studies

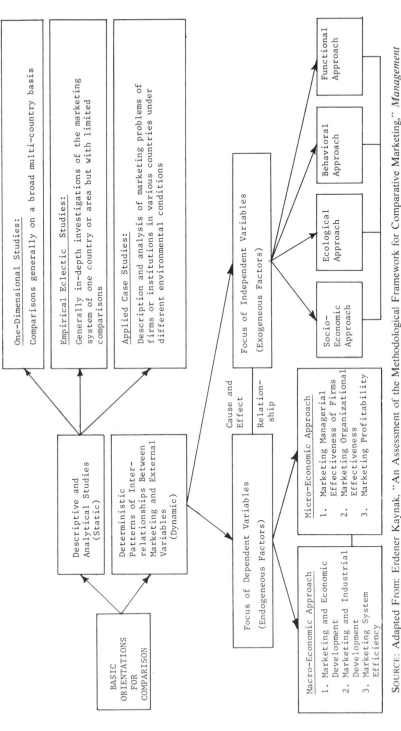

SOURCE: Adapted From: Erdener Kaynak, "An Assessment of the Methodological Framework for Comparative Marketing," *Management Decision*, Vol. 20, No. 4, 1982, p. 10.

2) Determining the basis for comparing the properties or dimensions studied.[52] The objective of the comparative marketing analysis should be to provide the guidelines for determining the appropriate object (what) and method (how) of comparison.

Traditionally, comparative marketing studies have tended to compare certain entities (institutions, regions, or countries), their structure and functions. However, comparative marketing studies should focus on systems as a whole, or on the structure and functioning of such systems. Since most of the entities can be viewed and analyzed as systems, it is necessary to establish what to compare within the context of a system. What to compare should involve three specific steps:[53]

1) Determining the system to be compared.
2) Determining the unit of analysis.
3) Determining the relevant dimensions.

The decision concerning how to compare, on the other hand, will focus on both the logic and methodology of comparison. This is derived from both the aim of the analysis and from the selected object of comparison. It primarily involves three related tasks:

1) Determining the appropriate type of comparison.
2) Determining the specific research technique and desired sample size.
3) Establishing the basis for the correspondence (translation) rule for comparison.

This author believes that a suitable group of scholars should map out the comparative marketing systems field by: (a) establishing some research priorities, e.g., what countries, what periods, what sectors, what problems, how and with what resources? (b) suggesting suitable conceptual and operational schemes of analysis; (c) designing conceptual frameworks and methodologies that can be used and applied in more than one country and one situation over a period of time; and (d) critically evaluating and interpreting existing research conducted across cultures and other countries. Table 16.1 illustrates the typology of comparative marketing studies discussed above. The search for normative principles leads to the development of anecdotal descriptions and eventually predictive and analytical studies that initially have limited scope. Normative principles also inspire and affect the development of more formal theories, which eventually should engender the system-oriented (longitudinal and holistic) studies this chapter has advocated.

TABLE 16.1
A Typology of Comparative Marketing Studies

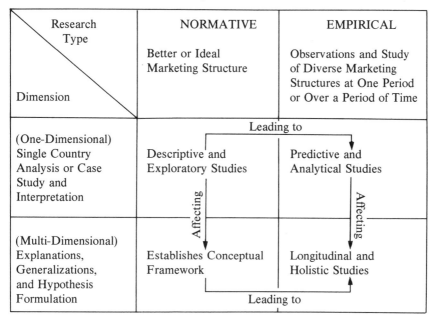

Research Type ⟍ Dimension	NORMATIVE — Better or Ideal Marketing Structure	EMPIRICAL — Observations and Study of Diverse Marketing Structures at One Period or Over a Period of Time
	Leading to	
(One-Dimensional) Single Country Analysis or Case Study and Interpretation	Descriptive and Exploratory Studies	Predictive and Analytical Studies
	Affecting	*Affecting*
(Multi-Dimensional) Explanations, Generalizations, and Hypothesis Formulation	Establishes Conceptual Framework	Longitudinal and Holistic Studies
	Leading to	

SOURCE: Erdener Kaynak, "An Assessment of the Methodological Framework for Comparative Marketing", *Management Decision*, Vol. 20, No. 4, 1982, p. 12.

Further Research Needed

The published research in comparative marketing indicates that the literature is lagging behind that of other areas in marketing. Most of the work done so far is exploratory in nature.

Comparative marketing studies require a generalized system of concepts that will enable the researcher to rigorously compare and contrast marketing phenomena in different countries.[54] Although a universal marketing taxonomy does not exist, this does not obviate the possibility of universal patterns of marketing behavior and structure. The identification of these patterns will help to develop a framework for comparative study.

Some theories have been developed by academics in recent years that attempt to explain or interpret basic developments in comparative marketing. However, the behavioral sources for such theories are weak, and applying them to comparative marketing merely confounds our search for universals.

So far, marketers have not developed a sufficient data base on which to construct such fundamental concepts.[55]

A perusal of the literature on marketing methods in foreign countries suggests that undue emphasis has been placed on the description of a marketing system in relation to its socioeconomic, cultural, physical and geographic environment, with suggestions as to the probable future pattern within this narrow context. What is needed is a conceptual framework for a comparative analytical approach to marketing that will enable the practical marketer to devise marketing strategies pertinent to the national environment. In facilitating future research comparative marketing could benefit greatly from the support of business, not only with respect to data gathering but also in the area of funding. Such collaborative efforts would open new avenues of development in the study of comparative marketing systems.

Notes

1. F. Kenneth Berrien, "Methodological and Related Problems in Cross-Cultural Research," *International Journal of Psychology*, Vol. 2, No. 1, 1967, pp. 33–43; Joseph W. Elder, "Comparative Cross-National Methodology," *Annual Review of Sociology*, Vol. 2, 1976, pp. 209–30; and Murray A. Straus, "Phenomenal Identity and Conceptual Equivalence of Measurement in Cross-National Comparative Research," *Journal of Marriage and the Family*, Vol. 31, No. 2, May 1969, pp: 233–39.

2. Robert Bartels, "Are Domestic and International Marketing Dissimilar?" *Journal of Marketing*, Vol. 32, July 1968, pp: 56–61.

3. For an excellent review of the developments in comparative marketing see: Jean J. Boddewyn, "Comparative Marketing: The First Twenty-Five Years," *Journal of International Business Studies*, Vol. 12, No. 1, Spring/Summer 1981, pp: 61–79.

4. David Carson, *"Present State of the Art of Comparative Marketing,"* in Thomas V. Greer, eds., *Increasing Marketing Productivity and Conceptual and Methodological Foundations of Marketing*, 1973, Combined Proceedings, AMA Series No. 35, 1974.

5. R. D. Carter, "Comparative Management: An Alternative Approach," *The Southern Journal of Business*, Vol. 5, No. 4, October 1970, pp: 51–57.

6. Adel El-Ansary, *The Development of International Marketing Thought and Its Contribution to the General Body of Marketing Thought*, Occasional Paper, Baton Rouge, Louisiana, College of Business Administration, Louisiana, College of Business Administration, Louisiana State University, 1971.

7. Eugene D. Jaffe, "Comparative Marketing Revisited," *Marquette Business Review*, Vol. 20, No. 4, Winter 1976, pp: 143–253.

8. Robert Bartels, *Comparative Marketing: Wholesaling in Fifteen Countries* (Chicago: Richard D. Irwin Inc., 1963).

9. David Carson, *International Marketing: A Comparative Systems Approach* (John Wiley & Sons Inc., 1967).

10. Stanley J. Shapiro, "Comparative Marketing and Economic Development," in George Schwartz, eds., *Science in Marketing* (New York, John Wiley & Sons Inc., 1965).

11. Eugene D. Jaffe, "A Flow-Approach to the Comparative Study of Marketing Systems", in Jean Boddewyn, ed., *Comparative Management and Marketing* (Scott, Foresman and Co., 1969), pp: 160–70.

12. Robert Bartels, "Methodological Framework for Comparative Marketing Study", in A. Greyser, eds., *Toward Scientific Marketing*, Chicago, American Marketing Association, 1964.

13. Jean A. Boddewyn, "Construct for Comparative Marketing Research," *Journal of Marketing Research*, Vol. 3, May 1966, pp: 149–153.

14. Richard N. Farmer and B. M. Richman, *Comparative Management and Economic Process* (Bloomington, Indiana: Cedarwood Publishing Co., 1970).

15. Anand R. Negandhi, "American Management Abroad: A Comparative Study of Management Practices of American Subsidiaries and Local Firms in Developing Countries," *Management International Review*, Vol. 11, Nos. 4–5, 1971, pp: 97–106.

16. B. D. Estafen, "System Transfer Characteristics: An Experimental Model for Comparative Management Research," *Management International Review*, Vol. 10, Nos. 2–3, 1970, pp: 21–43.

17. H. Koontz, "A Model for Analyzing the Universality and Transferability of Management," *Academy of Management Journal*, Vol. 12, No. 4, December 1969, pp: 415–30.

18. S. Chong, "Comparative Marketing Practices of Foreign and Domestic Firms in Developing Countries: A Case Study of Malaysia," *Management International Review*, Vol. 13, No. 6, 1973, pp: 91–98.

19. Gerard Albaum, *Research in International Marketing: Current Status and Future Directions*, Presented at the Annual Meeting of the Academy of International Business Conference, Las Vagas, Nevada, June 1979.

20. Reavis Cox, "The Search for Universals in Comparative Studies of Domestic Marketing Systems," in Peter D. Bennett, eds., *Marketing and Economic Development*, Chicago, AMA, 1965, pp: 143–53.

21. Yoram Wind and Susan Douglas, "Comparative Methodology and Marketing Theory," in *Theoretical Developments in Marketing*, Proceedings of the AMA, Chicago, 1980.

22. S. R. Prasad, *Management in International Perspective* (Appleton-Century-Crofts: New York, 1967).

23. Guy E. Swanson, "Frameworks for Comparative Research: Structural Anthropology and the Theory of Action," in Ivan Vallier, ed., Comparative Methods in Sociology: *Essays on Trends and Applications* (Berkeley: University of California Press, 1971), pp: 141–202.

24. George Katona, Strumpel and Zahn, *Aspirations and Affluence: Comparative Studies in the U.S. and Western Europe* (New York: McGraw-Hill Book Co., 1971).

25. M. Y. Yoshino, *The Japanese Marketing System* (Cambridge, Mass: The MIT Press, 1971).

26. Dole Anderson, *Marketing and Development: The Thailand Experience* East Lansing: Michigan State University International Business and Economic Studies, 1970.

27. Lee Preston, "Market Control in Developing Economies," *The Journal of Development Studies*, July 1968, pp: 481–96.

28. William Glade and J. G. Udell, "The Marketing Behavior of Peruvian Firms: Obstacles and Contributions to Economic Development" in Moyer and Hollander, eds., *Markets and Marketing in Developing Economies* (Richard D. Irwin Inc., Chicago, 1968), pp: 153–69.

29. Robert Green and Eric Langeard, "A Cross-National Comparison of Consumer Habits and Innovation Characteristics," *Journal of Marketing*, July 1975, pp: 34–41.

30. James Sood, "Marketing in Finland: An Entry to the East," *Columbia Journal of World Business*, Fall 1975, pp: 93–100.

31. D. Hawes, S. Gronmo, and J. Arndt, "Shopping Time and Leisure Time: Some Preliminary Cross-Cultural Comparisons of Time Budget Expenditures," *Proceedings of the 1977 Conference of the Association for Consumer Research*, 1977, pp: 151–59.

32. J. M. Carmen and R. M. March, "How Important for Marketing Are Cultural Differences Between Similar Nations?" *Australian Marketing Researcher,* Vol. 3, No. 1, Summar 1979, pp: 5–20.

33. R. Bendix, "Concepts and Generalizations in Comparative Sociological Studies," *American Sociological Review*, Vol. 28, No. 4, August 1963, pp: 532–37.

34. Jean Boddewyn and S. C. Hollander, *Public Policy Toward Retailing: An International Symposium*, Lexington Books, Lexington Mass., 1972.

35. Erdener Kaynak, "Transfer of Supermarketing Technology from Developed to Less-Developed Countries: The Case of Migros Turk," *The Finnish Journal of Business Economics*, Vol. 23, No. 1, 1980, pp: 33–49.

36. Erdener Kaynak, "A Refined Approach to the Wheel of Retailing," *European Journal of Marketing*, Vol. 13, No. 7, pp: 237–45.

37. Jean Boddewyn, *Belgian Public Policy Toward Retailing Since 1979*, Michigan State University, Division of Research, Graduate School of Business Administration, East Lansing, 1971.

38. Richard N. Farmer and B. M. Richman, op. cit.

39. Bentil Liander, *Comparative Analysis for International Marketing*, Boston: Allyn and Bacon Inc., 1967.

40. Ruel Kuhler, *International Marketing*, (5th ed.), Southwestern Publishing Co., Cincinnati, 1983, pp: 6–7.

41. Jean Boddewyn, "The Comparative Approach to the Study of Business Administration," *Academy of Management Journal*, Vol. 8, No. 4, December 1964, pp: 261–67.

42. Jean Boddewyn, *Comparative Management: Teaching, Training, and Research*, Proceedings of the Comparative Management Workshop, New York, 1970.

43. Susan P. Douglas, "Patterns and Parallels of Marketing Structures in Several Countries," *MSU Business Topics*, Vol. 19, No. 2, Spring 1971, pp: 38–48.

44. P. J. Gordon, "Editorial Comment," *Academy of Management Journal*, Vol. 8, No. 4, 1965, pp: 259–60.

45. Reed Moyer and S. C. Hollander, *Markets and Marketing in Developing Economies*, Richard D. Irwin Inc., 1968.

46. J. A. Howard and J. N. Sheth, *The Theory of Buyer Behavior* (New York: John Wiley & Sons: 1969); and J. F. Rychlak, *A Philosophy of Science for Personality Theory,* (Boston: Houghton Mifflin, 1968).

47. H. Hakanson and B. Wootz, "Supplier Selection in an International Environment," *Journal of Marketing Research*, February 1975, pp: 46–51.

48. R. Hoover, R. Green, and J. Saegert, "A Cross-National Study of Perceived Risk," *Journal of Marketing*, July 1978, pp: 102–08; E. Kaynak, "Difficulties of Undertaking Marketing Research in the Developing Countries," *European Research*, Vol. 8, No. 8, November 1978, pp: 159–65; E. Kaynak, "A Comparative Approach to the Study of Urban Food Distribution Systems in Latin America and the Middle East," Presented at the *Annual Meeting of the Academy of International Business*, Las Vegas, Nevada, 1979; and G. Leroy, *Multi-national Product Strategy: A Typology for Analysis of Worldwide Product Innovation and Diffusion* (New York: Praeger Publishers, 1976).

49. W. Straver, "The International Consumerist Movement," *European Journal of Marketing*, Vol. 11, No. 2, 1977; A. Urban, "A Cross-National Comparison of Consumer Media Use Patterns," *Columbia Journal of World Business*, Spring 1977, pp: 53–63; and G. Harris, R. Still, and M. Crask, "A Comparison of Australian and U.S. Marketing Strategies," *Columbia Journal of World Business*, Summer 1978, pp: 87–94.

50. W. Glade, W. A. Strang, and J. G. Udell, *Marketing in a Developing Nation* (Lexington, Mass.: Heath Lexington Books, 1970); M. Shumaguchi and W. Lazer, "Japanese Distribution Channels: Invisible Barriers to Market Entry," *MSU Business Topics*, Winter

1979, pp: 49–62; and A. Louden, "A Note on Marketing Research in Mexico," *Journal of Business Research*, Vol. 4, No. 1, February 1976, pp: 69–74.

51. Erdener Kaynak, "An Assessment of the Methodological Framework for Comparative Marketing," *Management Decision*, Vol. 20, No. 4, 1982, pp: 3–15.

52. R. Madox, K. Gronhaug, R. Homans, and F. May, "Correlates of Information Gathering and Evoked Set Size for New Automobile Purchasers in Norway and the U.S.," Proceedings of the 1977 *Conference of the Association for Consumer Research*, 1977, pp: 167–70; and Kemal Kurtulus, "Present Status of Marketing Research in Turkey," *European Journal of Marketing*, Vol. 12, 1978, pp: 529–40.

53. Yoram Wind and S. P. Douglas, "On the Meaning of Comparison: A Methodology for Cross-Cultural Studies," *Quarterly Journal of Management*, Vol. 2, No. 4, July 1971, pp: 105–23.

54. Erdener Kaynak, "Future Direction for Research in Comparative Marketing," *The Canadian Marketer*, Vol. 11, No. 1, 1980, pp: 23–28.

55. Jagdish N. Sheth and S. Prakash Sethi, "Theory of Cross-Cultural Buyer Behaviour" in the *Proceedings of ESOMAR Seminar on Developments in Consumer Psychology*, Maidenhead, U.K., May 30–June 2, 1973, pp: 219–38.

17

THE FUTURE DIRECTIONS OF COMPARATIVE MARKETING: AN AGENDA FOR RESEARCH PRIORITIES

Erdener Kaynak and Ronald Savitt

Introduction

As has been seen in the previous chapters, the field of comparative marketing is rich and varied. In the nearly 30 years since the area became recognized as a legitimate field for study, its contributions have grown greatly. The variety of literature since the introductory statements by Bartels, Boddewyn, and Cox has been immense.[1]

So far, marketing scholars have learned more about the conceptual frameworks and methodologies of undertaking comparative analysis than about making the results relevant to academics, public policy makers, and managers. Many of the early studies were descriptive in nature; so are many of the current ones, and it looks as though a great number of future studies shall also be. Description is the keystone to understanding any phenomenon. While comparative analysis may have once been looked upon as the result of the travel experiences of marketing scholars, this is no longer the case. While individual case studies still comprise much of the comparative marketing literature, they are undertaken with new levels of sophistication and insight. Recent literature on comparative marketing has attempted to incorporate quantitative methodologies; however, its impact on the development of the area has not been as substantial as once was expected. In recent years, the state of comparative studies in marketing has certainly been improved by the introduction of new ways of understanding quantitative data, though all too often researchers have paid more attention to the data and their analysis than the more pressing underlying issues and their policy implications.

The basic concepts of comparative analysis still hold, but, as has been pointed out before, the contemporary scholar has access to an increasingly more sophisticated research methodology. The central point for comparison is still the marketing system either in or between countries, with all of the component parts. As the concepts of marketing have expanded, and as the definitions of marketing itself have been extended and refined, so has the outreach of comparative analysis grown. The result is that there is great unevenness in the research and writing in the field. There has been little of the systematic investigation that has occupied scholars in a great number of disciplines from archeology to zoology. Comparative studies have a long way to go in marketing before they are recognized as an essential part of the discipline. Even the *Journal of Marketing* has yet to acknowledge comparative marketing as part of its topical classification scheme. While the recognition of a "class" is not the "be-all or end-all," it may have a significant influence on whether scholars will go into the field.

Comparative marketing systems as a subject area also needs business support not only in respect to data and, possibly, funding, but even more important, in helping to continually remind academics as well as practitioners that we are working in an applied field. Various approaches have been discussed in previous chapters in an effort to facilitate the development of theories and conceptual frameworks for future comparative marketing studies. This part of the book critically evaluates the literature of comparative marketing systems and suggests methodologies that provide an adequate framework on which to base future comparative marketing systems research.

Basic Methodological Concerns

Since 1957 comparative marketing issues have become the focus of a moderate research effort by a growing number of scholars. However, a large portion of it lacks the required vigor and has certain shortcomings necessary to mention here before one can move any further.[2]

1. So far most research studies conducted in comparative marketing are descriptive and exploratory in nature, rather than causal. Even the empirical studies are descriptive in nature and lacking in analytical rigor.

2. In the comparative marketing literature, experimental designs are practically nonexistent. Some of the research reflects substantial methodological deficiencies.

3. Many of the comparative studies undertaken ignore the existing literature and hence are of limited value.

4. Most comparative studies are cross-sectional in nature; relatively few are longitudinal. Very few of these studies have a historical perspective.

5. A significant amount of the research that has been reported in comparative marketing can be viewed as qualitative research, in that in-depth and somewhat unstructured interviews have been used. Insufficient attention is frequently paid to the planning and execution of the research effort.

6. It seems that empirical evidence is often gathered without much concern for the representatives of the data and without well-developed, appropriate methodological instrumentations. Judgement samples appear to be widely used in selecting countries for cross-national/cultural comparison studies. Usually, small sample sizes and convenience sampling are used.

7. A great portion of the on-going comparative marketing research is not aimed at theory/concept/model-building. There is also strong evidence of an inadequate linkage between empirical research and existing theoretical/ conceptual studies, and the two, in most cases, do not support each other.

8. A substantial percentage of the research in comparative marketing is one-dimensional, descriptive, and static in nature. There is, of course, an urgent need in the literature for one- as well as multi-dimensional, analytical-interpretive and generalizing-normative empirical studies.[3]

9. The single most popular technique used for collecting data is the survey. The personal interview appears to be the most widely used method of eliciting information from respondents.

10. With respect to measurement and scaling, Likert-type scales seem to be most popular for attitudinal measurements. However, the low literacy rate in less-developed countries would render the Likert- and Guttman-type scaling techniques difficult to use. Usually respondents with little or no education are unable to make the fine distinction between "strongly agree" and "moderately agree." A solution to this dilemma may lie in the use of three-point scales.[4] Some researchers have also used the semantic-differential scales in comparative marketing research but to a limited degree.

11. Most of the comparative marketing studies compare the urban markets of countries with very little attention paid to rural marketing systems or comparison of rural and urban markets.

12. In these economically hard times, marketing productivity and efficiency both at firm and country levels gain tremendous importance. When one looks at the comparative marketing literature, one sees scarcity of studies on marketing productivity and efficiency across nations.

13. Very little of the current comparative marketing research effort goes into the development of case material. This is an area that requires more attention from marketing scholars.

As it was pointed out in previous chapters, there is an abundance of descriptive studies concentrating on marketing in particular countries. There is clearly no shortage of normatively oriented studies pertaining to marketing in general as well as to such elements of marketing as advertising and distribution. There is no shortage either of general procedural frameworks. A number of them were cited in this book and there are others. Yet, the comparative marketing discipline, as far as one can detect, lacks the universal taxonomy of marketing and the general propositions and hypotheses that might serve as both the inspiration and the intellectual basis for holistic or system-oriented and longitudinal studies. There is, moreover, a void in comparative marketing literature of the diagnostic type. It may be that we confront an example of the proverbial "chicken or the egg" conundrum here. Perhaps we cannot have a universal taxonomy or general propositions before a number of system-oriented studies have been attempted and completed.

Still, global marketing has arrived. Its arrival has made it abundantly evident not only that many of our principles of marketing are merely culture-bound practices, but also that without a set of truly general or universal principles of marketing, international marketers must function like the novice language student: speaking in one language while thinking in another.

There is, then, an urgent need for innovative and general comparative studies of marketing systems. A truly general theory of comparative marketing cannot be a North American theory or a European theory. It must be a world theory or a theory with global applicability tested on a global scale.

Comparative marketing research should not be influenced by the advancement in research techniques; rather it should provide the framework in which techniques can be applied. Since much of managerial marketing has been influenced by developments in the developed world rather than the developing world, comparative marketing has not found a place in the mainstream of the marketing discipline. In part, this is a result of the general association of comparative marketing with issues of economic development in the developing world rather than with managerial problems in a developed economy. Comparative marketing, in part, has been overlooked as an analytic and synthetic process since it is associated with qualitative rather than quantitative analysis. These perceptions about the field are not true, as the present collection clearly indicates.

An Agenda for Research

The variety of topics and issues for further research in comparative marketing is literally boundless. What the editors have attempted to do here is discuss some of the issues in the hopes of stimulating further research. Clearly, there are a variety of unanswered questions that can be found in the current collection. Admittedly there are research areas which require immediate attention. We are leaving these to the reader as a possible further research topic.

1. *Research Methods*. While a basic set of elements has been developed, there are limitations to its use. Quantitative analysis has not provided the insight needed to undertake comparative studies. All too often, the methods themselves have been allowed to overshadow the purpose of comparison, as well as the available data. A starting point for comparative research is description based on good observation. Scholars working in comparative analysis may have to sharpen their observational abilities by undertaking more frequent and more systematic field research. This in fact may be the distinguishing factor between comparative research and traditional marketing research. There is also need for a smooth transition from descriptive to more normative and diagnostic studies in comparative marketing.

2. *Data Collection and Development of a Classification Scheme*. If field research is going to characterize the direction of comparative studies, then new traditions in the development of data will be required. These will be especially critical if comparative marketing hopes to go beyond the traditional criticism, "but your data are not comparable." Researchers are going to have to expand their conceptions of the type of data used and the ways in which they are collected. The development of comparative research is expected to move along with historical research. In this process the deterministic models found in contemporary marketing as well as the research methods used in other fields will play a facilitative role. If the data are to be truly comparable, researchers must actually involve themselves in the environments from which the data come. Only in this way will the standard criticism be minimized.

The development of classification schemes must come first if there is to be an appreciable increase in the quality of the data collected and used in comparative marketing. Included in this task is reformulation of marketing functions, processes, and institutions. If comparative studies are to help in understanding the differences in and among marketing systems, thought will have to be given to what different distributive institutions really include and what are the differences and similarities and types of distributive institutions. Marketing scholars in their work within a single system such as the United States have given inadequate attention to such issues. Marketing scholars all acknowledge there are many versions of "the drugstore," but have not revised definitions to keep pace with marketing realities. The development of more adequate classification schemes will not only enrich the understanding of a single economy's marketing system, but is absolutely required if significant comparative research is to be undertaken.

3. *Descriptive Studies*. Though some contemporary researchers avoid

descriptive studies, since they are often viewed as nonanalytical, these studies are the basis of comparison. Understanding can be gained through description. However, unlike some of the early work in comparative research, descriptive studies will have to be more comprehensive. They will have to clearly identify elements that can be used in subsequent comparison. To the extent that market researchers to not want to engage in description as the starting point, they will have to draw upon the work of others, especially those in anthropology, economics, geography, history, psychology, and sociology. The problem will be one of transferability of concepts from other disciplines to marketing. To this end, a priority research effort should focus on an analysis of existing descriptive studies, as comparison without solid descriptive data might end up dealing with skeletons.

4. *Marketing Systems.* The central set of concepts to be compared will be the marketing systems in and among diverse and similar cultural/national settings. The components of such systems can range in diversity and complexity from the environmental setting to individual types of retail establishments. The work in macro-marketing to data has not been totally helpful in establishing connections for classifying different components of the marketing system, nor has it been showing the relationship between marketing systems and their environment. To be certain, there is general agreement about the size and form of the marketing channel, but more research needs to be undertaken before more substantial comparative work can take place in other parts of marketing.

While most of the research has centered on the comparison of marketing in various economies, the past should not indicate that all comparative research must have an international flavor. Indeed, there is much to be done within domestic marketing systems. For example, there has been little recent work on comparative channels or comparative marketing practices. While much emphasis will focus on international comparison, there is still much to be learned from intranational comparative research.

5. *Multidimensional Areas of Research.* As was indicated in Table 1.3 in Chapter 1, there is an absence of multidimensional research. Primarily, this gap is found in two areas: a) generalizing normative studies and b) analytical-interpretative studies—though further work still needs to be done in the descriptive area.

6. *Some Substantive Areas of Research.* It is not possible to describe all of the substantive areas, however, some seem of higher importance and we hope by listing them in this fashion researchers will begin to work on them.

a. *Pricing Structures and Price-Making.* Pricing takes place in each marketing transaction. Still, very little is known about the structural and behavioral elements present. Beyond economic theory, there is little normative direction that can aid in price-setting. Prices are everywhere about us, yet there has been only limited empirical study of price-setting in and among firms. Comparative research could provide important insights.

b. *Consumer Behavior*. The generally accepted models of consumer behavior are applied vigorously without question as to their applicability. Perhaps one of their weaknesses is that little attention has been paid to behavioral patterns among a variety of groups. There are two important dimensions. One relates to the decision-making process itself, the other to how buyers actually behave or use the products that are purchased.

c. *Public Policy*. In spite of the great amount of attention to public policy issues in marketing, less attention has been paid to comparative public policy research than might be expected. To be certain, there are studies which compare consumers' attitudes about regulations and laws and comparative studies of specific laws, most notably antitrust laws; less attention has been paid to the comparative roles of governments as influencers and participants in a variety of marketing systems.

d. *Market Information and Decision Processes*. In the decision-making context, little is known about what information is used and how it is evaluated in making marketing decisions. While there is a strong normative literature of what should be collected and how it should be used, there is still no comparative marketing research that examines the use of marketing data either at the level of marketing systems or at the level of the firm.

Afterthoughts

It is not presumptuous to view comparative research and analysis as a central part of the development of marketing theory. Indeed, it is appropriate to suggest that continued comparative research may serve as a more productive foundation for the creation of a body of coherent marketing theory than some of the piecemeal work currently underway. Comparative analysis demands answers to the question: relevant compared to what?

Notes

1. Robert Bartels, "A Methodological Framework for Comparative Marketing Study," in Stephen A. Greyser, ed., *Toward Scientific Marketing*, (Chicago: American Marketing Association, 1964), pp: 383–90; J. J. Boddewyn, "A Construct for Comparative Marketing Research," *Journal of Marketing Research*, III, 1966, pp: 149–53; and Reavis Cox, "The Search for Universals in Comparative Studies of Domestic Marketing Systems," Peter D. Bennet, ed., *Marketing and Economic Development* (Chicago: American Marketing Association, 1965, pp: 143–62.

2. G. Albaum, "Research in International Marketing: Current Status and Future Directions." Presented at the Annual Meetings of the Academy of International Business, Las Vegas, Nevada, June 19, 1979.

3. H. Schollhammer, "Current Research on International and Corporative Management Issues," *Management International Review*, 15: 2–3, 1975, p. 35.

4. C. Chu Godwin, "Problems of Cross-Cultural Communication Research," in S. Prakash Sethi and Jagdish N. Sheth, eds., *Multinational Business Operations: Marketing Management*, Goodyear, 1973, p. 152.

5. For an excellent recent article on the topic see: E. C. Nevis, "Cultural Assumptions and Productivity: The United States and China," *Sloan Management Review*, Vol. 24, no. 3, Spring 1983, pp: 17–29.

BIBLIOGRAPHY

Anderson, R. D., J. L. Engledow and H. Becker. "Advertising Attitudes in Germany and the U.S.A., An Analysis Over Age and Time." *Journal of International Business Studies*, Winter 1978, pp: 27–38.

Anderson, R. D. and J. L. Engledow. "A Factor Analytic Comparison of U.S. and German Information Seekers." *Journal of Consumer Research*, Vol. 3, March 1977, pp: 185–96.

Anderson, R. D. and J. L. Engledow. "Perceived Importance of Selected Product Information Sources in Two Time Periods by United States and West German Consumers." *Journal of Business Research*, Vol. 9, No. 4, December 1981, pp: 339–51.

Arndt, J. "Comments on Cross-Cultural Consumer Research," in H. Hunt (ed.). *Advances in Consumer Research*, Vol. 5, Ann Arbor, MI: Association for Consumer Research, 1978.

Arndt, J. "Temporal Lags in Comparative Retailing." *Journal of Marketing*, Vol. 36, October 1972, pp: 40–45.

Arndt, J., H. C. Barksdale, and W. D. Perreault. "Comparative Study of Attitudes Toward Marketing, Consumerism and Government Regulation: The United States vs. Norway and Venezuela." Mimeographed. Bergen, Norway, Norwegian School of Economics and Business Administration, 1980.

Arndt, J., S. Gronmo, and D. K. Hawes. "The Use of Time as an Expression of Life-style: A Cross-National Study." Mimeographed. Bergen, Norway: Norwegian School of Economics and Business Administration, 1979.

Arnold, S. J., J. S. White and D. J. Tigert, "Canadians and Americans: A Comparative Analysis," *Working Paper Series*, Faculty of Management Studies, University of Toronto, October 1972, No. 72–73, 25 pages.

Barksdale, H. C. and L. M. Anderson. "Comparative Marketing: A Review of the Literature." *Journal of Macro-Marketing*, Vol. 2, No. 1, Spring 1982, pp: 57–62.

Barksdale, H. C. and L. M. Anderson, "Towards a Conceptual Framework for Comparative Marketing Studies." Presented at Fifth Macromarketing Seminar, University of Rhode Island, August 1980.

Barnard, P. "Conducting and Coordinating Multicountry Quantitative Studies Across Europe." *Journal of the Market Research Society*, Vol. 24, No. 1, January 1982, pp: 46–64.

Bartels, R. "A Methodological Framework for Comparative Marketing Study," in A.

Greyser, ed., *Toward Scientific Marketing*. Chicago: AMA, 1964, pp: 383–90.

Bartels, R. "Are Domestic and International Marketing Dissimilar?" *Journal of Marketing*, Vol. 32, July 1968, pp: 56–61.

Bartels, R. *Comparative Marketing: Wholesaling in Fifteen Countries*. Homewood, Illinois: Richard D. Irwin, 1963.

Bartels, R. *Global Development and Marketing*. Columbus, Ohio: Grid, 1981, p. 117.

Bartels, R. "Marketing and Economic Development." in P. D. White and C. C. Slater, eds., *Macro-Marketing: Distributive Processes from a Societal Perspective*, University of Colorado, Boulder, 1977, pp: 211–17.

Bartels, R., "National Culture-Business Relations: United States and Japan Contrasted," *Management International Review*, Vol. 22, No. 2, 1982, pp: 4–12.

Becker, H. "Is There a Cosmopolitan Information Seeker?" *Journal of International Business Studies*, Vol. 7, No. 1, Spring 1976, pp: 77–89.

Berien, F. K. "Methodological and Related Problems in Cross-Cultural Research." *International Journal of Psychology*, Vol. 2, No. 1, 1967, pp: 33–43.

Boddewyn, J. J. "A Construct for Comparative Marketing Research." *Journal of Marketing Research*, Vol. 3, May 1966, pp: 149–53.

Boddewyn, J. J. "Advertising Regulation, Self-Regulation and Self-Discipline Around the World: Some Facts, Trends and Observations." *Journal of International Marketing*, Vol. 1, No. 1, 1981, pp: 46–55.

Boddewyn, J. J. *Belgian Public Policy Toward Retailing Since 1789: The Socio-Politics of Distribution*. M.S.U. International Business and Economic Studies, East Lansing, 1971, 274 pages.

Boddewyn, J. J. *Comparative Management: Teaching, Training and Research*. Proceedings of the Comparative Management Workshop, New York University Press, 1970.

Boddewyn, J. J. *Comparative Management and Marketing*. Glenview, Ill: Scott, Foresman and Co., 1969.

Boddewyn, J. J. "Comparative Marketing: The First Twenty-Five Years." *Journal of International Business Studies*, Vol. 12, No. 1, Spring/Summer 1981, pp: 61–79.

Boddewyn, J. J. "The Comparative Approach to the Study of Business Administration." *Academy of Management Journal*, Vol. 8, No. 4, December 1965, pp: 261–267.

Boddewyn, J. J., H. L. Engberg, J. Fayerweather, P. G. Franck, A. Kapoor, and W. L. Ness. *World Business Systems and Environments*. International Textbook Company, 1972.

Boddewyn, J. J. and S. C. Hollander. *Public Policy Toward Retailing: An International Symposium*. D. C. Heath and Co., 1972.

Boddewyn, J. J. and R. Nath. "Comparative Management Studies." *Management International Review*, Vol. 10, No. 1, 1970, pp: 3–5.

Berien, J. K. "Methodological and Related Problems in Cross-Cultural Research." *International Journal of Psychology*, Vol. 2, No. 1, 1967, pp: 33–43.

Bucklin, L. P. "Trade Productivity: Comparison Between Japan and the U.S.A.," in Dov Izraeli et. al., eds., *Marketing Systems for Developing Countries*. New York: John Wiley, 1976, pp: 101–10.

Bucklin, L. P. *Vertical Marketing Systems*. Glenview, Illinois: Scott, Foresman and Company, 1970.

Buxton, G. "The Role of the Comparative Analysis Approach in Social Marketing." *European Journal of Marketing*, Vol. 7, No. 1, 1973, pp: 55–63.

Carmen, J. M., R. M. March. "How Important for Marketing Are Cultural Differences Between Similar Nations?" *Australian Marketing Researcher*, Vol. 3, No. 1, Summer 1979, pp: 5–20.

Carson, D. "Comparative Marketing—A New Old Aid." *Harvard Business Review*, May–June 1967, pp: 22–34, 38.

Carson, D. *International Marketing: A Comparative Systems Approach*, New York: John Wiley and Sons, Inc., 1967.

Carson, D. "Present State of the Art of Comparative Marketing" in T.V. Greer, ed., *Increasing Marketing Productivity and Conceptual and Methodological Foundations of Marketing*. Chicago: AMA 1974, pp: 67–70.

Cuvusgil, S. T. and Y. M. Godiwalla. "Decision-Making for International Marketing: A Comparative Review." *Management Decision*, Vol. 20, No. 4, 1982, pp: 47–54.

Chadabra, Pond R. O'Keefe. "Cross-National Product Value Perceptions," *Journal of Business Research*, Vol. 9, 1981, pp: 329–37.

Chong, Sin-Jee. "Comparative Marketing Practices of Foreign and Domestic Firms in Developing Countries: A Case Study of Malaysia." *Management International Review*, Vol. 13, No. 6, 1973, pp: 91–98.

Chu, G. C. "Problems of Cross-Cultural Communication Research" in S. P. Sethi and J. N. Seth, eds., *Multinational Business Operations: Marketing Management*, Goodyear Publishing Co., Pacific Palisades, California, 1973, pp: 146–153.

Cox, R. "The Search for Universals in Comparative Studies of Domestic Marketing Systems" in P. D. Bennett, ed., *Marketing and Economic Development*, Proceedings of the Fall Conference, AMA, Chicago, Illinois, 1965, pp: 143–62.

Cox, S. M. "A Comparison of Industrial Information Source Usage: Mexico vs. U.S." in H. W. Berkman and J. K. Fenyo, eds., *Selling to the Global Shopping Center, Academy of Marketing Science Journal*, Vol. 5, 1977, pp: 13–16.

Cundiff, E. W. "Concepts in Comparative Retailing." *Journal of Marketing*, January 1965, pp: 53–63.

Cundiff, E. W. and L. D. Dahringer. "Comparative Retailing Revisited." Mimeographed; Atlanta, GA: School of Business, Emory University, 1982.

Cundiff, E. W. and M. T. Hilger. "The Consumption Function: Marketing's Role in Economic Development." *Management Decision*, Vol. 20, No. 4, 1982, pp: 36–46.

Dahringer, L. D., "Public Policy Implications of Reverse Channel Mapping for Lesotho," *Journal of Macro Marketing*, Vol. 3, No. 1, Spring 1983, pp: 69–75.

Darling, J. R. "A Study of the Attitudes of Finnish Consumers Toward the Products and Associated Marketing Practices of Various Selected Countries." *Finnish Journal of Business Economics*, Spring 1976, pp: 3–19.

Darling, J. R. "The Competitive Marketplace Abroad: A Comparative Study." *Columbia Journal of World Business*, Vol. 16, No. 3, Fall 1981, pp: 53–62.

Davis, H. L., S. P. Douglas, and A. J. Silk. "Measure Unreliability: A Hidden Threat to Cross-National Marketing Research?" *Journal of Marketing*, Vol. 45, Spring 1981, pp: 98–108.

Davis, S. M. Comparative Management: *Organizational and Cultural Perspectives*. Englewood Cliffs, New Jersey: Prentice-Hall Inc., 1971, p. 593.

Demetrescu, M. C. "Comparative Marketing Systems—Conceptual Outline" in D. Izraeli, D. N. Izraeli, and F. Meissner, eds., *Marketing Systems for Developing Countries*, New York: Halsted Press, 1976, pp: 111–17.

Dholakia, N. and R. R. Dholakia. "A Framework for Analyzing International Influences on Third World Marketing Systems." Presented at Fifth Macro-Marketing Seminar, University of Rhode Island, August 1980.

Dholakia, N. and R. R. Dholakia. "Marketing in the Emerging World Order." *Journal of Macromarketing*, Vol. 2, No. 1, Spring 1982, pp: 47–56.

Dholakia, N. and R. Khurana. *Public Distribution Systems: Evolution, Evaluation and Prospects*, New Delhi: Oxford and IBH, 1973.

Dholakia, R. R., "Towards a Concept of an Ideal System for Comparative Marketing," Faculty Working Papers, No. 80-11, College of Business Administration, Kansas State University, June 1980, 11 pages.

Dolich, I. J. "A Cross-Cultural Comparison of Consumer Evaluations of Product Information Sources." Mimeographed. Lincoln, NE: College of Business Administration, University of Nebraska—Lincoln, 1980.

Douglas, S. P. "Adjusting for Sample Characteristics in Multi Country Survey Research" in M. A. Saren and M. J. Baker, eds., 9th Annual Meeting of the European Academy for Advanced Research in Marketing, Edinburgh 1980, pp: 190–98.

Douglas, S. P. "Cross-National Comparisons and Consumer Stereotypes: A Case Study of Working and Non-Working Wives in the U.S. and France." *Journal of Consumer Research*, Vol. 3, June 1976, pp: 12–20.

Douglas, S. P. "Patterns and Parallels of Marketing Structures in Several Countries." *M.S.U. Business Topics*, Vol. 19, Spring 1971, pp: 38–48.

Douglas, S. P. and B. Dubois. "Looking at the Cultural Environment for International Marketing Opportunities." *Columbia Journal of World Business*, Vol. 12, No. 4, Winter 1977, pp: 102–09.

Douglas, S. P. and R. Shoemaker. "Item Non-Response in Cross-National Attitude Surveys." *European Research*, Vol. 9, No. 3, July 1981, pp:124–32.

Douglas, S. P. and C. D. Urban. "A Cross-National Exploration of Husband-Wife Involvement in Selected Household Activities," in W. L. Wilkie, ed., *Advances in Consumer Research*, Vol. 6, Ann Arbor, MI: Association for Consumer Research, 1979, pp: 50–57.

Douglas, S. P. and C. D. Urban. "Life-style Analysis to Profile Women in International Markets." *Journal of Marketing*, Vol. 41, No. 3, July 1977, pp: 46–54.

Dowling, G. "Information Content in U.S. and Australian Television Advertising." *Journal of Marketing* Fall 1980, pp: 34–37.

Ehrenberg, A. S. C. and G. J. Goodhardt. "A Comparison of American and British Repeat-Buying Habits." *Journal of Marketing Research*, Vol. 5, 1968, pp: 29–34.

Elder, J. W. "Comparative Cross-National Methodology." *Annual Review of Sociology* Vol. 2, 1976, pp: 209–30.

El-Shervini, A. A., "Behavioral Analysis of the Role of Marketing in Economic Development," *Journal of Macro Marketing*, Vol. 3, No. 1, Spring 1983, pp: 76–79.

England, G. W. "Managers and Their Value Systems: A Five Country Comparative Study." *Columbia Journal of World Business*, Summer 1978, pp: 35–44.

Estafen, B. D., J. Anzizu, J. Hernandez, A. Laskos and R. Zimmerman. "The Systems Transfer Characteristics of Firms in Spain: A Comparative Study of U.S. and Spanish Firms." *Academy of Management Proceeding*, August 1969, pp: 161–67.

Etgar, M., "A Failure in Marketing Technology Transfer: The Case of Rice Distribution in the Ivory Coast," *Journal of Macro Marketing*, Vol. 3, No. 1 Spring 1983, pp: 59–68.

Farley, J. U., J. M. Hulbert and D. Weinstein. "Price Setting and Volume Planning By Two European Industrial Companies: A Study and Comparison of Decision Processes." *Journal of Marketing*, Winter 1980, pp: 46–54.

Farmer, R. N. and B. M. Richman. *Comparative Management and Economic Progress*. Bloomington, Indiana: Cedarwood Publishing Co., 1970.

Fisk, G. "Comparative Analysis of Macromarketing Systems and Distribution Channels Organization, Current Status, and Future Prospects." Presented at Sixth Macromarketing Seminar, Emory University, August 1981.

French, N. D., D. D. Showver, and D. W. Scotton. "A Comparative Analysis of Channel Structures for Two Major Household Appliances in the United States, Italy, and West Germany," in H. W. Berkman and J. F. Fenyo, eds., Academy of Marketing Science Monograph Series I, No. 1, 1978, p. 28.

Frijda, N. and G. Jahoda. "On the Scope and Methods of Cross-Cultural Research." *International Journal of Psychology*, Vol. 1, No. 2, 1960, pp: 109–27.

Ghosh, A. and M. L. McNulty. "Locational Analysis and Spatial Planning of Marketing Systems in Developing Countries." Paper presented at the International Geographical Union Working Group on Market-Place Exchange Systems Symposium, Zoria, Nigeria, July 27–30, 1978.

Gill, R. W. T. and D. L. Brady, "A Comparative Study of U.S. Department of Commerce Directors' Attitudes Towards Their Ability to Provide Export Assistance to Small and Large Businesses in Selected States," *American Journal of Small Business*, Vol. 7, No. 1, July-September, 1982, pp: 1–7.

Goldman, M. I. "A Cross-Cultural Comparison of the Soviet and American Consumer" in R. Mozer, ed., *Changing Marketing Systems*. AMA 1967 Winter Conference Proceedings, Washington, D. C. December 1967, pp: 195–99.

Green, R. T. and I. C. M. Cunningham. "Family Purchasing Roles in Two

Countries: United States and Venezuela." *Journal of International Business Studies*, Spring/Summer 1980, pp: 92–97.

Green, R. T., I. C. M. Cunningham, and W. H. Cunningham. "Cross-Cultural Consumer Profiles: An Exploratory Investigation" in S. Ward and P. Wright, eds., *Advances in Consumer Research*, Vol. 1, 1973, pp: 136–44.

Green, R. and E. Langeard. "A Cross-National Comparison of Consumer Habits and Innovation Characteristics." *Journal of Marketing*, Vol. 39, No. 3, July 1975, pp: 34–41.

Green, R. T. and E. Langeard. "Comments and Recommendations on the Practice of Cross-Cultural Marketing Research." Mimeographed. Brussels, European Institute for Advanced Studies in Management, 1979.

Green, R. T. and P. D. White. "Methodological Considerations in Cross-National Consumer Research." *Journal of International Business Studies*, Vol. 7, No. 2, Fall 1976, pp: 81–87.

Guilhaus, F. W., "A Comparative Study of Industrial Power, Control and Conflict: Australian Petroleum, Automobile and Fast Food Retailing," *Management Forum*, Vol. 7, No. 3, September 1981, pp: 168–193.

Gurol, N. N. and E. Kaynak, "The Effects of Corrective Advertising on Company Image: A Cross-Cultural Study of the U.S.A. and Canada," Unpublished Working Paper, Department of Business Administration, Mount Saint Vincent University, Halifax, 1982, 29 pages.

Hackett, D. W. "The International Expansion of U.S. Franchise System—Status and Strategies." *Journal of International Business Studies*, Vol. 7, No. 1, Spring 1976, pp: 65–75.

Hall, M. J. Knapp and C. Winsten. *Distribution in Great Britain and North America* London: Oxford University Press, 1961.

Halliday, M. I., H. C. Barksdale, and W. D. Perrault. "A Preliminary Analysis of Consumer Attitudes Toward Marketing and Consumerism in Australia and U.S.A.." *Australian Marketing Researcher*, Vol. 5, No. 1, March 1981, pp: 34–49.

Harris, C., R. Still, and M. Crask. "A Comparison of Australian and U. S. Marketing Strategies." *Columbia Journal of World Business,* Spring 1980, pp: 36–46.

Hawes, D., S. Grommo, and J. Arndt. "Shopping Time and Leisure Time: Some Preliminary Cross-Cultural Comparisons of Time-Budget Expenditures." Proceedings of the 1977 Conference of the Association for Consumer Research, pp: 151–59.

Hempel, D. J. "Family Buying Decisions: A Cross-Cultural Perspective." *Journal of Marketing Research*, Vol. 11, August 1974, pp: 295–302.

Hilger, M. T. "Factors Inhibiting the Development of Comparative Marketing." Paper presented at the 7th Annual Macro-Marketing Seminar, University of Colorado, August 1982.

Holloway, R. J. and R. S. Hancock. "The Nature of Comparative Marketing" in *Marketing in a Changing Environment*. New York: John Wiley and Sons, 2nd edition, 1973, pp: 64–76.

Hoover, R. J., R. T. Green, and J. Saegert. "A Cross-National Study of Perceived Risk." *Journal of Marketing*, July 1978, pp: 102–08.

Hornik, J. "Comparative Evaluation of International vs. National Advertising Strategies." *Columbia Journal of World Business,* Spring 1980, pp: 36–46.

Izraeli, D., D. N. Izraeli and F. Meissner, *Marketing Systems in Developing Countries,* Vols. I & II, New York: John Wiley and Sons, 1976.

Jaffe, E. D. "A Flow Approach to the Comparative Study of Marketing Systems," in J. Boddewyn, ed., *Comparative Management and Marketing.* Glenview, Illinois: pp: 160–70.

Jaffe, E. D. "Are Domestic and International Marketing Dissimilar?" *Management International Review,* Vol. 20, No. 3, 1980, pp: 83–86.

Jaffe, E. D. "Comparative Marketing Revisited." *Marquette Business Review,* Vol. 20, No. 4, Winter 1976, pp: 143–53.

Jaffe, E. D. *Towards a System Approach to the Study of Domestic Marketing Abroad: A Case Study of Israeli Food Distribution.* Unpublished Ph.D. Dissertation, University of Pennsylvania, 1966.

Kaikati, J. G., "Marketing Practices in Iran Vis-à-Vis Saudi Arabia," Management International Review, Vol. 19, No. 4, 1979, pp: 31–37.

Karp, R. E. and A. Gorlick. *Cross-Cultural Considerations of Marketing and Consumer Behavior,* MSS Information Corporation, New York, 1974.

Kaynak, E. "A Cross-National Comparison of Ghetto Market Shopping Habits in Two Different Cultures." Proceedings of the Academy of International Business, Honolulu, Hawaii, December 18–20, 1979, pp: 738–51.

Kaynak, E. "An Assessment of the Methodological Framework for Comparative Marketing Studies." *Management Decisions,* Vol. 20, No. 4, September 1982, pp: 3–15.

Kaynak, E. and L. A. Stevenson. "Comparative Study of Home Buying Behavior of Atlantic Canadians." *Management Research* Vol. 4, No. 3, 1981, pp: 3–11.

Kaynak, E. "Food Distribution Systems: Evolution in Latin America and the Middle East," *Food Policy,* Vol. 6, No. 2, May 1981, pp: 78–90.

Kaynak, E. "Future Directions for Research in Comparative Marketing." *The Canadian Marketer,* Vol. 11, No. 1, 1980, pp: 23–28.

Kaynak, E. "Shopping Practices for Food: Some Cross-Cultural Comparisons," in M. J. Baker, ed., *Buyer Behavior.* Proceedings of the Marketing Education Group Conference, Glasgow, Scotland, June 1976, pp: 107–41.

Kaynak, E. and S. T. Cavusgil. "The Evolution of Food Retailing Systems: Contrasting the Experience of Developed and Developing Countries." *Academy of Marketing Science Journal,* Vol. 10, No. 3, Summer 1982, pp: 249–68.

Kaynak, E. and L. A. Mitchell. "Analysis of Marketing Strategies Used in Diverse Cultures." *Journal of Advertising Research,* Vol. 21, No. 3, June 1981, pp: 25–32.

Kaynak, E. and L. A. Mitchell. "A Study of Comparative Media Usage in Canada, the United Kingdom and Turkey." *European Journal of Marketing* Vol. 15, No. 1, 1980, pp: 1–9.

Kaynak, E. and L. A. Mitchell. "Comparative Analysis of Advertising Agency Systems in Multiple Environments in V. V. Bellur et. al., eds., *Developments in Marketing Science.* Proceedings of the Academy of Marketing Science, Miami Beach, Florida, April 29–May 2, 1981, pp: 247–52.

Kaynak, E., L. A. Mitchell, and S. T. Cavusgil. "The Comparisons of Role and Function of Advertising Agency-Client Relationships in Turkey and Canada." *Journal of International Marketing and Marketing Research*, Vol. 6, No. 1, February 1981, pp: 3–11.

Kaynak, E. and A. Meidan. "Home Buying Behavior: A Comparison of Canadian vs. British Attitudes." *Management International Review*, Vol. 20, No. 4, 1980, pp: 53–63.

Kaynak, E. and A. C. Samli "A Conceptual and Methodological Approach to the Study of Marketing Practices in LDC's," *Journal of Business Research*, Vol. 11, No. 4. December 1983.

Kaynak, E. and U. Yavas. "Home Buying Behavior: Do Canadians Differ from Americans?" The Canadian Business Review Vol. 8, No. 3, Autumn 1981, pp: 34–36.

Kaynak, E. and U. Yucelt. "A Comparative Study of Credit Card Usage Behaviors: Canadian Versus American Credit Card Holders," in J. S. Burton, ed., Northeast AIDS 1983 Annual Meeting, Philadelphia, Pennsylvania, April 7–8, 1983.

Kelley, L. and R. Worthley. "The Role of Culture in Comparative Management: A Cross-Cultural Perspective." *Academy of Management Journal*, No. 1, 1981, pp: 164–73.

Kobayashi, N. "The Present and Future of Japanese Multinational Enterprises: A Comparative Analysis of Japanese and U.S.-European Multinational Management." *International Studies of Management and Organization*, Vol. 12, No. 1, 1982, pp: 38–58.

Lamb, C. W. "Domestic Applications of Comparative Marketing Analysis." *European Journal of Marketing*, Vol. 9, No. 2, 1975, pp: 167–72.

Lasserre, P. "The New Industrializing Countries of Asia—Perspectives and Opportunities," *Long Range Planning*, Vol. 14, No. 3, 1981, pp: 36–43.

Lehtinen, U. "Marketing Mix in Export: A Comparative Analysis." A paper read at the European Academy for Advanced Research in Marketing, Tenth Annual Conference, Copenhagen, Denmark, March 1981.

Leroy, G. *Multinational Product Strategy: A Typology for Analysis of Worldwide Product Innovation and Diffusion*. New York: Praeger Publishers, 1976.

Liander, B. V. Terpstra, M. Y. Yoshino and A. A. El-Sherbini. *Comparative Analysis for International Marketing*. Boston: Allyn & Bacon, Inc. 1967, p. 198.

Linton, A. and S. Broadbent. "International Life-style Comparisons—An Aid to Marketers." *Advertising Quarterly*, No. 44, Summer 1975, pp: 15–18.

Luqmani, M., A. Z. Quraeshi, and L. Delene. "Marketing in Islamic Countries: A Viewpoint," *M.S.U. Business Topics*, Summer 1980, pp: 17–25.

Maddox, R. N., K. Homans, and F. May. "Correlates of Information Gathering and Evoked Set Size for New Automobile Purchasers in Norway and the U.S.," in H. K. Hunt, ed., *Advances in Consumer Research*, Vol. 5, Ann Arbor, MI. Association For Consumer Research, 1978, pp: 167–70.

Marketing East-West: A Comparative View, Report on the Work of the ESOMAR East-West Working Group Amsterdam, ESOMAR, 1973, p. 248.

Mayer, C. S. "Multinational Marketing Research: The Magnifying Glass of Methodological Problems." *European Research*, Vol. 6, No. 2, March 1978, pp: 77–83.

Merritt, R. L. and S. Rokkan. *Comparing Nations: The Use of Quantitative Data in Cross-National Research*, Yale University Press: New Haven, Conn., 1966.

Mintz, S. W. "The Role of the Middleman in the Internal Distribution System of a Caribbean Peasant Economy," *Human Organization*, Vol. 15, No. 2, Summer 1956, pp: 18–23.

Miracle, G. E. "A Two-Nation Comparison of Advertising Law and Regulation: Norway and the U.S.A." A paper presented at the 1974 National Conference of American Academy of Advertising, Newport, Rhode Island, April 30, 1974.

Miracle, M. "Comparative Market Structures in Developing Countries." *Nebraska Journal of Economics and Business*, Vol. 9, No. 4, Autumn 1970, pp: 33–46.

Munson, J. M. and S. H. McIntyre. "Developing Practical Procedures for the Measurement of Personal Values in Cross-Cultural Marketing," *Journal of Marketing Research*, February 1979, pp: 48–52.

Munson, J. and S. McIntyre. "Personal Values: A Cross-Cultural Assessment of Self Values and Values Attributed to a Distant Cultural Stereotype." Proceedings of 1977 Conference of the Association for Consumer Research, 1977, pp: 160–66.

Nagashima, A. "A Comparison of Japanese and U.S. Attitudes Toward Foreign Products." *Journal of Marketing*, Vol. 34, January 1970, pp: 68–74.

Nagashima, A. "A Comparative 'Made In' Product Image Survey Among Japanese Businessmen." *Journal of Marketing*, Vol. 41, No. 3, July 1977, pp: 95–100.

Nambudiri, C. N. S. and M. S. Saiyadain. "Management Problems and Practices—India and Nigeria." *Columbia Journal of World Business*, Summer 1978.

Nevis, E. C., "Cultural Assumptions and Productivity: The United States and China," *Sloan Management Review*, Vol. 24, No. 3, Spring 1983, pp: 17–29.

Nuttal, J., "Marketing—The Swedish, British, and German Styles," *European business*, No. 35, Autumn 1972, pp: 64–71.

Organization for Economic Development Center (OED), *Critical Issues in Food Marketing Systems in Developing Countries*. Paris: Development Centre, OECD/FAO Joint Seminar, 1977.

Padberg, D. I. and D. Thorpe. "Channels of Grocery Distribution: Changing Stages in Evolution—A Comparison of U.S.A. and U.K.." *Journal of Agricultural Economics*, Vol. 25, No. 1, June 1974, pp: 1–22.

Plummer, J. T. "Consumer Focus in Cross-National Research." *Journal of Advertising*, Vol. 6, No. 2, Spring 1977, pp: 5–15.

Przeworkski, A., and H. Teune, "Equivalence in Cross-National Research," *The Public Opinion Quarterly*, Vol. 30, No. 4, Winter 1966–1967, pp: 551–68.

Ronkainen, I. A. and A. G. Woodside. "Cross-Cultural Analysis of Market Profiles of Domestic and Foreign Travellers." *European Journal of Marketing*, Vol. 12, No. 8, 1978, pp: 573–87.

Ruff, H. J. and G. I. Jackson. "Methodological Problems in International Comparisons of the Cost of Living." *Journal of International Business Studies*, Vol. 5, No. 2, Fall 1974, pp: 57–67.

Samli, A. C. "A Comparative Analysis of Marketing in Romania and Yugoslavia." *The Southern Journal of Business*, Vol. 5, No. 3, July 1970, pp: 108–13.

Samli, A. C. "An Approach for Estimating Market Potential in East Europe." *Journal of International Business*, Vol. 8, No. 2, Fall/Winter 1977, pp: 49–53.

Samli, A. C. *Marketing and Distribution Systems in Eastern European Economies*, New York: Praeger Publishers, Inc., 1978.

Samli, A. C. and J. T. Mentzer. "A Model for Marketing in Economic Development." *Columbia Journal of World Business*, Vol. 16, No. 3, Fall 1981, pp: 31–101.

Savitt, R. "A Historical Approach to Comparative Retailing." *Management Decision*, Vol. 20, No. 4, 1982, pp: 16–23.

Seaton, B. and R. H. Vogel. "Cross-National Comparison—Are They Relevant?" in S. Raveed and Y. R. Puri, eds., Proceedings of the Academy of International Business, Chicago, Illinois, August 1978, pp: 121–24.

Sekaran, U. "Methodological and Theoretical Issues and Advancements in Cross-Cultural Research," Presented at Cross-Cultural Symposium, McGill University, October 1981.

Sethi, S. P. "Comparative Cluster Analysis for World Markets," *Journal of Marketing Research*, August 1971, pp: 348–54.

Shapiro, S. J. "Comparative Marketing and Economic Development," *Marketing Horizons*, Vol. 15, No. 8, August 1976, pp: 14–19.

Sheth, J. N. and S. P. Sethi "A Theory of Cross-Cultural Buyer Behavior," in A. G. Woodside, J. N. Sheth and P. D. Bennett, eds., *Consumer and Industrial Buying Behavior*, New York: North Holland Publishers, 1979, pp: 369–86.

Shipchandler, Z. E. "A Cross-Country Study of Annual Unit Sales and Ownership Patterns of Three Consumer Durables." Unpublished DBA Dissertation, Indiana University, 1972.

Slater, C. C. "Marketing Processes in Developing Latin American Societies." *Journal of Marketing*, Vol. 32, July 1968, pp: 50–55.

Smith, C. A., "Economics of Marketing Systems: Models from Economic Geography," in B. J. Siegel; A. R. Beals; and S. A. Tyler eds., *Annual Review of Anthropology*, Vol. 3, 1974.

Sommers, M. S. and J. B. Kernan. *Comparative Marketing Systems*. New York: Appleton-Century-Crofts, 1978.

Stern, L. W. and Reve. "Distribution Channels as Political Economies: A Framework for Comparative Analysis." *Journal of Marketing*, Vol. 44, Summer 1980, pp: 52–64.

Straus, M. A., "Phenomenal Identity and Conceptual Equivalence of Measurement in Cross-National Comparative Research," *Journal of Marriage and the Family*, Vol. 31, No. 2, pp: 233–239.

Thompson, D. N. *Contractural Marketing Systems*, Lexington, Mass: Heath Lexington Books, 1971.

Thorelli, H. B., H. Becker, and J. Engledow. *The Information Seekers: An International Study of Consumer Information and Advertising Image*. Cambridge, Massachusetts: Ballinger, Publishing Co., 1975.

Thorelli, H. B. and S. V. Thorelli. *Consumer Information Systems and Consumer Policy*. Cambridge, Massachusetts: Ballinger Publishing Co., 1977.

Tiegert, D. J., C. W. King, and L. J. Ring. "Fashion Involvement: A Cross-Cultural

Comparative Analysis," in J. C. Olson (ed.) *Advances in Consumer Research*. pp: 17–21.

Tolhurst, J. "Multicultural Marketing in the 1980's," *Australian Marketing Researcher*, Vol. 4, No. 2, October 1980, pp: 57–64.

Urban, C. D. "A Cross-National Comparison of Consumer Media Use Patterns." *Columbia Journal of World Business*, Winter 1977, pp: 53–54.

Urban, C. D. "Life-style Patterns of Women, United States and United Kingdom." Paper presented at the American Academy of Advertising, Knoxville, Tennessee, 20 April 1975.

Van Raaij, W. F. "Cross-Cultural Research Methodology as a Case of Construct Validating," in H. K. Hunt, ed., *Advances in Consumer Research*, Vol. 5, Ann Arbor, MI: Association For Consumer Research, 1978, pp: 693–701.

Wadinambiaratchi, G. "Channels of Distribution in Developing Economies." *Business Quarterly*, Winter 1965, pp: 74–82.

Webster, L. L. "Comparability in Multi-Country Surveys," *Journal of Advertising Research*, Vol. 6, No. 4, December 1966, pp: 14–18.

Wierer, K. "A Comparative Analysis of Fertilizer Marketing in Selected Countries." Cento Seminar on Key Management Problems in the Marketing, Distribution and Use of Fertilizers, Islamabad, Pakistan, January 7–10, 1974, pp: 171–84.

Wilson, F. A., "The Development of Small Scale Marketing Systems: Some Observations on Intermediary Activities in the Perishable Trade," *Agricultural Administration*, Vol. 3, 1976, pp: 263–269.

Wind, Y. "Cross-Cultural Analysis of Consumer Behavior," in R. Moyer, ed., *Changing Marketing Systems*. American Marketing Association, Chicago, 1967, pp: 183–85.

Wind, Y., and S. P. Douglas. "Comparative Consumer Research: The Next Frontier." *Management Decision*, Vol. 20, No. 4, 1982, pp: 24–35.

Wind, Y. and S. P. Douglas. "Comparative Methodology and Marketing Theory," in *Theoretical Developments in Marketing*, Proceedings of the American Marketing Association, Chicago, Illinois, 1980, pp: 30–33.

Wind, Y. and S. P. Douglas. "On the Meaning of Comparison: A Methodology for Cross-Cultural Studies." *Quarterly Journal of Management Development*, Vol. 2, No. 4, June 1977, pp: 108–10.

Yavas, U., "Marketing Research Usage by Domestic and Foreign Manufacturing Firms in Turkey," *Management International Review*, Vol. 23, No. 2, 1983, pp: 56–64.

Yavas, U. and W. D. Rountree, "Turkish Students' Perceptions of Marketing and other Major Fields in Business: A Comparative Study," *Der Markt*, No. 1, 1980, pp: 31–35.

INDEX

ABOUT THE CO-EDITORS
AND CONTRIBUTORS

Erdener Kaynak is Associate Professor of Marketing and Chairman at the Department of Business Administration and Public Relations Degree Program of Mount Saint Vincent University, Halifax, Nova Scotia, Canada. Prior to this, he held teaching positions with Acadia University, Wolfville, Nova Scotia and Hacettepe University, Ankara, Turkey. Dr. Kaynak holds a B. Econ. degree from Istanbul University, an M.A. degree in Marketing from the University of Lancaster, and a Ph.D. from Cranfield School of Management. Furthermore, he has conducted post-doctoral research studies at Michigan State University, U.S.A. and Lund University, Sweden, and has lectured and held executive training programs in Europe, North America, the Middle East, and Latin America. He is the founder and president of a Halifax-based company, Cross-Cultural Marketing Services Incorporated; and Vice-President Research and Development for Tomarket International Limited.

Dr. Kaynak has served as a consultant to business as well as a number of Canadian and international organizations. He has published over 50 articles in scholarly and professional journals and published books, monographs, and mimeographed marketing reports. His articles have appeared in the *Journal of Advertising Research, Journal of Business Research, European Journal of Marketing, Management International Review, Academy of Marketing Science Journal*, and many other publications. In addition to this, he has read papers and chaired sessions in more than ten countries at over 30 conferences. Dr. Kaynak is Associate Editor of the *Journal of Management Decision* and serves on the editorial board of the *Journal of Enterprise Management, Academy of Marketing Science Journal, International Journal of Marketing and Marketing Research* and *Management Research*. He was the organizer and chairman of three international congresses: one on tourism, one on housing development, and one on international marketing.

Ronald Savitt is Chairperson and Professor of Marketing at the Department of Marketing and Transportation Administration, Graduate School of Business Administration of Michigan State University, East Lansing,

Michigan. Prior to this, he has taught at the University of Alberta, Canada; University of Edinburgh, Scotland; Boston University, Massachusetts; and worked as senior economist for National Economic Research Associates Inc., a New York-based company. During the 1972–73 academic year, he was a Senior Fulbright Lecturer in Marketing at the School of Administrative Sciences of Bogazici University, Istanbul, Turkey. Dr. Savitt holds A.B. and M.B.A. degrees from the University of California, Berkeley, and a Ph.D. from the University of Pennsylvania. He is the author or coauthor of a number of books and research monographs, and has published articles in the *Journal of Marketing, European Journal of Marketing, Academy of Marketing Science Journal, California Management Review, Journal of Contemporary Business*, and many other publications. Dr. Savitt has also served in an advisory capacity to government agencies as well as to business firms both in Europe and North America.

L. Mctier Anderson is a doctoral student in Marketing at the Department of Marketing of the University of Georgia, Athens, Georgia.

Hiram C. Barksdale is Professor of Marketing at the Department of Marketing of the University of Georgia, Athens, Georgia.

S. Tamer Cavusgil is Associate Professor of Marketing at the College of Business and Economics of the University of Wisconsin-Whitewater, Wisconsin.

C. Samuel Craig is Associate Professor of Marketing at the Graduate School of Business Administration of New York University, New York.

John A. Dawson is the Fraser-Allender Professor of Distributive Studies, University of Stirling, Stirling, Scotland, United Kingdom.

Susan P. Douglas is Associate Professor of Marketing and International Business at the Graduate School of Business Administration of New York University, New York.

Adel I. El-Ansary is Professor of Business Administration at the School of Government and Business Administration of the George Washington University, Washington, D.C.

Michael Etgar is Professor of Marketing at the Graduate School of Business Administration of New York University and on leave from Hebrew University of Jerusalem, Jerusalem, Israel.

Arieh Goldman is Professor of Marketing at the School of Business Administration of Hebrew Unviersity of Jerusalem, Jerusalem, Israel.

John L. Hazard is Professor of Marketing and Transportation Administration in the Department of Marketing and Transportation Administration of Michigan State University, East Lansing, Michigan.

Mun Kin-Chok is Professor of Marketing and Dean of Faculty of Business Administration at the Chinese University of Hong Kong, Shatin, Hong Kong.

Douglas M. Lambert is a Professor of Marketing in the Department of Marketing and Transportation Administration of Michigan State University, East Lansing, Michigan.

William Lazer is Professor of Marketing at the Department of Marketing and Transportation Administration of Michigan State University, East Lansing, Michigan.

Marilyn L. Liebrenz is Assistant Professor of Business Administration at the School of Government and Business Administration of the George Washington University, Washington, D.C.

James T. Rothe is Professor of Marketing at the Department of Marketing of the Southern Methodist University, Dallas, Texas.

A. Coskun Samli is Professor of Marketing at the School of Business Administration of Virginia Polytechnic Institute and State University, Blacksburg, Virginia.

James R. Stock is an Associate Professor in the Division of Marketing in the College of Business Administration, University of Oklahoma, Norman, Oklahoma.

Laszlo Szabo is Professor of Marketing at Karl Marx University of Budapest and the Managing Director of the Hungarian Institute for Market Research, Budapest, Hungary.